Burford

buildings and people
in a Cotswold town

An England's Past for Everyone paperback

Institute of Historical
Research

In association with the VCH Oxfordshire Trust and
Oxfordshire County Council

Burford

buildings and people
in a Cotswold town

ANTONIA CATCHPOLE,
DAVID CLARK AND
ROBERT PEBERDY

with contributions from Simon Townley and Nicholas Cooper

edited by Simon Townley

Phillimore

First published 2008
Reprinted 2009

A Victoria County History publication
Published by Phillimore & Co. Ltd, Chichester, West Sussex PO20 2DD,
England in association with the Institute of Historical Research at the
University of London.
www.phillimore.co.uk

ISBN 978-1-86077-488-1

British Library Cataloguing in Publication Data. A cataloguing record for this
book is available from the British Library.

Typeset in Humanist 521 and Minion

We wish particularly to thank the following EPE and VCH staff for their efforts
during the production of this volume:

John Beckett – Director of the Victoria County History
Matthew Bristow – Historic Environment Research Manager
Catherine Cavanagh – Project Manager
Nafisa Gaffar – Finance and Contracts Officer
Aretha George – Education and Skills Manager
Mel Hackett – Communications Manager
Neil Penlington – Administrator
Andrew Stokes – Web Manager
Alan Thacker – Executive Editor of the Victoria County History
Kerry Whitston – Publications Manager
Elizabeth Williamson – Architectural Editor of the Victoria County History

Printed and bound in Malta

Cover image: Burford's annual hiring fair in 1895 (detail), photographed by
Henry Taunt. (Oxfordshire County Council Photographic Archive)

Contents

Foreword

If you wish to know the history of Des Moines, Iowa – and I speak as someone who has spent some time on this – the definitive work is *Des Moines: The Pioneer of Municipal Progress and Reform of the Middle West, Together with the History of Polk County, Iowa, the Largest, Most Populous and Most Prosperous County in the State of Iowa*, written in 1911 by a man with the interestingly back-to-front name of Johnson Brigham.

Mr Brigham's book, though pleasingly hefty and thorough, has two unfortunate drawbacks: it is almost unreadable and it is about a century out of date. Yet it remains the definitive history of Des Moines, because it is the only one. If you were to search in a similar fashion for the histories of Omaha or Topeka or Kankakee, I fear you would experience similar disappointments.

Local history, I'm afraid, is not always regarded with much reverence, or even attention, in the world I grew up in. So when I come across a book like this, about a lovely little town that I hardly know, and find myself charmed and enthralled from the first page, I can barely express my admiration.

You are of course immensely lucky in this country to have such a wealth of history all around you, but you are also very wise to keep track of it so devotedly. Living alongside the past is a wonderful satisfaction; understanding it is even better. I can't think of a more rewarding demonstration of both those qualities than this delightful volume.

Bill Bryson

Preface

The picturesque town of Burford, on Oxfordshire's western edge at 'the gateway to the Cotswolds', will need little introduction to the visitors who throng its streets every year, attracted by its up-market shops and visual charm. Probably only a few, however, pause to look at the fabric of the town in detail, or to give any thought to how and why it acquired its present-day character. This book is about the origins of the Burford we see today: its buildings, streets and townscape, explored in the context of the town's wider history and of the lives of the people who helped shape it. The main chronological chapters are followed by a house-by-house historical gazetteer, which visitors can use to explore the buildings along its main streets. Through the book as a whole we hope that residents, visitors and specialists alike will see Burford with new eyes, and deepen their understanding of its complex growth and rich architectural history.

In working on the town's history we have benefited enormously from earlier books about Burford, which are listed under Further Reading. This latest addition, however, draws on considerable new research and differs from its predecessors in two ways. First, though the book is wide-ranging it is not a standard chronological overview. The approach throughout has been to combine close examination of the town's buildings and physical layout with documentary research into its history and people, in an attempt to understand Burford's development over the centuries. As such it builds on a long-standing Victoria County History (VCH) tradition. Behind it stands the pioneering work of Michael Laithwaite, whose stimulating 1973 essay on Burford's buildings is also listed in Further Reading.

Second, the approach has been collaborative. The Victoria County History's England's Past For Everyone project (EPE) presented an opportunity to examine Burford's buildings and townscape in more depth than we could normally hope to do, and in 2002 we accordingly established a partnership with the Oxfordshire Buildings Record (OBR), a voluntary group which encourages active involvement in building recording. Over the next few years OBR volunteers, coordinated by the OBR's Secretary David Clark, participated in a series of Burford 'recording days', collecting a mass of information on buildings along the main streets. At a later stage a small photography group was established to create a complete visual record of the buildings and of particular architectural details. This complemented the professional photography undertaken by Mike Hesketh-Roberts and James Davies of English Heritage, and James also led two highly successful training days for the photography group out in the town. A third volunteer strand was the Burford Probate Group, set up by Mary Hodges in 2004 and later coordinated by Heather Horner, which transcribed and analysed nearly a thousand Burford wills and other probate documents for the period 1530-1699.

Meanwhile, VCH staff and contributors researched particular aspects of the town's history. David Clark, as architectural consultant, investigated many of Burford's buildings in greater detail, combining his work with OBR material to draft the architectural chapters and the building descriptions in the Gazetteer. He also arranged for tree-ring dating of some roof timbers, providing the first scientific dating evidence for buildings in Burford. The architectural historian Nicholas Cooper, another consultant, researched The Priory, The Great House, and the parish church. Among VCH staff, Robert Peberdy painstakingly researched individual house histories for the Gazetteer and wrote the post-medieval social and economic history (Chapters 6-7). Antonia Catchpole, funded by the Heritage Lottery Fund, unravelled Burford's medieval and modern layout (Chapters 2 and 8), and wrote the medieval historical sections and the religious history (Chapters 3, 5, and 9). Simon Townley, as County Editor and EPE Team Leader, contributed the opening chapter and Afterword, oversaw the image selection, and undertook final editing and redrafting, in consultation with the contributors and VCH Central Office. Elizabeth Williamson and Matthew Bristow, architectural editors for EPE, made suggestions throughout, and the project also benefited from work by Veronica West-Harling and Eleanor Chance, both formerly of VCH Oxfordshire. John Steane, Rob Parkinson, Terry Slater and David Sturdy gave valuable help, and James Nash kindly gave access to his D Phil thesis on 19th-century Burford.

Such a book could not have been written without the support of people in Burford, who gave information, access to documents or photographs, and above all access to their homes. Particular thanks are due to Christopher Baines, Abbot Stuart Burns, Derek Cotterill, Hugh Ellis-Rees, John Horner, and John and Julia Melvin. By far the greatest local debt is to Raymond and Joan Moody, historians of Burford, whose friendship, hospitality, and generosity in sharing their unrivalled knowledge helped to make the project so pleasurable.

Some of the data on which the book draws, including photographs, buildings information, wills, transcripts, and fuller

versions of the Gazetteer, are being made available on the EPE
website (*www.ExploreEnglandsPast.org.uk*). When complete, the
website will provide all those interested in local history, from the
school teacher to the researcher, with a rich bank of resources on
which to draw. Information will be searchable in a variety of ways,
and has been designed to complement the EPE paperback series.

The project is also feeding into work with schools. Pupils from
Mabel Prichard School in Oxford are comparing industries and
buildings in Burford and Henley, focusing on the wool and river
trades. Starting at the Henley River & Rowing Museum, pupils will
have the opportunity to investigate Burford and Henley through
field trips, engaging with artefacts and discovering 'treasures' in
both towns and along the river.

Simon Townley
County Editor and EPE Team Leader, VCH Oxfordshire

*VCH Oxfordshire is supported by Oxfordshire County Council, the
VCH Oxfordshire Trust, Oxford University Library Services, and
the University of Oxford, without whom this project would not have
been possible. We are also grateful to the VCH Oxfordshire Trust
for a subvention towards the cost of producing this book and to the
Oxfordshire Architectural and Historical Society for contributions
towards the cost of tree-ring dating.*

Note to the Second Edition
*For the reprinting of this book in 2009, we have taken the opportunity
to incorporate additional information supplied by readers and to
correct a few small errors.*

Understanding Burford

Figure 1 The Windrush
valley from the A40
(the ancient Cotswold
ridgeway), with Burford
nestling in the distance
beyond the trees.

THE SETTING

Driving westwards from Oxford along the modern A40 (part of
the ancient ridgeway towards Gloucestershire and the Cotswolds),
the first glimpse of the small former market-town of Burford is of
a distant stone spire down to the right, protruding from clumps
of trees scattered along the Windrush valley. Below, the river
snakes along the wide valley floor on its way to join the Thames at
Newbridge, a few miles downstream. Above the river, flat meadows
give way to a patchwork of hedgerows and gently undulating
pasture, occasionally still dotted with the sheep for which the area
was once famous.

   A mile or so further on, not far from the Oxfordshire-
Gloucestershire boundary, the road into Burford branches off
to the right. The few buildings visible up here at the town's edge
are not especially striking, but, as the road drops sharply to the
valley bottom, the scene is transformed. Ahead, the broad expanse
of High Street, even though usually clogged with cars, four-by-
fours and shoppers, opens out impressively, leading down to the
medieval stone bridge at the town's end. On the right the 15th-
century church spire is still visible, while in the near distance the
far slope of the river valley rises up towards the village of Fulbrook.
The countryside encroaches from every side. With a population
of around a thousand Burford is, in fact, little larger than most
neighbouring villages, and has never exceeded 2,000 people.

   But what really gives the town its character (and what, along
with the tourist and antique shops, attracts so many visitors)
are the buildings lining the street. Higher up these are mostly of
stone, a continuous run of small cottages and houses featuring the
odd Cotswold gable, an occasional smart front with smooth-cut
ashlar and sash windows, and in one case a carved medieval head.
Further down on the right is a remarkable run of large, timber-
framed and clearly high-status medieval houses, intermixed with
an 18th-century classical mansion, a large brick-fronted inn, and
on the opposite side an intriguing miscellany of stone-fronted
cottages and houses, shopfronts, alleyways, and medieval stone
archways. The rich variety of frontages continues down to the river
and along the two main side roads of Witney Street and Sheep
Street, a jumble of changing rooflines, patched stonework, and

Figure 2 Burford High Street, characteristically choked with traffic. Even so the vista is impressive, with its rich variety of Cotswold stone, timber framing, and the distant view across the valley.

Figure 3 The county of Oxfordshire in the SE of England.

much-altered window or door openings which together hint at the complex histories of the buildings within.

This book is an attempt to understand those buildings and the townscape of which they form a part, within the context of the town's wider history and of the lives and aspirations of the people who lived and worked there. Perched at 'the gateway to the Cotswolds', Burford is often depicted as a quintessential 'Cotswold town'. The term has become synonymous with heritage-industry connotations of picturesque stone gables, mullioned windows, and rolling countryside, and like many stereotypes this one contains some elements of truth. As the description above implies, Burford has plenty such buildings, and shares much in common with other 'Cotswold' towns such as Northleach, Chipping Campden or Stow-on-the-Wold – their early prosperity based on wool, and their building traditions reflecting the prevalence throughout the Cotswolds of hard-wearing oolitic limestone, which lends the area so much of its visual character. But ultimately every place is unique, and the picture of Burford which emerges from the following pages is richer, more varied, and more specific. The first chapters look at the medieval town, discussing its creation by medieval planners and exploring how its economic, social and religious life were reflected in its striking array of medieval buildings. Later chapters adopt a similar approach for more recent periods, up to and including the 20th and early 21st centuries. The final section is a historical gazetteer of all the buildings along Burford's main streets, which draws on a broad range of documentary and architectural evidence to summarise who lived there, how the buildings were used, and how this is reflected in what we see today.

BURFORD THROUGH TIME

Like many small towns, Burford owes its origins to medieval planning and entrepreneurship. The existing pattern of streets and house-plots was laid out between the late 11th and mid-13th centuries by a succession of enterprising manorial lords who, like many of their contemporaries, hoped to capitalise on expanding trade and commerce. This was, across much of Europe, the classic period of new town foundations, which were designed to attract traders, merchants and craftsmen and consequently to increase landlords' profits. In Burford the venture was clearly successful, as devotees of Cynthia Harnett's classic children's tale *The Woolpack* (set in a semi-fictional 15th-century Burford of underhand

Map 1 Burford in its locality, showing county boundaries, rivers, chief roads, and the most important neighbouring towns and villages.

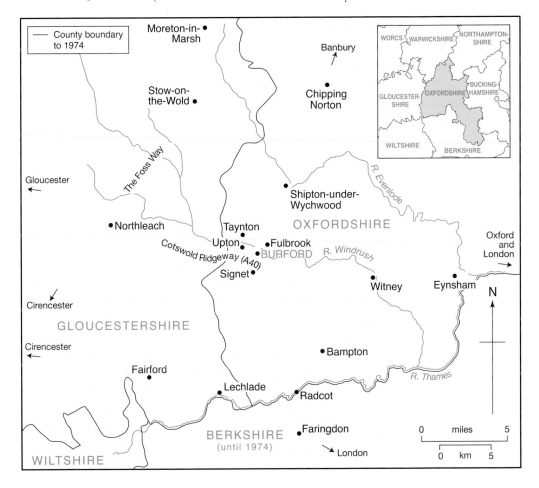

business-dealings and intrigue) will know. By the 13th and 14th centuries the town was emerging as an important medieval wool town, its prosperity based on the international trade in wool and cloth in which the Cotswolds played a major part.

Documentary evidence for these earliest phases is limited, but, as so often, use of physical evidence can amplify the picture. Chapter 2 shows how analysing streets, plots, and frontages allows us not only to reconstruct the medieval town, but to recover elements of the earlier, late Anglo-Saxon settlement which underlay it. Only scattered fragments now remain of the earliest medieval buildings, but substantial structures from the 15th century onwards survive in much larger numbers. Combined with information from similar towns, such evidence brings us closer to understanding what the medieval town may have looked like, how its buildings were constructed, and how they were used and adapted over time. Though very few of the most prominent late-medieval buildings can be tied to particular owners, houses such as Calendars on Sheep Street, now firmly dated to 1473, show that Burford's late medieval merchants were making substantial investments in new buildings. Public buildings, too, reflected the town's economic vitality, among them the existing Tolsey or market house (built in 1525) and the town's numerous medieval inns.

From the 17th century Burford lost its medieval pre-eminence, slipping slowly into the role of an undistinguished but modestly successful market town serving its immediate locality. The wool merchants and clothiers who had dominated the medieval town were replaced by a new town élite of prosperous traders and innkeepers with narrower horizons, supplemented by a few professionals such as surgeons or lawyers and by a smattering of gentry. As might be expected, new building on a grand scale became less common – indeed this very decline accounts for the survival of so much of Burford's medieval fabric, compared, for instance, with nearby Witney, where the prosperity generated by the local cloth and blanket industry prompted an almost complete rebuilding. By contrast, Burford was mainly remodelled rather than rebuilt, with old buildings modernised and refronted, new, more fashionable windows and doorcases inserted, and outbuildings or workshops rebuilt or adapted. There were, of course, some notable exceptions, such as The Great House on Witney Street (built for the local surgeon John Castle), or most strikingly The Priory, a grand Elizabethan mansion erected by the lawyer and politician Sir Lawrence Tanfield on the site of a dissolved medieval hospital, on the town's western edge. The development of coaching, too, brought a further burst of prosperity to the town's major inns, and several were remodelled: the *Bull*, for instance, was strikingly

Figure 4 The Tolsey or market house at the junction of High Street and Sheep Street. Built in 1525, it may have replaced an earlier building; nonetheless its construction reflects the town's continuing prosperity in the early 16th century.

Map 2 (opposite) Burford's streets: a simplified plan showing the town today, with key buildings marked.

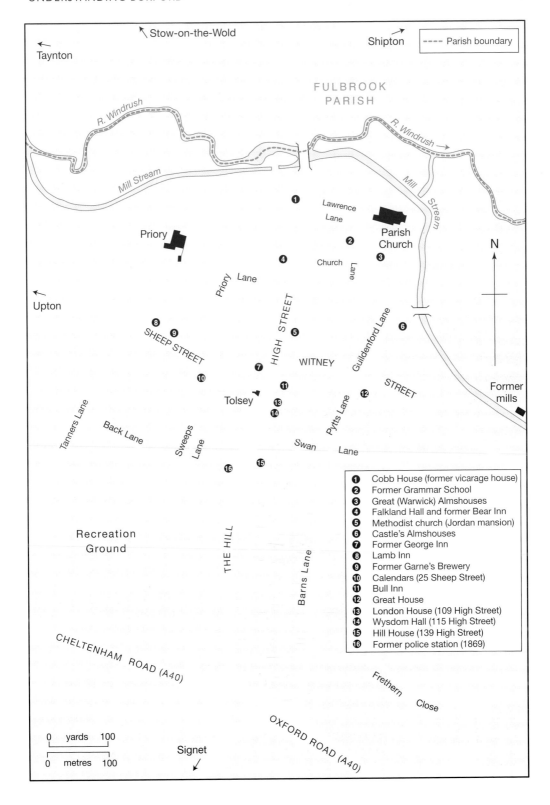

Taynton
Stow-on-the-Wold
Shipton
- - - - Parish boundary

FULBROOK
PARISH

R. Windrush

R. Windrush

Mill Stream

Mill Stream

❶
Lawrence
Lane

Priory

Parish
Church

N

❷

❹
Church
Lane

❸

Priory   Lane

Upton

HIGH STREET

❽   ❾

❺

SHEEP STREET

Guildenford Lane

❻

WITNEY

❼

STREET

Former
mills

❿

❶❶

Tolsey

❶❷

Tanners Lane

Back Lane

Sweeps
Lane

❶❸

❶❹

Pytts Lane

Swan   Lane

❶❻   ❶❺

Recreation
Ground

THE HILL

Barns Lane

❶	Cobb House (former vicarage house)
❷	Former Grammar School
❸	Great (Warwick) Almshouses
❹	Falkland Hall and former Bear Inn
❺	Methodist church (Jordan mansion)
❻	Castle's Almshouses
❼	Former George Inn
❽	Lamb Inn
❾	Former Garne's Brewery
❿	Calendars (25 Sheep Street)
❶❶	Bull Inn
❶❷	Great House
❶❸	London House (109 High Street)
❶❹	Wysdom Hall (115 High Street)
❶❺	Hill House (139 High Street)
❶❻	Former police station (1869)

CHELTENHAM   ROAD (A40)

Frethern   Close

0   yards   100

0   metres   100

Signet

OXFORD ROAD (A40)

refronted in brick, presumably to maximise its impact on travellers passing through the town. Yet, despite such improvements, the town failed to reinvent itself as a fashionable social centre, and the numerous medieval and 16th- or 17th-century buildings discovered behind remodelled façades confirm that many of Burford's inhabitants had only limited means.

From the 19th century, bypassed by a redirected turnpike road and by the railways, the town entered what must have seemed a period of terminal stagnation. Increasing numbers of labouring poor, some of them newcomers driven into the town by rural poverty, put increasing pressure on accommodation, prompting the division of many older houses into cramped cottages, and the development on back plots of the crowded cottage yards typical

Figure 5 The Mermaid on High Street is typical of Burford's complex building history. Much of it is 17th-century and later, but inside are some medieval cruck timbers. The doorway (possibly reset) is 14th-century. Its external 'Tudor' appearance is largely the result of a 20th-century remodelling.

Figure 6 Burford church from the south. Much of the visible work (including the spire and three-storey porch) is 15th-century, but 12th-century Norman window openings can be seen below the clock.

of so many small towns in this period. (Remains of a few, now smartened up and gentrified, can still be seen around the town.) A small professional element remained, and a significant proportion of the population continued to be engaged in crafts and services. But from the 1870s agricultural depression exacerbated Burford's problems, and by the First World War population had slumped and employment in traditional crafts had shrunk. Only with Burford's early 20th-century discovery by tourists, artists, and the Arts and Crafts movement did its fortunes begin, in a small way, to revive – the first stage in its transformation into the Burford of today, with its commuters and second-home owners, its clothing and antiques shops, its popular pubs, and its tourists and shoppers.

Intertwined with these developments was Burford's rich religious history, which is similarly reflected in some striking buildings. The exceptionally fine parish church, yet another manifestation of the town's medieval prosperity, formed a major focus of medieval town life, with its freestanding guild chapel (now embedded within the church) and its side altars and chantries, several of them supported by pious leading townsmen. Yet even before the Reformation Burford seems to have been a focus of new religious ideas, and from the 17th and 18th centuries several small nonconformist chapels were built, including the surviving Quaker meeting house on Pytts Lane. Most striking of all is the Methodist church on High Street, adapted around 1850 from one of the town's most imposing 18th-century houses.

PERCEPTIONS OF BURFORD

Like earlier visitors, we approach Burford's townscape with the concerns of our own age. Today we recognise that buildings can be read as historic documents: investigated to shed light on their original form and function and on their development over time. Students of vernacular architecture deal not with architect-designed houses but with the buildings of ordinary people, which have usually evolved piecemeal over centuries and whose owners' lives and motives (if they are recoverable at all) have to be teased from the buildings themselves and from a variety of obscure documents. This has been very much the approach adopted in this book.

Earlier writers, however, came to the town with different perceptions. Burford has been much described, drawn and photographed over the past two centuries, and before plunging into its history in more depth it is worth briefly surveying how it has been understood and represented in the past. Travel writers from the 16th century to the 18th, concerned primarily

Figure 7 Nos. 111-113
High Street *c*.1840:
one of several Burford
drawings by the antiquary
Sir Henry Dryden
(1818-99).

with the unusual or with grand historical landmarks, paid
it scant attention, commenting only on its large agricultural
market, the attractions of nearby horse-racing, and occasionally
on the church or The Priory, Burford's only grand country
house. By the mid-19th century the town's apparently terminal
decay was attracting less favourable comment, its houses
dismissed as 'ancient, irregular and ill-built', and the town itself
'insignificant', a place 'proverbial for its dullness'.[1]

And yet, as early as 1802, those with an eye for the picturesque
were beginning to see Burford's drift into 'languid rural torpor' as
an asset. An anonymous contributor to the *Gentleman's Magazine*
commented that he knew 'no town in this kingdom that has so
well escaped the general sweep of alteration, and where so many
ancient stone buildings (mansions) are to be found'. By 1905
Burford's seeming detachment from the modern world was
being promoted as its greatest charm: the town was 'fortunate in
having escaped the invasion of the railway', remaining 'exclusive,
select, aristocratic … It is a real pleasure to reflect upon the fate

which this venerable town has escaped'. By the 1980s this myth
of a timeless semi-rural idyll had degenerated into the typically
clichéd late 20th-century view peddled in numerous tourist guides,
setting Burford in aspic as a 'lovely old town [with] an impressive
main street lined with a series of old houses'. Perhaps surprisingly,
similar sensibilities underpinned the remodelling of many Burford
buildings during the 1920s and 1930s, playing to an early 20th-
century ideal, distantly informed by Arts and Crafts principles,
of what a 'medieval' Cotswold town *ought* to look like. Although
anathema to modern ideas about conservation, such remodellings
are an essential part of the fabric of modern Burford, part of the
centuries-old process of change, adaptation and development
which produced the town we see today.[2]

As with writers and architects so, too, with artists, who from the
early 19th century were attracted both by Burford's picturesque
charm and by its medieval buildings. Joseph Skelton's engravings in
the 1820s still concentrated on The Priory and church, but several
others recorded the townscape, among them G. Shepherd (*c.*1815),
John Chessell Buckler (1820s), Sir Henry Dryden (*c.*1840), and in
the 1890s the Oxford photographer Henry Taunt. Such images are
often a crucial source for the history of buildings which in some
cases have changed beyond recognition, although like written
descriptions they were sometimes distorted by the sensibilities of
their own time. Buckler, a practising architect deeply interested
in Gothic, is valued for the draughtsmanship and accuracy of his
topographical views, and it is surprising to find that his drawings
of some prominent Burford buildings apparently contain fanciful
reconstructions. This is an important reminder of the pitfalls
inherent in some of the evidence we regularly use (Panel 1).[3]

With the 1960s and 1970s came the first systematic examination
(by Michael Laithwaite) of Burford's vernacular buildings, the first,
too, to recognise just how complex the story is. Are the timber-
framed buildings in key locations on High Street, for instance,
the last remaining vestiges of a timber-framed medieval town, or
attempts to express status and individuality at a time when the
common building material was stone? Hidden within a collection
of academic essays, this and other perceptive observations
remained unexplored for over thirty years. Now, with vernacular
architecture well established as a discipline, we have the benefit of
studies of other medieval towns for comparison, and the detailed
building investigations carried out for this book with members
of the Oxfordshire Buildings Record. By combining this evidence
with Burford's broader history and with what we can uncover
about the lives of its townspeople, we can begin to understand the
town anew.[4]

The Mystery of Falkland Hall

Figure A   *J.C. Buckler's drawing of 1821.*

No. 42-44 High Street, now called Falkland Hall, is one of Burford's most intriguing buildings. The received story is straightforward: (1) the house was built by the clothier Edmund Silvester in 1558, as shown by a lost datestone inscribed ES 1558; (2) a drawing of 1821 by J.C. Buckler confirms the Silvester connection, and shows the house before modern changes; (3) comparing the drawing with the existing building shows how it was subsequently altered. Closer investigation has called much of this into question, illustrating the complexities of the evidence we use in unravelling building histories.

The Silvester Connection and the Datestone The earliest evidence unequivocally connecting the building with the Silvester family is Buckler's drawing, captioned 'A mansion of the Silvesters'. But Buckler must simply have been told this, and though he drew a datestone he filled it only with a squiggle. Local memory states that the datestone was reset to face inwards during early 20th-century building work, but no firm record of the inscription has been found, and early photographs are too murky to help.

Moreover, Edmund Silvester's will of 1569 mentions houses only on the other side of High Street. The location of his own 'dwelling house' is unfortunately not given, and *could* have been Falkland Hall, where a descendant held 'the Corner House' in 1594. But the family owned several other properties including an imposing timber-framed house at 109 High Street, which could equally have been where Edmund lived.

The Buckler Drawing Buckler is valued by building historians for his accurate draughtsmanship. Yet close inspection of his Falkland Hall drawing suggests that he added fanciful details. Instead of showing the 18th-century sash windows that face the street today, and which must have been there by 1821, he apparently substituted windows that he thought more appropriate to a Tudor building. Buckler was an architect who specialised in restoration of historic buildings, and tried to interpret the original designer's intentions.

The Building Investigation of the building has shown that this is not simply a 16th-century house altered after 1821 (see Gazetteer). Though some 16th-century features remain at the back, the building's façade *overlaps* the gateway to the former *Bear Inn* to the north, built in the 1640s. Whatever stood on the site of Falkland Hall must therefore have been substantially altered in the 17th century. This ties in with other building evidence, which shows that adjoining cottages on Priory Lane were remodelled to connect with Falkland Hall in the 1650s. All in all, the evidence suggests that Falkland Hall was rebuilt about that time as a lodging range for the *Bear*, with which it formed a single property in the early 19th century. The general configuration of the buildings (Figure C) supports this, and recalls a similar arrangement at the *Bull Inn* in Dorchester-on-Thames where an extension was built in 1610.

What, then, remains of the received story? In place of a 16th-century merchant's house, we have a complex multi-phase building remodelled in the 17th century as an extension to the *Bear*. Buckler's drawing is shown to have limited value as objective evidence, which calls into question his other Burford drawings: that of 25 Sheep Street (Calendars), for instance, also seems not to fit the building. Whether Edmund Silvester built or lived at Falkland Hall remains unknown – the possibility has not been ruled out, but neither can it be taken as proven.

Figure B *The existing front, showing 18th-century windows.*

Figure C *This unsigned 19th-century view of the back of Falkland Hall shows its close relationship to the* Bear Inn *(left) and Priory Lane range (right). The large stack, stair tower, and covered external stair (all now gone) fit its use as a lodging range.*

Planning Medieval Burford

Chapter 2

Figure 8 God as surveyor, measuring and designing the cosmos much as medieval planners surveyed new towns. To medieval people, planned landscapes were both hard-headedly practical and an extension of the Divine Plan.

Like many towns across England and Europe, Burford emerged not from piecemeal organic growth but from deliberate medieval planning. As such it fits into a broad range of medieval towns established by enterprising lords, bishops or monasteries, who were keen to capitalise on the expanding trade and commerce which characterised the period.

Though few medieval documents survive for this early period we can learn a great deal about the origins and growth of medieval towns from their present-day layouts, which usually retain elements from the town's earliest phases. This is the approach adopted in this chapter, which combines analysis of Burford's modern layout with a few key documents to help us understand how and when the town was created, what may have preceded it, and how it developed during the Middle Ages.

Responsibility for laying out a medieval new town seems normally to have been delegated from landowner to agent, and from the agent to a planner or surveyor who undertook the actual work. Edward I, planning his new town of Winchelsea in 1281, explicitly commissioned three men to 'plan and give dimensions for streets and lanes, and assign places suitable for a market and two churches', and similar procedures were probably followed with most new towns. The purpose of such planned development was to establish a framework within which trade and industry could flourish, and which would make the town attractive to incomers. The most common elements were a large central market area to which additional markets could be added as required; house or 'burgage' plots along the main streets; back lanes providing access to the backs of the plots, which could be redeveloped as secondary streets if demand for housing increased; a church for the spiritual well-being of the townspeople; and sometimes a residence for the lord of the manor (Map 3). But as no two medieval towns are identical, clearly there were no blueprints or pattern books: rather there was a set of general design principles adaptable to particular sites, and capable of expansion. The burgage plots themselves – long, narrow strips of land lying parallel to each other and roughly at right angles to the street – would be marked out by the planners, although construction of buildings on them was left to the owners or tenants (Panel 2). Standard measurements (usually 'perches', where one perch equals 16½ft or 5.03m) were used for the plots,

13

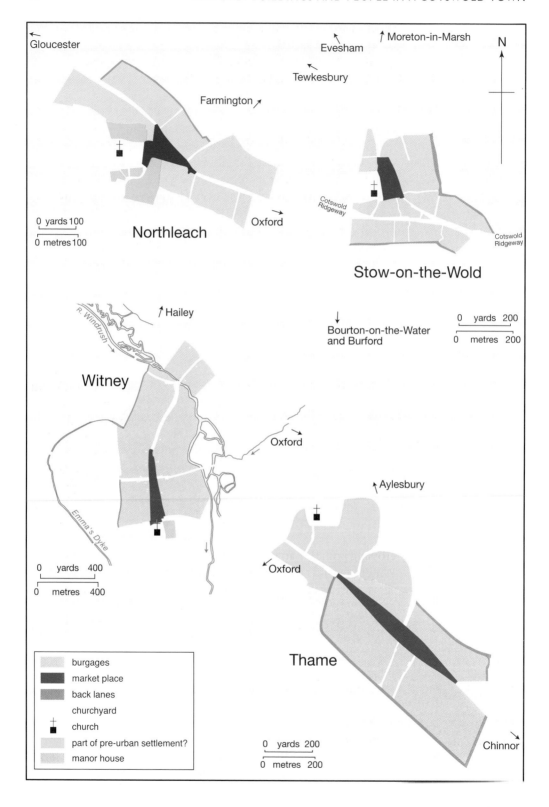

which eased the regulation of urban landholding since each could be let at standard rents.[5]

The foundation of medieval towns was thus an organised and co-ordinated process. The form of any particular town reflects decisions taken by individuals and corporate bodies, and the restrictions imposed by local geography, existing settlement or administrative boundaries. Town-plan analysis looks at the relationship between such factors, allowing the medieval planning process to be understood. Not all towns were laid out in one go, and the configuration of streets and plots in a particular part of the town will often have particular characteristics. Each such area comprises one 'plan unit', distinct from its neighbours and probably laid out at one time; each unit therefore represents a particular phase in the town's evolution. Looked at together, such units help to show which elements followed which as the town expanded.

THE ANGLO-SAXON SETTLEMENT: BURFORD BEFORE THE TOWN

Like most planned medieval towns, Burford was developed over a period. The earliest part, towards the river and church, was laid out probably in the late 11th or early 12th century, as explained below, and over the succeeding hundred years was enlarged through a series of carefully planned extensions. Few towns, however, were laid out on virgin 'green field' sites, while even those that were were constrained by geographical features. What, therefore, can we learn about the landscape or settlement which preceded the planned town?

Among the earliest and most significant features was the ford from which the town is named. Presumably it originated as a crossing point for an important north-south route over the River Windrush, and chance finds of Prehistoric and Roman material suggest it was in use from an early date. Recent excavation in the town itself points to Roman occupation in the vicinity – unsurprising given the well-attested presence of Roman farms, roads and villas in this part of west Oxfordshire – though as yet there is nothing to suggest any major settlement at Burford itself.[6]

Map 3 Planned medieval towns share common elements, particularly market areas and burgage plots. The details vary, however, as seen here at Thame and Witney in Oxfordshire, and Northleach and Stow-on-the-Wold in Gloucestershire.

For the Anglo-Saxon period we might expect to find more, since Burford's place name is of Anglo-Saxon origin. The name translates as 'ford by or leading to the *burh* (or defended enclosure)', but archaeological evidence is scanty, and the name alone does not necessarily mean there was a *burh* here by the river. It could, for instance, have referred to the important Anglo-Saxon centre at Bampton to the south-east, which would have been

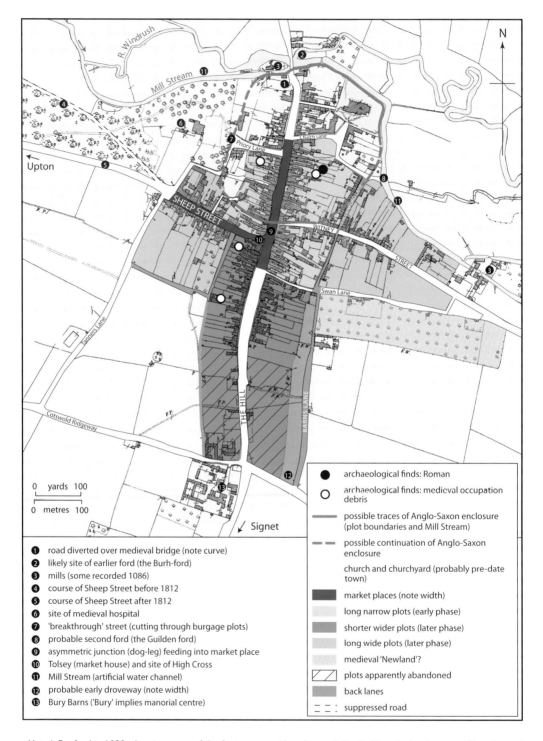

Legend:

● archaeological finds: Roman

○ archaeological finds: medieval occupation debris

— possible traces of Anglo-Saxon enclosure (plot boundaries and Mill Stream)

-- possible continuation of Anglo-Saxon enclosure

church and churchyard (probably pre-date town)

market places (note width)

long narrow plots (early phase)

shorter wider plots (later phase)

long wide plots (later phase)

medieval 'Newland'?

plots apparently abandoned

back lanes

suppressed road

❶ road diverted over medieval bridge (note curve)
❷ likely site of earlier ford (the Burh-ford)
❸ mills (some recorded 1086)
❹ course of Sheep Street before 1812
❺ course of Sheep Street after 1812
❻ site of medieval hospital
❼ 'breakthrough' street (cutting through burgage plots)
❽ probable second ford (the Guilden ford)
❾ asymmetric junction (dog-leg) feeding into market place
❿ Tolsey (market house) and site of High Cross
⓫ Mill Stream (artificial water channel)
⓬ probable early droveway (note width)
⓭ Bury Barns ('Bury' implies manorial centre)

Map 4 Burford in 1899, showing some of the features considered in analysing its historic development. Plot-size and shape, road layout, artificial watercourses, and historic or archaeological sites are all crucial to understanding how towns have evolved.

approached by the road from the ford. Analysis of Burford's layout strongly suggests, however, that there was a Saxon enclosure or *burh* on the site of the modern town (Map 5), which was probably marked by hedges, banks and ditches of which no trace now remains. Its southern boundary is preserved in the curving course of George Yard and the western end of Witney Street, while the northern and eastern boundaries may be preserved in the course of the present mill stream, an artificial watercourse of uncertain date. Fewer traces survive of the western boundary, which probably ran northwards towards the river. The main north-south route would thus have forded the Windrush and passed through the enclosure along the line of High Street, carrying travellers from the Foss Way and Banbury in the north, and continuing south on two separate routes to the ancient Thames crossings at Lechlade and Radcot.[7]

Similar enclosures elsewhere all pre-date the Norman Conquest, and as well as having defensive functions were often associated with early religious sites. Examples (some of them excavated and others, like Burford, suggested by field or plot boundaries) include Winchcombe or Bisley in Gloucestershire, Inkberrow in Worcestershire, and Bampton in Oxfordshire. At Burford, as at these other sites, the enclosure almost certainly contained an important early church, the evidence for which is discussed below. But the enclosure's size and location also point to a military function, most likely protecting the ford and the north-south route. If so it may have been constructed during the 10th century,

Map 5 The conjectural Anglo-Saxon enclosure at the north end of Burford, showing possible tofts (or house plots). These features pre-date the 11th- or 12th-century planned town.

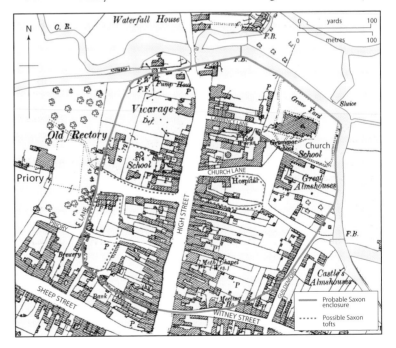

when the Anglo-Saxon kingdom of Wessex (south of the Thames) was expanding into that of Mercia to the north. Either way, the presence of a man-made enclosure indicates an Anglo-Saxon settlement of some standing. A few tofts (or house plots) associated with it appear to have been preserved in the surviving town plan, since they are of varied size and shape and are considerably larger than the burgage plots of the medieval town. Some may have been adopted as burgage plots when the planned town was established, as happened at Brewood in Staffordshire.[8]

This pre-urban settlement lay within an ancient agricultural landscape, of which other traces survive. The route preserved in the line of Barns Lane, Pytts Lane and Guildenford probably originated as a droveway down to the river from the fields south of the Burford ridgeway (now the A40). This is supported by the considerable original width of Barns Lane, which has been partly preserved in the rear boundary of the medieval plots fronting onto the east side of The Hill, and which would have helped to funnel flocks being herded down to the riverside meadows. The droveway led towards a second ford recorded at Burford, the Guildenford. Though the name does not appear in surviving documents before the mid-15th century, the crossing is likely to have originated considerably earlier, deriving its later name from the Burford 'guildsmen' (or townsmen) who owned and controlled it. The ford itself lay somewhere on Burford's eastern side, perhaps carrying travellers and their flocks across the mill stream rather than the River Windrush itself.[9]

Figure 9 Burford millstream (left) possibly began as an 11th- or 12th-century canalised watercourse, similar to those identified at Bampton, Wallingford, or Abingdon (the Swift Ditch, shown right).

The construction date of the mill stream has been controversial, with suggestions ranging from the mid-to-late 14th century to the early 18th. Comparison with similar examples, however, suggests that it is earlier than any of those dates, and that it relates to the immediate pre- or post-Conquest settlement at Burford. Recent work has shown that canal-building was a regular feature of the 11th and 12th centuries, intended to improve the navigation of particularly tortuous stretches of water. Such artificial watercourses were relatively flat-bottomed and wider than they were deep, averaging 7m in width. The Burford mill stream is of a similar scale to the canals identified at Abingdon, Wallingford and Bampton, and it may be that the section to the north and west of the church made use of the pre-existing enclosure ditch to ease its construction.[10]

Churches are not recorded in the Oxfordshire sections of Domesday Book. Nonetheless, it seems likely that the enclosure preserved in the town plan can be linked to an early church at Burford. Circumstantial evidence (discussed in Chapter 5) suggests that this may have been the site of a late Anglo-Saxon minster, a type of central church served by a group of priests and with jurisdiction over a wide area. If so, the presence of church, river crossing and defended enclosure may (as at many other early centres) have acted as a stimulus to informal trading, the most basic requirements for trade being a recognised meeting place and a set time of day at which buying and selling could take place. The presence of a predictable crowd at Burford on Sundays would have attracted pedlars and petty traders, the church and churchyard providing open spaces where business might be conducted. Many markets in England were first held on a Sunday when people met at church, and were only later moved to Saturday or weekdays under pressure from reforming churchmen. Though Burford's market was held on Saturday by 1314 it could therefore have originated as a Sunday market. Possibly there was also a livestock market outside the southern entrance to the enclosure, in the area through which Sheep Street later passed and from which it was perhaps named.[11]

CREATION OF THE MEDIEVAL TOWN

After the Norman Conquest Burford formed part of the vast estates given by William I to his half-brother Odo of Bayeux. In 1088, however, Odo rebelled against his nephew William II, and his lands were given to Robert FitzHamon, who remained loyal to the king. Some time between then and his death in 1107 FitzHamon granted the men of Burford a charter, which established a merchant guild (or corporate body), and gave them all the liberties usual when creating a new town or borough: the right to hold property for money rent instead of feudal service, the right to sell or devise property by will, the right to hold a weekly market, and other customs matching those of the men of Oxford. FitzHamon clearly recognised the possibilities offered by the proto-town he had been granted, and intended to capitalise upon them.[12]

The granting of the charter was accompanied by the planned development of the new town. The ridgeway, which ran along the high ground to the south of the settlement, was diverted to

Reconstructing Medieval Towns

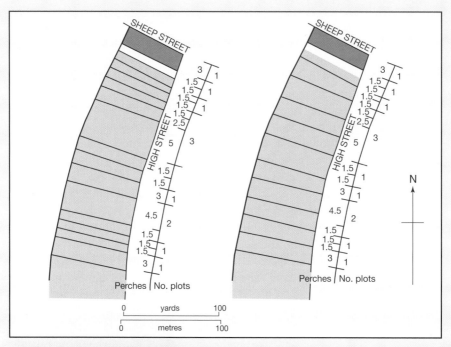

Nos. 128-132 (coloured red on the plan) still fill a complete 3-perch burgage plot. No. 134 next door (coloured yellow) was recorded as a half-burgage c.1250.

Town-plan analysis relies on the fact that the property boundaries which define urban house-plots (usually known as *burgages* in medieval towns) are extremely conservative and change very slowly. Thus, while ownership of a burgage plot might change through inheritance and purchase, and while it might be sub-divided or otherwise developed by various owners, its original, primary boundaries are unlikely to alter. This is due partly to the difficulties of moving boundaries in a built-up area without modern construction machinery, and partly to the legal rights associated with burgage tenure. Excavations in cities such as York and Southampton have shown that some plot boundaries survived unchanged for a millennium or more, carefully marked out using hedges, fences or walls.

Through examination of a town plan, therefore, the original dimensions of the burgages in various areas of a town can be determined. This involves measuring the width of each building in a plot-series to the nearest foot, with separate measurements taken for the gaps created by alleyways and post-medieval roads. The measurements are recorded onto a modern large-scale plan of the town, and analysed to see whether the distances between the primary boundaries form multiples or fractions of the statute perch of 16½ft (5.03m) – since studies have shown that burgages in planned towns were laid out according to standard measurements based on the perch. From this, it is possible to recreate the original plot-boundaries in any plan unit. At Burford, the earliest (11th- or 12th-century) plots were 1½ perches wide and between 22 and 28 perches deep (7.5 x 110-140m), while those laid out in the later 12th century were three perches wide and 14-19 perches deep (15 x 76-90m). This shows that

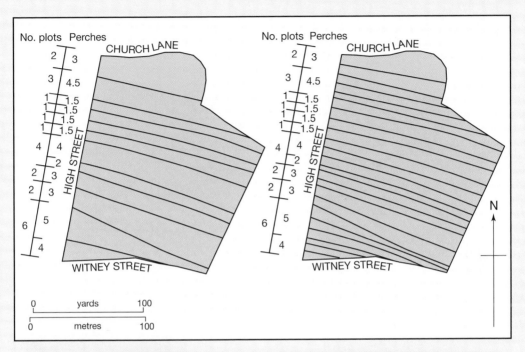

No. plots	Perches		No. plots	Perches
2	3	CHURCH LANE	2	3	CHURCH LANE
3	4.5		3	4.5
1	1.5		1	1.5
1	1.5		1	1.5
1	1.5		1	1.5
1	1.5	HIGH STREET			HIGH STREET
4	4		4	4
	2			2
2	3		2	3
2	3		2	3
6	5		6	5
	4	WITNEY STREET		4	WITNEY STREET

N

| 0 | yards | 100 |
| 0 | metres | 100 |

No. 33 High Street (coloured green on the plan) straddles two original 1½-perch plots.

Burgage plots along High Street, running south from Sheep Street (opposite page), and between Church Lane and Witney Street (above). Modern boundaries are shown on the left, and reconstructed medieval plots on the right.

The numbers show (a) the modern frontage measurement in perches, and (b) the number of medieval burgage plots which would originally have fitted into these spaces.

In the stretch shown opposite, medieval plots were three perches wide. South of Church Lane (above) they were 1½ perches.

there was a distinct and deliberate difference between the shapes of plots laid out in different periods.

In most towns, the pattern of medieval burgages was changed almost as soon as they were laid out to suit the needs of the inhabitants. At Burford it is still possible to find plots which have retained their original dimensions, as at Nos. 170-172, 188-192 and 139 High Street, all of which retain the three-perch frontage of the late 12th-century plots. However, sub-division and amalgamation of plots was common, resulting in properties such as 134 High Street (which occupies half the original three-perch plot), or 91 High Street (where the surviving five-bay medieval house has a frontage of 11m or 37ft, indicating that it was built on a site comprising one-and-a-half plots of 1½ perches each).

Analysing urban plots shows the care taken by the medieval urban planner in laying out a new town. The plots did not form areas of irregular development, but ranged along the main street frontages in a regular and ordered pattern. They did not come in a variety of shapes and sizes, but adhered to statute measurements on a scale that allowed speculative development by burgage holders, through sub-division and subletting. In addition, the wealthy could display their status through the construction of impressive houses occupying several adjoining plots.

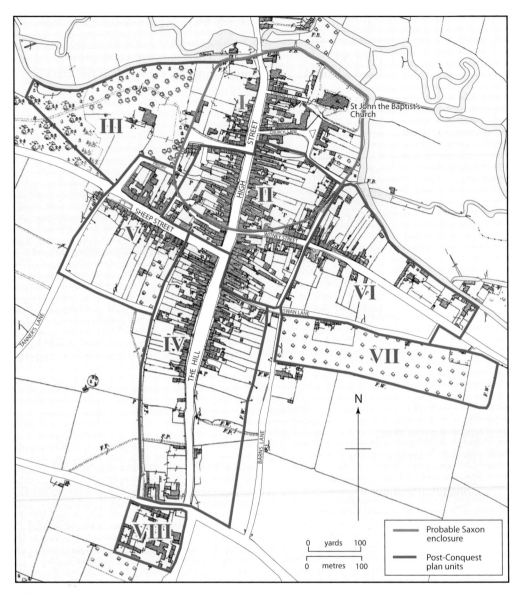

Map 6 The likely phases of Burford's medieval development, based on town-plan analysis. Phase I (the Anglo-Saxon enclosure) is the earliest, followed by Phase II (the earliest part of the planned town). Phase VII is the latest, probably early 13th-century. The site numbered VIII is Bury Barns just outside the town, centre of the lord's agricultural estate.

run down White Hill and what is now Witney Street, passing immediately south of the earlier enclosure. It then continued west along what is now Sheep Street, through Priory Woods, and back towards the ridge-line past Upton Quarries. Previous studies have shown that such diversions can often be recognised from sharp bends or 'dog-legs' in the course of a road, close to or at the point where it enters a town, which were intended to force travellers to pass through the commercial heart of the new settlement. At Burford the diverted road dog-legs across High Street, so that the junction of High Street with Sheep Street and Witney Street does not form a perfect cross-roads. The considerable width of High Street shows that it was designed to serve as the principal market place, while Sheep Street served or continued as the site of a livestock market, also demonstrated by the width of the street.[13]

Figure 10 Sheep Street's name and considerable width reflect its original use as a livestock market, probably similar to that which continued at Chipping Campden in 1895 (below).

Figure 11 This 19th-century view of High Street shows its great width, designed to accommodate markets, traders and fairs. The 16th-century Tolsey or market house, on the left, stands near the site of the medieval high cross, overseeing the medieval market area. The building beyond the Tolsey was an inn in the 15th century.

The High Cross, which in the later Middle Ages stood opposite the Tolsey in High Street, may have originated at this early date and served several functions. To travellers approaching Burford from the south it announced that they were about to enter a town (the ford and later the bridge serving a similar function on the north). It also marked the entrance to the markets in High Street and Sheep Street, perhaps acting as a point at which tolls were collected on goods brought for sale. Later it played a role in the punishment of religious heretics (Chapter 9), and presumably served other social functions. Around 1525 the cross was superseded by the Tolsey or market house, which partly blocked the entrance to Sheep Street, and which acted as a toll booth for goods being traded in the markets, as a market hall for the sale of delicate or perishable goods, and as a space where equipment used on market days might be stored, such as the pens for livestock set up in Sheep Street. In addition it served as a town lock-up, with the stocks and whipping post nearby. The High Cross survived until the end of the Civil War, when it was removed as a 'superstitious relic'.[14]

At the same time as the ridgeway was diverted, plots of specific dimensions were laid out along either side of the main street (Map 6, Plan Unit II). These early plots were long and narrow, measuring 1½ by 22-28 perches (7.5m by 110-140m). This is characteristic of early urban foundations of the late 11th or early 12th centuries, and suggests that this phase was contemporary with the granting of the Burford charter. The plots to the east of High Street were provided with back lanes now known as Guildenford and Pytts Lane, which re-used part of the existing droveway. The church, too, may have been rebuilt around the same time, reflecting the settlement's new urban status. The plots' length shows that the Anglo-Saxon enclosure had fallen out of use by the later 11th century, as they extend over the line of the defences.[15]

The next major addition was the Hospital of St John the Evangelist, built immediately west of the new town (Map 6, Plan Unit III). Medieval hospitals generally lay outside the core of the towns to which they were attached, as here at Burford where the hospital marked the western fringe of the urban area. The hospital is thought to have been founded by William, earl of Gloucester (then lord of Burford) between 1147 and 1183, although the first documentary reference is from 1226. The buildings stood on the site of the modern Priory and, before Sheep Street was altered to follow its present course in the early 19th century (Map 4), the attached grounds must have been considerably smaller than those of the house today. Probably the original line of Sheep

Figure 12 High Street from the air, looking north to the church and river. The long burgage plots running back from it are clearly visible, many with buildings now running along their length.

Street and Priory Lane marked their southern and eastern extent. Within this area lay pasture, orchards, garden plots and a large barn, while just over its southern perimeter was a late-medieval lodging house known later as Ivy House, probably now part of the *Lamb Inn*. Access to the hospital was along St John's Street (now known as Priory Lane), which leads west from High Street; before the hospital's construction this was probably an area of burgage plots, which were deliberately cut through to create this new 'breakthrough street'.[16]

LATER MEDIEVAL EXPANSION

Some earlier writers on Burford, misled by the lack of early documentary references to houses on The Hill, suggested that the medieval town ended at the junction of Sheep Street and Witney Street. Examination of the burgage plots, however, makes it clear there was another phase of planned urban development at Burford in the late 12th or early 13th century. This extended the urban area along High Street up to Bury Barns at the top of The Hill, and along Sheep Street and Witney Street (Map 6, Plan Units IV-VI). The new stretch of High Street (south of the crossroads) was as wide as the original street market, showing that it was designed as an extension to the existing market area. The new burgages on either side of The Hill were again laid out to specific dimensions: 3 by 14 perches (15m x 70m) to the west, and 3 by 19 perches (15m x 96m) to the east. The shape of these plots is therefore quite different from those of the first phase of development, reflecting the change of plot-use from semi-agricultural to entirely urban as the town developed. The new burgages were provided with back lanes to provide rear access. The lane to the west has been partially lost, while that to the east, partly preserved as Barns Lane, again made use of the existing droveway.[17]

The burgage plots along Sheep Street and Witney Street were also of specific dimensions, but were larger than those of High Street. Those fronting Sheep Street's south side measured 4 by 49 perches (20m x 149m). Those on Witney Street were also four perches wide, but as the planner had to incorporate the pre-existing mill stream their depth to the north varied from 10 to 21 perches (50m to 106m). The plots' larger size reflects their location away from the main market area in High Street and the landlord's consequent need to attract tenants, by making it possible to sub-divide and sublet the plots for a cash income. Once again, back lanes were provided for the Sheep Street plots and for those south of Witney Street, though the presence of the mill stream prevented such access for Witney Street's northern plots.

Figure 13 Burford bridge, documented from 1323 but almost certainly of earlier origin. It replaced a ford (from which Burford is named) a little further east.

The replacement of the ford by a bridge may also have taken place around this time, the curve in the northern end of High Street indicating that the ford remained in use while the bridge was being built a little further west. The earliest documentary evidence for the bridge dates from 1323, when Edward II granted the inhabitants a levy on goods carried over it to help pay for its repair. Possibly this was when the bridge was first rebuilt in stone, though it could equally mark a period of repairs to existing stonework.[18]

The final phase of medieval planned development at Burford saw the creation of a 'Newland' suburb on the town's eastern side, south of Swan Lane (Map 6, Plan Unit VII). Newlands were a distinct type of planned development, usually consisting of a single street lined with plots, and have been identified at numerous medieval small towns including Pershore, Witney and Eynsham. All those extensions have been dated to the 13th century, and there is every reason to date the Burford development to the same period. A single original plot may survive at the eastern end of the Burford Newland: if so the plots measured 9½ by 17 perches (48m by 86m), and eight would have fitted into the available space. As on the main side streets, the plots' large size was intended to encourage settlers to move into this part of the town.[19]

Map 7 'Newland' developments at Pershore (Worcs.) and Eynsham (Oxon.), both dated to the 13th century.

Unlike many medieval towns Burford had no resident lord, and therefore no manor house. In its absence Bury Barns (Map 6, Plan Unit VIII) may have played a similar role. Bury Barns was the focus

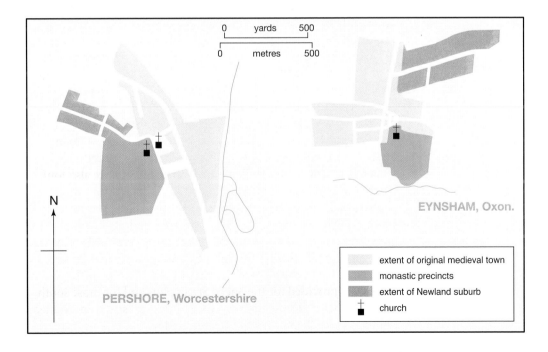

0   yards   500

0   metres   500

N

EYNSHAM, Oxon.

PERSHORE, Worcestershire

extent of original medieval town

monastic precincts

extent of Newland suburb

✝ church

of the agricultural part of Burford manor, site of the lord's barns
and the place where his officials held the manor court. It lay at the
southern extent of the town at the top of The Hill, and may have
been deliberately intended to mark the boundary between the town
and the surrounding agricultural land. Its position also suggests
an overseeing function, if only in a symbolic sense: manor officials
would have been able to 'oversee' the activities of the townspeople
below on behalf of the lord of the manor.[20]

ADAPTATION AND SHRINKAGE

Almost as soon as the burgages were laid out in different parts of
the town, they were altered to suit the needs and preferences of
their owners. 'Medial' division of plots (dividing a single plot along
its full length into halves, thirds or quarters) was commonplace,
and can be easily traced in the plots along High Street. The earliest
documentary evidence comes from 1250, when a half-burgage
plot was mentioned: this has been identified as 134 High Street,
in the part of the town laid out with three-perch wide plots in the
late 12th or early 13th century (Panel 2). The present plot does
indeed have a street frontage of 1½ perches (i.e. half the original
width); the other half of the plot lies to the south and is occupied
by part of 142 High Street. Another example of subdivision can be
seen at 166-168 High Street, whose frontage measures 11m (37ft):

Map 8 Burgage plots
were combined or
subdivided from an early
date. Those at 134 and
166-168 High Street were
divided in the Middle
Ages; Nos. 111-113
and 154-158 occupy
combined plots.

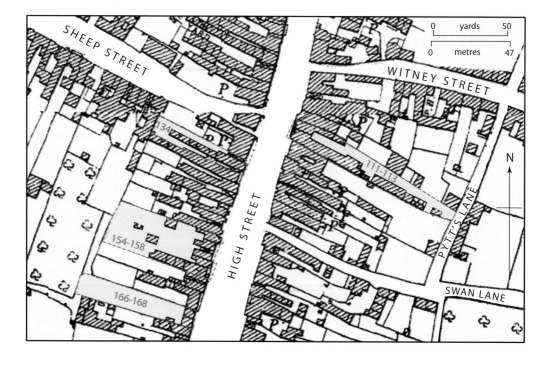

Map 9 'Medial' and 'transverse' plot subdivision: the original burgage-plot boundaries are in black, and later medieval subdivisions in red.

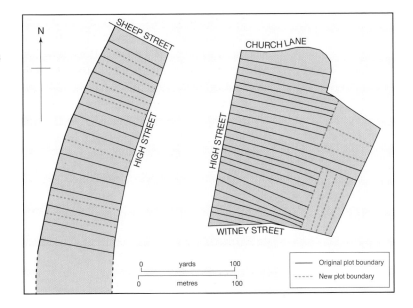

three-quarters of a three-perch plot. 'Transverse' subdivision also took place, whereby a plot was split across its width to produce two shorter plots arranged back-to-back. Most commonly it involved the earliest, extremely long plots in the town centre, allowing construction of the cottages fronting Guildenford, and creating a short series of plots on the north side of Witney Street.[21]

Wealthier inhabitants also amalgamated contiguous plots, allowing them to build much larger and more impressive houses on the street frontages. The men responsible for such relatively large-scale developments are likely to have been those involved in the wool trade, upon which much of the town's wealth was based (Chapter 3). Documentary evidence is scarce, although in 1552 John Hannes was said to own a burgage and a half apparently at 111-113 High Street, which has a frontage measuring 11 metres. Since plots in this part of the town were originally laid out with widths of 1½ perches (7.5m), a frontage of 11m would indeed have occupied one and a half burgages. Away from the market area, 154-158 The Hill originally formed a single hall-house (see Gazetteer), whose frontage was about 18m (3.75 perches) wide. In this part of the town the street frontages were originally three perches (about 15m), and it would thus appear that the property sat in the centre of a large (perhaps six-perch or 30-m.) plot formed by the amalgamation of two adjacent burgages.[22]

Plot division and amalgamation reflected not only individual fortunes, but the town's overall population and economic vitality. The size of Burford's medieval population is hard to gauge. In 1086 Domesday Book noted 43 tenants living on the manor, suggesting a total population of 200 or more, although the survey made no attempt to distinguish between urban and rural. Early 14th-century taxation lists suggest similar numbers to nearby Witney, a town which on other evidence contained 300 houses and a total population of over 1,000. Certainly, analysis of Burford's layout indicates a minimum of 143 separate plots along the main streets by the later 13th century, many of them subdivided: there could, therefore, have been well over 200 individual properties in the town, and a population of 900 or more. This seems a reasonable estimate, given that many typical 14th-century small towns had populations in the region of 500-1,000. By contrast the poll tax of 1377, some 30 years after the Europe-wide catastrophe of the Black Death, was paid by only 343 inhabitants aged over 14, suggesting a

Map 10 The likely extent of the medieval borough. Some riverside meadows may also have been included from an early date. By the 19th century those areas abandoned in the later Middle Ages had been excluded from the town, most obviously at the top of The Hill (Map 16).

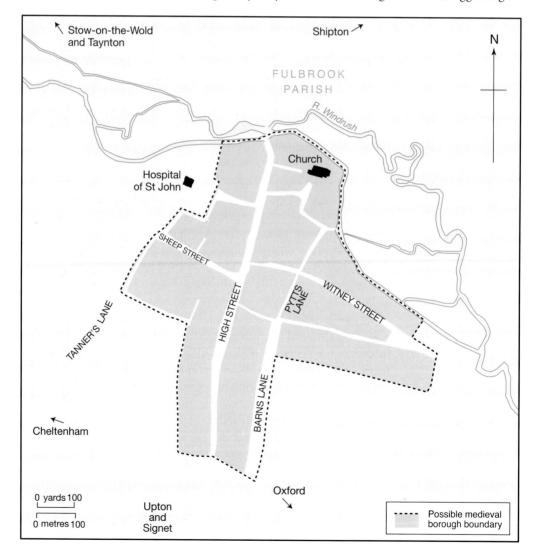

smaller population than Witney, Henley or Thame, but larger than Chipping Norton. Allowing for evasion there may by then have been around 700 inhabitants in all: a fall of well over 20 per cent, almost certainly attributable to the lasting effects of plague.[23]

As in many towns this late-medieval reduction in population was reflected in shrinkage of the occupied area, with plots farthest from the commercial heart of the town (along Sheep Street, Witney Street and The Hill) being apparently abandoned in favour of those with a more central location. The original urban plots in these abandoned areas reverted to agricultural use, surviving as closes and orchards until they were gradually built up again from the 17th century (Chapter 8). The town's shrinkage is well illustrated by changes to the medieval urban boundary. No documentary evidence survives for the line which divided the medieval urban area from the agricultural part of the manor, but almost certainly it encompassed the entire early 14th-century town, stretching from the ridgeway on the south to the river on the north, and from the Hospital of St John on the west to Witney Street mill on the east. By the time the boundary was officially mapped in the 19th century the urban area was much smaller: omitting precisely those areas (most notably the upper part of The Hill) which had been abandoned in the later 14th century. [24]

CONCLUSION

As this chapter has shown, present-day Burford emerged from a long and complex history of medieval planning and replanning, which is recoverable through the sort of painstaking analysis described above. Innumerable market towns (and indeed many villages) show similar signs of planning, which in turn reflect the sophistication of late Anglo-Saxon and medieval government and society.

But as in any age, the creation and expansion of planned towns represented a considerable risk and investment. The intention was to create a framework for trade and marketing from which both lord and traders might benefit. In the next chapter we shall look at how medieval townspeople exploited the new town's potential, and how its society and economy developed in the centuries following its creation. This in turn provides the key to understanding its surviving medieval buildings.

Chapter 3

A Medieval Wool Town

As we have seen, the creation of a planned town at Burford was undertaken for hard-headed commercial reasons. Some such ventures throve while others failed to fulfil their potential, a few planned towns becoming little more than large, predominantly agricultural villages or even disappearing altogether. Burford's physical expansion during its first hundred years suggests, however, that Robert FitzHamon's gamble was largely successful, and from the 13th and 14th centuries, with the survival of fuller documentation, we can begin to trace its economic and social development in more detail. This chapter examines the basis of the town's medieval wealth and the structure of its society, before we turn in more detail to its medieval buildings.

Until the 19th century Burford's economy, like that of most small towns, was primarily concerned with the marketing and processing of surplus produce from the countryside, and depended on regular sales and purchases by inhabitants of a clearly defined hinterland. These included gentry, clergy, and farmers, but most importantly the thousands of small tenants, wage-earners and rural artisans who sold goods and spent cash in return for manufactured goods and services. The products sold generally reflected their modest requirements, concentrating on inexpensive clothing, shoes, ironware and basic foods and drink.[25]

Alongside these everyday transactions, in the Middle Ages Burford's position at a nodal point on Oxfordshire's communication network, and at the edge of the wool-growing Cotswolds, made it an important centre in the international trade in raw wool and finished cloth. This trade attracted foreign merchants, especially Italians, to the town, generating above-average wealth for a small number of prosperous resident merchants with broader horizons than most inhabitants. The trade in wool was already an important feature of Burford's economy in the 13th and 14th centuries, although most evidence comes from the 15th century, when the export of raw wool peaked.

From the 15th century English cloth manufacture began to eclipse the sale of raw wool on a national scale. This was reflected in Burford by the presence of weavers and other clothworkers in the 16th century, and of a few wealthy clothiers involved in the retail of cloth. This phase was, however, short-lived, and by the later 16th and early 17th centuries Burford was reverting to its more traditional market functions: acting as a service and redistribution centre for the surrounding rural area, while neighbouring towns such as Witney took over its role as a manufacturing centre.

SOCIAL HIERARCHY

In the 14th century Burford was dominated by a small wealthy élite who were probably mostly merchants. Below them were less wealthy but more numerous craftsmen, artisans, and traders of varying fortunes, followed by labourers, agricultural workers and urban poor. Most evidence for the social hierarchy comes from taxation (or subsidy) records, which record the amount paid by each taxpayer based on the estimated value of their movable goods (Figure 15). Even so, many poorer inhabitants fell below the tax threshold, so that the recorded names represent only a proportion of the population. The earliest subsidy list for Burford (dating from 1316) names 57 taxpayers, and suggests that taxed wealth was relatively evenly distributed, with 70 per cent paying less than 5s. in tax. Of the rest four people paid more than twice this sum, however, with John le Napper contributing 10s., the master of the Hospital 11s. 2d., Thomas Corbet 13s. 4d. and Isabel de Clare 16s. 6d. [26]

Of the wealthy few, le Napper's surname suggests involvement in cloth production ('napping' being part of the finishing process). Isabel de Clare held Burford manor in 1316, and may have been taxed not only on town property but on agricultural stock outside it, while the same applies to the master of the Hospital. Other leading tax-payers are most likely to have been merchants, however, perhaps involved in the wool trade, participating in town government through the guild (see below),

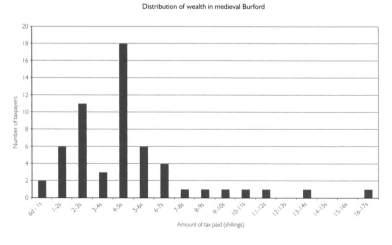

Figure 15 The distribution of wealth in medieval Burford, as reflected in the lay subsidy (or taxation) of 1316. Most people paid less than five shillings (representing goods worth £4), but a few were much wealthier. The poorest were not taxed at all.

and enriching religious life through bequests or additions
to the church. Presumably these were also the people who
accumulated building plots and commissioned high-status houses
along the main streets, although for this period little building
evidence survives.[27]

By the 15th century such people had been succeeded by better-
documented merchants such as Richard Lavington (recorded 1419-
56), William Stodham (died 1461), William Bishop (died 1485) and
John Pinnock (died 1486 or 1487), who traded in wool and luxury
goods. Their wealth is reflected in their wills. Bishop left over £700
in cash (a vast sum), plus lands and property in the town. Pinnock
left around £200 and household goods including silverware,
amber vases and tapestry bed covers, as well as tenements and
land. Clearly Pinnock's home, on a prime High Street site, was
furnished in some luxury, and it was townsmen like these who
were responsible for the flurry of late medieval rebuilding which
produced houses such as Calendars or 109 High Street (Figure 33),
as well as aggrandising the church. Yet as well as advertising their
wealth within Burford, such men had wide horizons. Many traded
through Southampton, where some of the wealthiest seem to have
maintained houses. In the early 14th century 'John of Burford' held

Figure 16 A physician
with his patient, late
14th century. The
elaborate bed hangings
and tapestries left by
some wealthy Burford
townsmen would have
been similar to those
shown here.

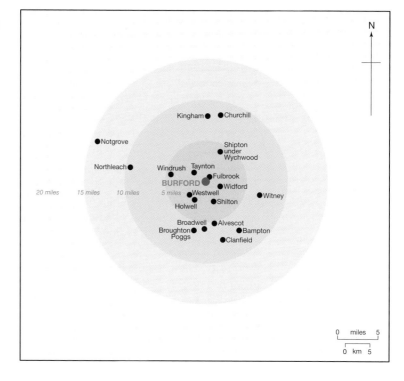

Map 11 Immigration into Burford, as indicated by medieval surnames. Most incomers seem to have come from within a narrow 10-mile radius, the same area as used Burford's medieval market.

a property in French Street there, and in the 15th century another house was said to have 'once belonged to John Pynnoc', possibly John (died 1486/7) or his father John (died 1473 or 1474), both of Burford.[28]

By contrast the vast majority of Burford's inhabitants, accommodated probably in the modest cruck cottages described below, had a narrower experience of life. Surnames derived from place of origin in 13th- to 15th-century Burford documents suggest that many townspeople came from within a 10-mile radius, the range of the town's market (Map 11). A far smaller proportion arrived from greater distances: 25-40 miles in several cases, and over 100 miles in the case of Thomas of Lincoln.[29]

MARKET, TRADE AND COMMERCE

Market, Trades and Crafts

The charter allowing Burford a weekly market, granted between 1088 and 1107, was one of the earliest market grants in Oxfordshire, and in fact the market is, as we have seen, likely to have originated much earlier. Map 12 shows the markets held around Burford in the medieval period, their market days, and the dates at which they were first recorded. As one of the oldest markets

Map 12 Medieval markets in the Burford area, showing when they were founded and the day on which they were held. As a Saturday market and one of the longest-established, Burford's market enjoyed a double advantage.

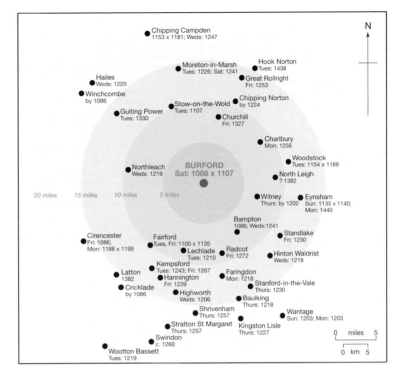

Burford was clearly at an advantage, and as the only Saturday market may have stood at the end of a market circuit. This would allow traders to sell on goods they had bought at other markets during the week, making Burford a point of sale for goods from a variety of areas including the Thames valley, the High Cotswolds, Wychwood Forest, and the farming regions of west Oxfordshire.[30]

Tradesmen were recorded sporadically in the period *c.*1250-1400, and included butchers, bakers, smiths, farriers, shoemakers and a chandler, suggesting that Burford was providing everyday goods and services to its inhabitants through the weekly market, and to its rural hinterland. In 1323 the townspeople were granted a toll on certain goods to pay for bridge repairs; listed merchandise included livestock, hides, fleeces, meats and fish, textiles and edible goods. Mid-16th-century court rolls provide comparable information about goods sold and consumed, including bread, ale, meat and fish, both fresh and preserved. The sale of fresh fish was a high-profit, high-risk trade in a period without refrigeration or rapid transport networks, and appealed to more wealthy entrepreneurs such as the 16th-century Burford merchants Simon Wisdom and Edmund Silvester.[31]

By the 16th century, fuller documentary sources enable Burford's trading hinterland to be mapped (Map 13). While this information relates only to the later medieval period, it suggests

Figure 17 Bakers at work, 15th century. Traces of similar brick-lined ovens, though much later in date, survive in some Burford buildings, for example at 35-39 High Street or in the former *Bear Inn*.

there was a well-established pattern of trade between Burford and people living within a 10-mile (16km) radius: beyond this zone other market centres predominated. But not all trade took place in the formal weekly market. Shops and semi-permanent stalls must have been part of the Burford streetscape from the town's earliest phases (Panel 3), and from the later 15th century documentary references become increasingly frequent. Some probably sold prepared food and drink: as in all towns, as inhabitants

Map 13 Burford's 16th-century market area, based on records of debts owed by or to Burford traders.

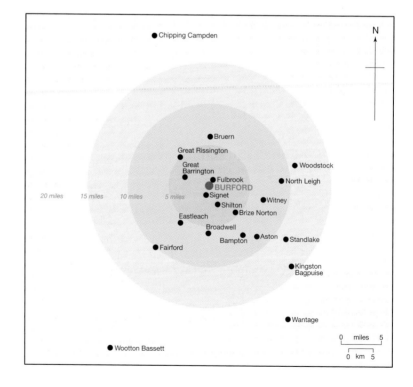

Medieval Shops

As in other towns, Burford's earliest shops were probably market stalls. Some may have stood in the centre of the street or under the Tolsey colonnade, others in front of the house where the owner worked: a craftsman or butcher, for example. Over time, such stalls became permanent structures: lock-up booths at first, then part of the main building. Fifteenth-century shops are recognisable by their wide four-centred arched windows (Figure A), which allowed display of goods and provided good light for the interior. Wooden shutters often opened upwards and downwards, the lower shutter (or 'stall-board') acting as a counter when opened.

Some evidence of such a shopfront survives in Castle's butcher's shop at 111 High Street (Figure B). The framing still includes the empty mortices and rebates of the medieval shop windows, brackets for the jetty bressumer (a long horizontal timber which would have supported the projecting first-floor jetty), and the site of hinges for shutters. Constant rebuilding has destroyed the evidence for Burford's other early shopfronts, though in the Middle Ages many of the houses in the centre probably had a shop facing the street. These would have sold the goods made or marketed by the craftsman or merchant living on the premises.

Lock-up shops also existed, and can often be found along popular routes. A pair of blocked 14th-century arches at the *George Inn* (Figure C) may once have opened to such small shops or booths: a shop and cellars there were mentioned in 1495.

Figure A *Fifteenth-century shopfront at Lavenham (Suffolk); note the typically narrow 'coffin' doorway, which increased security. Many Burford shopfronts probably looked much like this.*

Figure B *Evidence of a medieval timber shopfront inside 111 High Street. The modern shopfront is several feet forward, typical of the way many shopfronts have been progressively extended out onto the pavement.*

Figure C *Blocked 14th-century arches under the carriageway of the George Inn. Possibly they lit small lock-up shops.*

Further Reading: Clark, D R, 'The Shop Within? An Analysis of the Architectural Evidence for Medieval Shops', *Architectural History*, 43 (2000), 58-87.

concentrated increasingly on crafts and trade for their livelihoods so they were less able to produce their own food.[32]

Fairs and the Wool Trade

By the 13th century raw wool was the most important and lucrative English export, with around 30,000 sacks (the fleeces of 7¼ million sheep) exported each year. Sheep bones excavated at Burford suggest the existence of a local wool-trade by the 11th or 12th century, and Burford merchants certainly dealt in wool by the later 13th century. The scale of business is hard to quantify, but by the 14th century Burford's wool trade was evidently well established. The 1323 grant of tolls included fleeces and wool fells, and in 1378 an enquiry was held into the forestalling and regrating of wool at Burford and other Cotswold towns.[33]

Burford's annual 15-day fair was first recorded in 1323, but must have considerably pre-dated this. Medieval fairs differed from markets in the goods sold, concentrating on livestock, hides, skins, farming equipment and ironmongery, and attracting traders and visitors from far beyond the market hinterland. The date of Burford fair (24 June) allowed the town to specialise in the sale of wool, as the annual summer shearing took place immediately before. A 1403 letter to an Italian wool merchant mentioned the 'good and fine fair of Boriforte [Burford]', where the wool was 'very fine and white and better than expected'; 120 sacks of wool were purchased there before the agent moved on to the fair at Northleach, held over 29 June, at which the clip from the Gloucester Abbey flocks was sold. Henry VII granted a second fair to Burford's townspeople in 1497, to be held for seven days over the Feast of St Cross (14 September). Autumn fairs often specialised in the sale of surplus livestock not intended to be kept over the winter months, and the second fair is thus likely to have fed the town's wool and leather industries.[34]

Townsmen involved in the wool trade were variously called merchant, clothier, woolman or woolmonger, and in the 15th century included some of Burford's wealthiest inhabitants, such as Henry Bishop (recorded 1431-78) and John Pinnock father and son (recorded 1438-86). Italian and English wool buyers certainly visited Burford. In 1482 the prominent wool merchant Richard Cely of Calais wrote to his brother that he had just arrived in Northleach from Burford, while the accounts of some Italian wool merchants indicate the quantities of wool being traded by local men. In the late 15th century an agent bought over 45 sacks from William Fludgate for £425, 35 sacks from Henry Bishop, and 58½ sacks from John Pinnock, representing the fleeces of almost 33,800 sheep.[35]

Sheep and Wool Processing

'Wulle is chief tresour in this land growing' (John Lydgate, *Horse, Goose and Sheep*, c.1436-40)

Sheep farming was an important part of the Cotswolds economy by the Roman period. Medieval Cotswold sheep were a distinctive breed, producing fine white wool which was highly valued for cloth manufacture: in the 15th century, out of 50 grades of wool produced by English sheep, that of the Cotswold ranked third. Probably they were smaller than modern breeds: long-necked and fine-limbed, with short curly fleeces and a woolly forelock from which the nickname 'Cotswold Lion' derived. Certainly their fleeces weighed far less than their modern counterparts, about 1½ pounds compared with nine pounds or more. Medieval fleeces were sold by the sack, each of which weighed 364 pounds and contained the wool of some 240 sheep.

Sheep were washed and shorn in June and the wool sorted for sale. To be used for cloth manufacture it was carded and spun, either on a spindle and distaff or, from the early 14th century, on a spinning wheel. The woollen yarn produced was then woven. The earliest medieval looms were narrow, limiting the size of the finished cloth, but in the mid-13th century the broadloom was introduced, allowing cloths measuring 24 by 1¾ yards (21.9 x 1.6m) to be produced by two weavers sitting side by side. By the 15th century just over four cloths could be made from a single sack of wool, each cloth using the wool of about 50 sheep. Two cloths were equivalent in value to one sack of wool, which indicates the importance of broadcloth in the medieval economy.

Figure A *A modern Cotswold sheep. Since the medieval period the breed has developed to produce a lustrous long wool, but the characteristic forelock remains.*

Figure B *Illustration from a 15th-century manuscript, showing the various stages of wool processing: spinning on a distaff (front left), carding (front centre), combing (front right) and weaving (back).*

Figure 18 Loading ships at a quayside, 15th-century. To Burford merchants such as John Pinnock, trading through Southampton, this must have been a familiar scene.

Figure 19 Memorial brass to the Northleach woolman John Fortey (died 1458), showing a medieval Cotswold sheep under his right foot, and a wool sack under his left. Burford church may have contained similar memorials, though if so all are now lost.

In the early 15th century much of the wool sold at Burford was exported to Italy via Southampton. The destination of Burford wool before this date is unknown, although it probably left England through London or Bristol: fragments of medieval pottery from the Bristol area have been excavated at Burford, which suggests early trade links. The Southampton records do not name the individuals whose wool passed through the port, but it is tempting to think that it was dispatched by the people to whom luxury goods were transported by return, and who included several prominent Burford merchants. Some of them, as mentioned above, seem to have actually kept houses in Southampton, presumably to maintain local contacts and to keep a close eye on their businesses. The most common luxuries imported to Burford from Southampton were wine, oil, salt and dyestuffs, while other consignments included large quantities of garlic and dried or salted fish.[36]

The success of these Burford woolmen can be seen in the town's buildings: the period *c.*1450-1550 saw a significant amount of new construction, as discussed in Chapter 4. Much wool must have been stored in the town, though there is little surviving architectural evidence to suggest where. The south wing of Calendars (25 Sheep Street) could have been a wool store, and later documentary evidence includes occasional references to wool houses or storage. Nonetheless, by the 16th century national exports of raw wool were in decline, and though the wool trade seems to have continued in Burford in the early part of the century, the local manufacture and sale of woollen cloth was becoming more important. Thereafter references to woolmen in Burford records become increasingly sparse: the last mentioned was Simon Levell in 1620, and after the 17th century raw wool was seemingly unimportant.[37]

Figure 20 (left) The rear south wing of Calendars on Sheep Street, one of several structures around the town possibly used as wool stores.

Figure 21 (right) Part of the probate inventory of Susan Paty (died 1641), mentioning wool stored in her 'wood chamber' (*sic*).

Cloth Manufacture

There is evidence for cloth manufacture in Burford by *c*.1400, based on the presence of a fulling mill on Witney Street (Panel 5) and occasional references to weavers and dyers, although the size of the industry is impossible to gauge. The scale of manufacture probably increased in the mid-to-late 15th century, coinciding with a national rise in cloth exports. Woad and other dyes were regularly imported from Southampton, and packages of broadcloth were sent back by return; among them was a bale which arrived at the port in 1448/9, perhaps dispatched by John Pinnock.[38]

More evidence for cloth manufacture survives from the 16th century, by which time there had been a marked increase in the scale of manufacture. A few clothiers were operating on a grand scale, employing workers in Burford and well beyond. An exceptional example is John Jones of Burford (died 1544), who in 1538 was said to employ

> 'daily 500 of the king's subjects … Weekly need constrains him to send to Abingdon his cart laden with wool to be carded and spun or else many times his workmen should lack work, likewise he sends to Stroudwater'.

Jones's will shows that some of his workers were certainly based in Burford, as he left nine broadlooms scattered through various houses in the town. Like some other clothiers he may have leased out looms, and since he also left tuckers' shears in the fulling mill at Burford and drying racks in the nearby meadow, clearly a

Fulling and Finishing

Clooth that cometh fro the wevyng is noght
comly to were
Til it be fulled under foot or in fullyng stokkes,
Wasshen wel with water and with taseles
cracched [scratched],
Ytouked and yteynted and under taillours
hande

(William Langland, The Vision of William
concerning Piers the Plowman, written
c.1376-77)

After weaving, cloth had to be fulled to shrink and
strengthen the fabric, providing greater resistance to wear
and weather. The process originally involved immersing
the cloth in a trough filled with water and chemicals (such
as fuller's earth and urine), which helped remove any
grease or dirt, and compressing it by foot or hand. The
introduction of water-powered fulling mills in the later
12th century mechanised and speeded up the process,
with two wooden hammers replacing human effort.

Fulling shrank the cloth considerably – in the early
16th century it was accepted that a 32-yard cloth would
shrink to 25 yards – so as it dried, the fabric had to be
stretched (or tentered) on fulling racks to restore some
of the length and remove wrinkles. The matted effect
of the cloth was often enhanced by raising the nap with
teasels (since iron-toothed combs were considered too
rough), and clipping the resulting fuzz with large shears.
This process might be repeated several times, especially
for broadcloth, with the intention of giving the fabric a
silk-like sheen. Dyeing could be carried out at any stage
from washed wool to finished cloth; medieval dyes such
as madder and woad (imported by Burford merchants
in the 15th century) were vegetable-based, and so had
to be fixed with alum and other chemicals.

Burford had two water-powered mills by the time
of Domesday Book (1086), though at that date they
were used for grinding corn. One was probably near
the bridge on the site of the later Town or Port Mill;
the other was perhaps at Upton (which had a mill by
1299), or at the end of Witney Street (where a mill was
first recorded c.1400). The Witney Street mill may have
been purpose-built for fulling in the later 14th century,
and was certainly so used in the mid-16th, when the
wealthy clothier John Jones owned it. Upton Mill was
probably also adapted for fulling, and in the 1560s
was leased to the clothier Edmund Silvester. With the
decline of cloth manufacture in Burford both became
corn-grist mills, continuing in use until the 20th century.

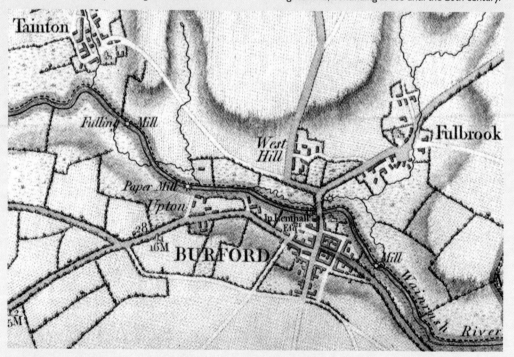

Figure A Watermills around Burford in 1797, as marked on Richard Davis's map of Oxfordshire. Witney St mill is shown east
of the town, and Upton mill (by then a paper mill) to its west. Burford town mill is marked east of the bridge. A mill further
upstream (towards Taynton) was still a fulling mill.

Figure B A 19th-century fulling mill. The large hammers or stocks for beating cloth are identical to those used in medieval water-powered fulling mills.

Figure C Nineteenth-century tenter-frames at Witney blanket mill, not far from Burford. The frames were used to stretch the cloth after fulling, and comprised two parallel horizontal bars fitted with tenterhooks, on which the cloth was hung. Medieval racks would have looked much the same.

Figure D Medieval dyers at work.

Figure E Nineteenth-century cloth shears, similar to those shown in medieval illustrations. As large and valuable items, shears were mentioned in several Burford wills.

considerable volume of cloth was being woven, fulled and finished in the town. No other Burford clothier appears to have operated on this scale, although as some local weavers left several looms they, too, perhaps ran small workshops.[39]

Other leading clothiers appear to have concentrated more on the sale of finished cloth, combining this with farming activities and investments in land and property. This is best illustrated by the will of Edmund Silvester (died 1569), who left seven properties in the town, over 52 acres of arable and meadow, the lease of Upton mill with fishing rights nearby, agricultural equipment including six cart horses, two iron-bound carts, and ploughs and harrows, and 12 quarts of barley for sowing, besides £172 in cash. Like the woolmen of the preceding century such men formed a wealthy urban élite, sharply demarcated from the bulk of the town's population in terms of wealth and possessions. Their status was further reflected in the buildings they added to the townscape. The merchant Simon Wisdom undertook considerable rebuilding around the town, including additions to his own house at 115 High Street (Figure 32), while the Silvester family has been associated with Falkland Hall (perhaps in error) and 109 High Street.[40]

Small-scale weaving continued into the 17th century, although by then local manufacture was in decline, eclipsed by the expansion of nearby Witney and the towns of the Stroudwater valleys. The decline is illustrated in the late 16th and early 17th centuries by the apprenticeship of young Burford men to Witney broadweavers: indeed what cloth production there was in 17th-century Burford may well have been largely organised and commissioned by Witney clothiers.[41]

Figure 22 No. 96 High Street was one of numerous premises remodelled by the wealthy merchant Simon Wisdom during the 16th century. His mark and the date 1578 appear over the doorway. (Decoration on the door itself dates from 1915 when this was the *Rose and Crown* inn.)

Inns and Brewing

Medieval inns provided accommodation for travellers and their horses, as well as venues for trade negotiations (see Panel 9). It is therefore not surprising that several substantial inns are documented in Burford from the early 15th century, when the wool and cloth trades were flourishing and visitors would have been arriving from across England and beyond. The *New Inn*, on the corner of High Street and Sheep Street, is documented from 1423, and seems to have been erected as a purpose-built inn *c.*1401. The *Bear* (later the *Angel*) and the *George*, both on High Street, were established by the 1480s and possibly much earlier. Despite the subsequent decline in the wool trade, the proliferation of inns continued through the 16th and 17th centuries, reflecting the continuing importance of the major east-west route through the town and the general expansion of inland trade in the late 16th century.[42]

Inns also provided food and drink, and ale was probably brewed on the premises. Smaller-scale brewing, for which no specialist equipment was needed, was undertaken by numerous townspeople in their own homes throughout the Middle Ages. Burford court rolls for 1547-9 illustrate the scale of the trade at that date, when 28 individuals were fined for brewing offences.[43]

Other Occupations

Among other trades carried out in medieval Burford was leather-working, in a variety of forms. Skins were one of the commodities in which the men of Burford were allowed to trade freely under the terms of the earliest charter, and excavated 11th- and 12th-century animal remains suggest that hides were being imported for processing. Tanning was again recorded in the 1430s. Most later-medieval leather-working was undertaken in small shops or outbuildings, and included shoemaking (recorded from 1385), glove-making (recorded from 1541), and particularly saddle-making (also recorded from 1541), for which Burford was known long after the Middle Ages. Some of the trade was on a more industrial scale, however. A new tannery was built in 1573 by William Symons, a bailiff of Burford, and in the 17th century the Silvesters ran another large tannery near the town bridge.[44]

Also important were the various building trades. Masons, glaziers, carpenters and others appear in town documents, though few are recorded before the 16th century. References to glaziers from the 1620s presumably reflect the increasing use of glass in ordinary buildings and houses, while some of Burford's higher-

Figure 23 The presence of glaziers reflected more widespread use of window glass by the 17th century, in contrast with the medieval period when it remained a luxury. Left: 15th-century mullioned window at Warwick's Almshouses, with metal casement and cross-leading. Right: an upper window at Cobb House, whose front was rebuilt in 1672.

status buildings may have been associated with specialist masons connected with Burford and Taynton quarries. Among the most eminent were Henry and Robert Janyns, who lived at Burford in the later 15th century and were master masons to Edward IV and Henry VII. Robert may have worked at Burford church, where some details of the Lady chapel show similarities to his work at St George's chapel, Windsor.[45]

Servants must have lived and worked in the town's wealthier houses and inns throughout the Middle Ages, but are almost invisible save for a few glimpses from the 16th century. Thus in 1545 William Hedges remembered six of his male servants in his will, while in 1577 William Silvester left money and clothing to his eight male and female servants, including two boys and a nurse. From just a little later comes the first evidence for professional classes servicing the town's wealthier inhabitants, among them barber surgeons or apothecaries, and attorneys such as Thomas Wright, who appeared before the Witney borough court in the early 17th century. Such men presaged a trend which was to become increasingly important in the town's later history.[46]

TOWN GOVERNMENT

The degree of self-government enjoyed by medieval towns varied considerably, depending on the rights and freedoms granted by the lord at the town's creation, and the extent to which his successors chose to interfere in town affairs. From the lord's viewpoint a balance had to be struck between making the town attractive to incomers, while still retaining some influence and maximising profits.

Market Houses and the Tolsey

Timber-framed and set on octagonal stone columns, the Tolsey is typical of a broad range of market houses, town halls, and moot- or guildhalls found in most small market towns. Tree-ring dating of its roof timbers has shown that it was built in or soon after 1525, though a similar building may well have stood here earlier.

Its primary function was as a market house – the name 'Tolsey', found particularly in the Cotswolds and Wiltshire, suggests a place where market tolls were collected, and the building overlooked the town's main medieval market area on High Street, allowing officials in the upper chamber to oversee the proceedings. Its location allowed it to face down Sheep Street as well as High Street, though in fact the building turns its back to Sheep Street: presumably by 1525 the market area there had become less significant. As with most such structures the open space beneath provided a covered area for stalls, particularly those selling products which required shelter – butter or cheese, which would deteriorate in the sun, or richer materials like silk, which needed protection from rain. A bell (added or replaced in 1651) sounded the market hours. As was commonly the case, the ground floor was later enclosed (here in the 1780s), and in 1797 housed the town's new fire engine; it was partly reopened in the 20th century. Other alterations at various dates included insertion of fireplaces and oriel windows.

Like similar structures elsewhere, the Tolsey had other uses. Town meetings may have been held in the upper chamber, and the back part housed the town lock-up, with the stocks, pillory, and 'couckinge stowle' standing outside in the 1580s. A reading room (lit by a gas chandelier) was opened here in the 1860s, and a town museum in 1960.

Figure A *The Tolsey in 1890, with the open trading area underneath blocked to house the fire engine. The large 19th-century clock underlines its public municipal functions.*

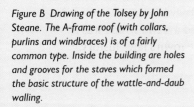

Figure B *Drawing of the Tolsey by John Steane. The A-frame roof (with collars, purlins and windbraces) is of a fairly common type. Inside the building are holes and grooves for the staves which formed the basic structure of the wattle-and-daub walling.*

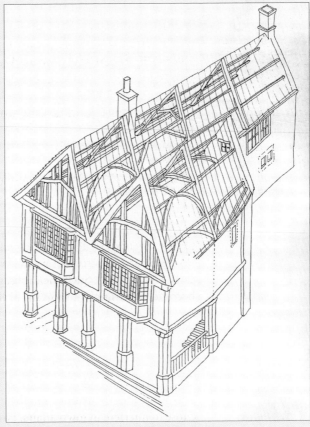

Figure 24 The former guild chapel from the south-west, remodelled and integrated with Burford church in the 15th century.

Figure 25 The guild or corporation seal was in use by *c.*1250. The 'Burford lion' was derived from Robert FitzHamon's own heraldic device; the inscription translates as 'common seal of the burgesses of Burford'.

In Burford, Robert FitzHamon gave the townspeople relatively wide-ranging rights which set them apart from the manor's 'unfree' agricultural tenants (Chapter 2). On his death in 1107 both manor and town passed to his daughter Mabel, and became, through her marriage to Henry I's illegitimate son Robert of Gloucester, a small part of his vast array of lands known as the Honour of Gloucester. As a result, Burford received little attention from its lord. There was no manor house, and no medieval lord is known to have stayed in the town, although a steward to oversee agricultural production may have been based at Bury Barns immediately to the south. Consequently Burford's inhabitants, though technically tenants, assumed increasing responsibility for the town's government, free from the lordly constraints and interference which characterised many small towns.[47]

FitzHamon's charter made provision for a town guild or assembly, perhaps acknowledging a pre-existing association of traders and artisans which had developed around the pre-Conquest market. By the later 14th century the guild comprised a distinct body of 13 to 15 townsmen (9-11 burgesses, an alderman, steward and two bailiffs). The term 'burgess' developed a specific meaning in Burford, referring only to members of the guild; men of the borough holding land by burgage tenure (the usual definition of a burgess) were simply called 'liberi tenentes' or freeholders. In the absence of a resident lord the guildsmen assumed the organisation of the market and fairs, the collection of tolls, subsidies and taxes, seizure of wrongdoers' possessions, election of town officers, holding of the town court, and the making of statutes and by-laws. Where the guild met is unknown, but may have been St Mary's chapel in the churchyard (mid-13th-century), or a building preceding the present-day Tolsey or market house (built in 1525).

Like most town guilds, the Burford guild also fulfilled religious and charitable functions. As well as funding the construction of St Mary's chapel, it employed priests to pray for its members' souls, supported members in hardship, administered lands bequeathed to guild and chapel for the support of its members and the poor, sponsored a small school in the chapel, and provided feasts and processions. Guild members bequeathed lands and properties to support such endeavours. The most conspicuous charitable act in late medieval Burford was the foundation in 1455-6 of the Great Almshouse (or Warwick Almshouses) for eight poor persons by the burgess and wool merchant Henry Bishop, under the aegis of the earl of Warwick (Figure 70). The initiative was part of a broader trend in late medieval England, which saw endowed almshouses founded in several small towns.[48]

COMMUNAL LIFE

As in most small towns, much of Burford's communal life would
have been based around the 'ritual year' of religious festivals
and associated secular activities, although in Burford these are
less well documented than for some places. The numerous side
altars, lights, chapels and chantries in the church suggest that
the townspeople experienced a rich religious life focused on the
rituals and processions common to most medieval town churches
from the later Middle Ages. Popular secular celebrations such as
May Day and Hockday must also have been marked, while the
two annual fairs would have provided further opportunities for
gatherings and merrymaking. The townsmen's right to spend
one day a year hunting in Wychwood Forest is recorded from
the later 16th century, but is likely to have originated much
earlier and was probably associated with ancient grazing rights.
Similarly, an annual Whitsun procession to Cap's Lodge in the
Forest, where there was further merrymaking, may have developed
from a medieval Church Ale, held to raise money for charitable
purposes and featuring games, entertainments, and the sale of
food and drink. The procession of the Burford Dragon (Figure

Figure 26 The annual
procession of a 'Burford
Dragon' on midsummer
eve was recorded in the
17th and 18th centuries,
and resurrected in 1971.
Possibly it developed
from a medieval guild
festival.

26) may be another medieval relict, originating perhaps from a guild-sponsored festival. Shrove Tuesday is also likely to have been marked by the ringing of the 'Pancake Bell' at midday, followed by an afternoon during which a variety of games, including football, were played. Less wholesome entertainment was afforded by numerous inns and alehouses: the 'gross drunkenness' complained of by 19th-century vicars is unlikely to have been new.[49]

CONCLUSION

The social hierarchy portrayed in the preceding pages was typical of many medieval small towns. What particularly characterised Burford, along with similar Cotswold wool towns such as Northleach or Chipping Campden, was the presence of so many wealthy merchants involved in the international wool trade and, slightly later, in cloth manufacture. Alongside them, the mix of small craftsmen and tradesmen, food and drink suppliers, and servants, labourers and poor formed part of the common fabric of medieval urban life.

Understanding the nature of Burford's medieval society is the key to understanding its earliest buildings. As we saw in the previous chapter, the physical layout of the town was the result of careful planning, designed to create an environment conducive to trade. Similarly the buildings which medieval townspeople erected, whether houses, shops, workshops or inns, reflected their means and needs and aspirations. It is to these buildings that we now turn.

Chapter 4

Medieval Secular Buildings

The medieval structures along Burford's streets grew out of the world described in the previous two chapters. As such they are also historical documents, which can be 'read' to tell us more not only about medieval town buildings, but about how Burford developed, how its townspeople lived, and how its better-off inhabitants chose to use and express their wealth.

Unravelling Burford's buildings, however, is not straightforward. The earliest survivals are often fragmentary and concealed behind later façades, while even the town's most obviously medieval houses have usually been greatly altered. Their original form and the ways in which they were used can be reconstructed only through detailed examination, underpinned by comparisons with similar buildings in other towns. For the later period, wills and probate inventories help to show how space was used and shed light on occupations, providing evidence which can sometimes be linked to particular buildings. But for the medieval period few buildings are fully documented, and both dating and function have to be deduced from the building itself, occasionally with the help of modern scientific dating methods such as dendrochronology (Panel 8).

This chapter is an attempt to understand Burford's medieval buildings. What form did the town's medieval houses take, and how were they used? What were the main building phases, and how do they relate to the town's broader history? What materials were used and why? These are just some of the questions to be asked of the buildings in any town. For Burford, intensive building investigation over several years has now provided some (but by no means all) of the answers. The building examples given below have been carefully chosen to make particular points, but are far from being exhaustive. Further details will be found in the Historical Gazetteer.

MEDIEVAL HOUSES

The Earliest Remains

A small number of Burford's medieval houses survive almost intact, albeit with major alterations and sometimes behind later façades. Nearly all date from the 15th century, however, by which

Figure 27 A Caernarvon arch, so called from its use at Caernarvon castle (1283).

Figure 28 Ballflower, a stone-carved decoration common in Gothic architecture, is found in some 14th-century Burford buildings including Bull Cottage. Its form is a flower with three (or sometimes four) petals, nearly closed over a central ball.

Figure 29 Bull Cottage (No.12 Witney Street) retains 14th-century archways, fireplaces, and decoration, all hidden behind a later, remodelled exterior.

time the town had already seen 300 years of building. For earlier periods the surviving fabric is much more fragmentary, hidden usually within later structures. Nothing remains of the town's 11th- and 12th-century houses, and perhaps the earliest identified feature is a shouldered-arched doorway in a rear outbuilding at Wychwood in Sheep Street. This is of a type often referred to as a 'Caernarvon arch', from its use in Edward I's castle at Caernarvon built in 1283.

The finest early example of medieval building is Bull Cottage in Witney Street, where a remarkable amount of fabric survives from the 14th century: arches, recesses, a fireplace, and ballflower decoration typical of the period. Ballflower can also be seen in a former doorway within a shop at Christmas Court (94 High Street), and the upper part of its cruck roof is smoke-blackened, showing that it was built as a medieval open hall. (For cruck frames and open halls see Panel 7.) In the wall between 49 and 51 High Street is a pair of ogee-headed arches, probably the doorways to the buttery and pantry of a high-status 14th-century hall house on the site, which previously extended across the two plots. There are also 14th-century two-centred stone archways at The College (behind 56 High Street), the *Mermaid* (78 High Street), *The Burford Gallery* (69 High Street), and 45 Witney Street, and inside 80 High Street, the *Swan Gallery* (127 High Street) and Glenthorne (174 The Hill).[50]

While many of these features clearly remain from earlier buildings on the site, some may have been reset. For example, a window at the rear of the front range of Hill House (139 The Hill), datable to *c.*1320, has flowing tracery of a type usually found in high-status ecclesiastical buildings. While it may have lit the dais end of a medieval open hall (Panel 7), there is no internal evidence to support this. On the other hand, there is a very fine roof over this part of Hill House, which on stylistic grounds is probably 15th-century.[51]

Perhaps more reliance can be placed on a combination of document and building evidence for the rear of the *Lamb Inn*, which along Priory Lane has a gabled range with a window of four cusped lancets, probably of the late 15th century (Gazetteer). There is a strong case that this was the 'tenement called Ivy House' listed in a rental of 1539, suggesting that the window could well be in its original place. A barn, once associated with the building, also survives in converted form.[52]

House Plans and Layout

Most medieval houses were centred on a hall open to the rafters, with private rooms (often storeyed) at one end, and an entrance and service rooms at the other. Usually the hall was heated by a central open hearth (Panel 7). Signs of such an arrangement survive at 124 High Street (Reavley's), built as the *New Inn* in 1401. The roof timbers are smoke-blackened and there is evidence of a ground-floor open hearth, where the hot stones have charred the timbers of the floor joists. As these were also joists for the cellar roof, this shows that the cellar is also medieval, and that hearths were not always built on packed-earth floors.[53]

But not everyone in medieval Burford had to put up with an open hearth. The town is notable for the number of surviving early fireplaces, although these are not always a reliable guide

Figure 30 An early 14th-century window at 139 The Hill (Hill House). Though possibly in its original position, it could equally have been reset or brought from another building. Part of the house's roof structure is 15th-century.

The Medieval House

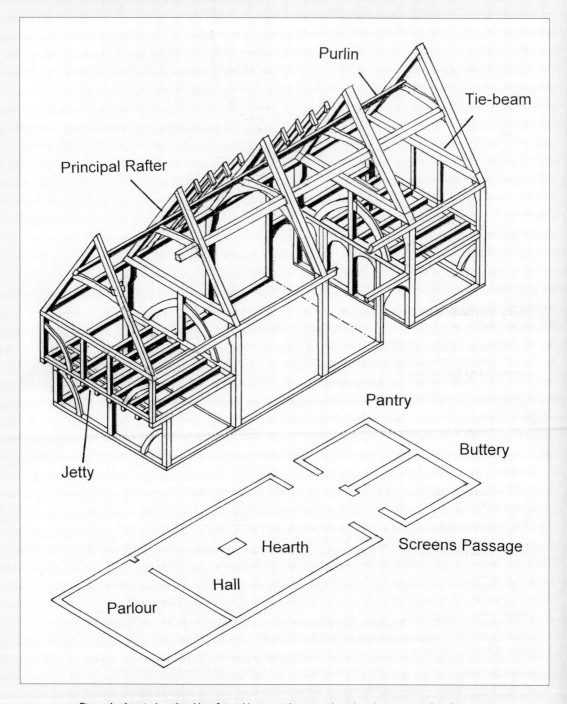

Figure A   *A typical medieval box-framed house, with an open hearth and a projecting first-floor jetty.*

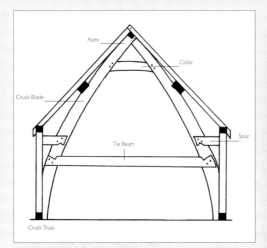

Figure B *Cross section of a cruck-framed house, showing the curved 'cruck' blades.*

The standard model of the medieval house is a three-unit plan centred on a hall, which was open to the roof and had a central hearth. Smoke rose through the thatch, depositing tell-tale soot on the roof timbers and covering. Entry was by means of a through- or screens-passage giving access to the hall and service rooms, while the parlour was a private room reached from the 'high' end of the hall. In many cases there would have been sleeping accommodation above the service rooms and parlour, reached by ladders or crude stairways. External clues to such hall-houses are off-centre doorways, tall high-end windows, and sometimes jettied wings (protruding at first-floor level) at right angles to the hall, where extra accommodation could be provided.

The hall house was the setting for a hierarchical lifestyle. The head of the household and his immediate family presided over communal meals, sitting at a 'high table', often on a raised dais, at the end of the hall furthest from the screens passage. Food was sometimes cooked on the central hearth, but in higher status households in a detached kitchen to the rear, to reduce the risk of fire and avoid unpleasant cooking smells. Dry foods were stored in the pantry (from the Norman-French 'pan' for bread) and liquids in the buttery (or bouteillerie).

In towns, houses built to this standard plan could be built on the street frontage of a burgage plot if it were wide enough. But where plots were narrow or subdivided because of pressure for space (e.g. in the central part of Burford near the Tolsey), this plan had to be modified. Some owners built a taller house, while others created space by building back along the plot. In both cases, a side passage provided light and access.

Figure C *A surviving cruck frame in Harwell (Oxfordshire).*

Structure

There are two main medieval timber-building traditions in England, the cruck and the box frame. For a box frame, carpenters hewed trees, cut and squared timbers and made the necessary joints. Numbers (usually in Roman form) were scratched on the pieces of timber so that they could be assembled in the correct way when brought to the house site for erection. The panels in the framework were then filled in, usually with wattle-and-daub. Medieval carpentry in England follows a basic 'grammar', whereby a number of two-dimensional frames fit firmly together to form a house. But there are regional differences (or 'dialects') and improvements in the joints used, which can be studied to place each building in the context of its time and locality.

In the cruck frame (found in England north and west of a line roughly from the Solent to the Wash), pairs of long curved 'cruck' blades form the trusses, and carry the weight of the roof down to ground level. The wall material can be anything which will fill in the area below the eaves. Fewer and less complex joints are found in cruck frames, but there are also some significant regional variations.

Figure 31 The first-floor fireplace at 109 High Street, a late 15th-century timber-framed house fronting the market area (Figure 35). Note the seven quatrefoils decorating the overmantel.

to dating buildings: styles continued in fashion for a long time, centuries rather than decades in some cases. An early example at 174 The Hill (Glenthorne) has a plain chamfered surround associated with a 14th-century archway. Elsewhere, three important 15th-century examples were recorded in Margaret Wood's classic book on the English medieval house. One, at Red Lion House (118-122 High Street), has a frieze of five quatrefoils, while at 109 High Street there are seven quatrefoils, with floral decorations within each. They are probably of the 1480s. There are plainer but similar openings to fireplaces at Hill House and at 4 Priory Lane. The former *Rose and Crown* (96 High Street) is one of the merchant Simon Wisdom's dated properties (1578), and has both 14th-century and 15th-century types of fireplace. Wisdom often remodelled earlier houses, and in this case probably retained existing fireplaces.[54]

A detailed study of Burford's medieval houses in the 1970s noted the remarkable number of surviving hall houses built along the front of wide plots. Such houses can be identified by their structure and plan: good examples include Hill House (139 The Hill), 154-58 The Hill, 166-168 The Hill, 188-192 The Hill, 15-17 High Street, the Golden Pheasant (91 High Street, a five-bay house), and 111-113 High Street (see Gazetteer). Some may represent amalgamations of plots by wealthy merchants, and it is striking that many are towards the town's southern edge, where space was at less of a premium and original plot sizes were larger (Chapter 2).

Nevertheless, the survival of these hall houses suggests that even in the medieval town the pressure on space was not sufficient to make plot subdivision essential. Burford has none of the large houses built sideways along the burgage plot that we find in York or Oxford, gable end to the street. Even so, space constraints in Burford's central part did sometimes force builders to adopt other plans, as at 80 High Street (*Orvis*) and 69 High Street (*The Burford Gallery*), where there were single-unit halls with side passages. Both houses were later extended to the rear, in the case of No. 80 as early as the 15th century. Off the High Street, Bull Cottage on Witney Street has a two-room plan, with a rear wing.

Some of the medieval houses had cross-wings at one end, providing accommodation on two floors. No. 154 The Hill is the remaining part of such a wing: the hall was where No. 156 is now, and No. 158 was probably the service end of the same house. The left-hand part of Hill House similarly once had a gable, and was a floored cross-wing containing a parlour with chambers above. Another house, 115 High Street, stands out as an example of a courtyard plan (Figure 32). A complex series of wings behind the

Figure 32 The medieval courtyard of 115 High Street with its timber-framed jetties, all concealed behind a grand 18th-century street front. In the 16th century the prominent merchant Simon Wisdom owned the house, and almost certainly lived there.

rebuilt façade includes 15th- and 16th-century rooms, and was almost certainly the house at the heart of Simon Wisdom's business empire in the second half of the 16th century. Larger domestic properties would have also had spaces for servants and business use, including warehousing. At 115 High Street the courtyard allowed a degree of separation of these different activities, with the hall range clearly identifiable by its high jetty and moulded bressumer (the horizontal supporting timber).[55]

Figure 33 No. 25 Sheep Street (Calendars), one of the prominent timber and stone buildings erected in late 15th-century Burford, probably for a wealthy wool merchant. The house's timbers have been dendro-dated to 1473, proving that it was all of one build.

The survival of such a wide range of 15th-century structures allows Burford to play a part in the wider study of medieval town buildings. It seems that, where possible, the medieval builder put a standard three-part hall house along the front of his plot. Over time, economic pressures meant that many of those in the centre of the town were replaced by more compact designs with side passages for rear access. To this general picture must be added the contribution of a few important townsmen who had the money to build inns and larger houses, extending well behind the street range. In these, the owner's personal inclinations may be a key to understanding the building. In the 16th century Simon Wisdom generally adapted and added to what was there before, while the builder of Calendars (25 Sheep Street) preferred in 1473 to build a complete living/working complex from scratch, and had the resources to do so.[56]

A further consequence of this constant plot-division and rebuilding was the development, possibly during the Middle Ages, of the so-called 'flying freeholds' so characteristic of Burford, where one property extends over another at first-floor level or above (e.g. 125 High Street). They can often be identified by looking at the paintwork of the windows: people don't paint their neighbours' windows. Study of the plot boundaries also shows some interlocking of buildings at ground-floor level.

STRUCTURE AND MATERIALS

The visitor to Burford may be surprised to see so much timber framing in a Cotswold town noted for its stone quarries. In the Middle Ages, builders in both traditions seemed to have worked together harmoniously. Many timber-framed buildings in Burford have stone rear walls, while some stone or rendered façades conceal earlier timber-framed structures. The high quality of the visible timber framing shows that this was not a second-class material. Indeed, in an area usually associated more with elm than with oak, sampling in preparation for this book (for tree-ring dating) uncovered a surprising number of good-quality oak roofs. Several of those have now been dated.

Timber

The student of vernacular buildings must look first at the structural system employed by the builders, rather than the 'fancy' elements possibly borrowed from elsewhere. In most buildings the roof contains important information because it is likely to be the least altered part, and often it can reveal the building's original structure.

Figure 34 Part of a raised cruck at 162 The Hill, with the elongated 'knee' found in several Burford buildings. Timbers here have been dendro-dated to 1459.

The two main medieval timber-building traditions in England were the cruck and the box frame, illustrated in Panel 7. Both are found in Burford. True crucks, where the full length of the supporting timber blade survives, are rare in the town, though examples remain in a barn behind Titcombs in Sheep Street (dated to 1571). More often, the lower part of the blade is embedded in a stone wall. Some of these may originally have been full-length crucks, which were perhaps raised later to create an upper floor for more living space. In other cases the feet of the crucks may have rotted over time, and have had to be cut off and the roof supported by a stone wall. Alternatively the house may have been built with pairs of these 'raised crucks', as at 162 The Hill (dendro-dated to 1459), the Masonic Hall behind 35 Sheep Street, and Fysshers Croft at Guildenford. The first two of these raised crucks have an unusual elongated 'knee', which seems to be a distinctive local feature of the Burford area. The wall material in such buildings can be anything which will fill in the area below the

Dating Vernacular Buildings

Vernacular buildings, constructed by local builders in local materials using local styles, have generally evolved piecemeal over centuries. Since they are not architect-designed, few leave any documentary record: even where a title deed mentions 'new building' this is often only an addition or alteration, and sometimes the phrase has been copied from earlier deeds. Maps are not usually accurate enough to provide detailed building information before the large-scale Ordnance Survey maps of the 1870s, which in any case pick up only major changes in plan. Dating vernacular buildings, therefore, relies on evidence from the building itself. This is done by finding for each building-phase a 'diagnostic' feature which can be pinned down to a particular date-range.

Stone walling, once weathered, is virtually impossible to date, but windows and window surrounds give clues – bearing in mind that, as insertions, these (like datestones) often relate to a remodelling rather than the building's 'original' construction. Fireplaces, too, are often later additions or replacements, while decorative mouldings have sometimes been reset from other buildings. Other clues are provided by plan-form. Medieval houses, for instance, usually followed a common arrangement (Panel 7), whose traces can sometimes be detected in what appear to be much later buildings. But the best way to date the original construction is through the internal roof structure. Where this remained structurally sound it was replaced less often than visible features, and can be roughly dated by comparing carpentry techniques – though as these changed slowly, particularly in country areas, the science is not precise. Timber-framed buildings can be dated by similar techniques.

Figure B *Stone-mullioned windows and dripmoulds at 27 Sheep Street suggest (with the gables) a date of c.1620. The frontage was heavily remodelled c.1907, however, and it is not fully clear how much is still original.*

Figure A *The medieval roof at 124 High Street (formerly the New Inn) survives within a later roof, which was built around it. Its structure suggests a 14th- or 15th-century date, which has now been confirmed by dendrochronology (felling date 1401).*

Figure C *The flat-headed 'Tudor' doorway of the Bay Tree Hotel on Sheep Street, part of a house built soon after 1649. The attic gables, two-room cross-passage plan, and contemporary fireplaces are other clues.*

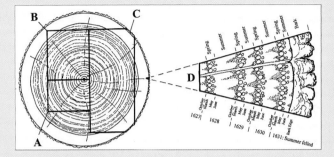

Figure D *Tree section, showing how different samples give different information. Area A will show that felling was after a particular date; B will give a felling date-range; and C a precise year. Area D (enlarged) shows the outermost rings of the sapwood, which can give the exact felling season (e.g. summer 1631). (Drawing by Dan Miles)*

Dendrochronology

These stylistic methods are subjective, since they rely on comparing recognised building features with more firmly dated examples from the same area. The greatest advance in building-dating has come from the development, over the last few decades, of scientific tree-ring dating or dendrochronology, which can provide an accurate date for when oak timbers used in a building were felled. Since timber was stockpiled only rarely in the Middle Ages, we can be fairly certain that the dates of felling are within a year or so of the date of the building.

The technique is based on the fact that each tree-ring (representing a year's growth) is of a different width, depending on growing conditions that year. Over many decades, local databases have been built up showing which growth patterns are associated with particular periods, based initially on samples taken from firmly dated buildings. A core is then taken from a timber in the building we wish to date, and the pattern of widths is compared with the database to obtain a 'best fit'. Where bark or sapwood is present an accurate dating is possible, even showing at what time of year the

tree was felled. Without sapwood, all we can say is that the tree was felled after a certain date (Figure D).

In Burford eight buildings were tree-ring dated as part of this project. The dates are given in the inset. Most broadly confirm the conclusions reached previously on stylistic grounds, though it is now known, for instance, that the front and back ranges of Calendars on Sheep Street, previously thought to represent two phases, were the result of a single building campaign in 1473.

Burford Dendrochronology (Felling) Dates

High Street:

No. 82 (roof, front)	1529-49
No. 84 (roof)	1432
No. 124 (roof)	1401
No. 162 (roof, part)	1459
Tolsey (roof)	1525

Sheep Street:

No. 25 (front and back)	1473
No. 25 (inserted floor)	1487
Titcombs (barn)	1571

Priory Lane:

No. 2 (floor)	1650

Dating by Dr Daniel Miles,
Oxford Dendrochronology Laboratory

Figure E *Calendars (25 Sheep Street), now dendro-dated to 1473.*

eaves. In Burford, where field stones are available, these may have been used with a crude mud mortar: such walls can be seen today in houses from the 17th century onwards, suggesting a continuity of the tradition. [57]

Crucks were probably a relatively common form of building in Burford in the 15th century, but the technology has serious limitations. Height is restricted by the availability of trees, and creating more space is virtually impossible without rebuilding. Consequently, the greater affluence of the late 15th and 16th centuries led to new buildings in stone or timber box-frames. The front range of Christmas Court (94 High Street) has a cruck roof, and is perhaps the only surviving single-storey example, although it now has an inserted floor.

Timber box-frames are in clear evidence in some Burford buildings. In High Street, No. 109 is three-storeyed and jettied (i.e. the upper storey protrudes beyond the ground floor), and the framing was meant to be seen. Further up on the same side, the House of Simon (No. 123) had a double-jettied front, which was under-built in the 1580s: the lower floors were extended forwards under the overhangs, creating a flat façade. The 16th-century first-floor framing is of poorer quality than the earlier work and was probably originally rendered, though the render has since been removed. Some other buildings, such as 124 and 134 High Street, have timber frames concealed behind later façades.

Most of Burford's surviving medieval buildings also have high-quality timber roof structures, featuring chamfered principal rafter trusses with collars (Panels 6 and 7). In Hill House there are two rows of chamfered purlins and wind-braces, and both there and at

Figure 35 Burford timber framing.
Left: 109 High Street, probably built *c.*1485 for a prominent merchant. Originally it had rows of windows to each upper floor, a high-status gesture at a time when glass was expensive.
Right: 123 High Street, whose original double jetty was underbuilt in the 1580s. The 16th-century first-floor timbering was probably originally rendered.

80 High Street the central hall-truss had arched braces to the collar. The roof of the *New Inn* (124 High Street), now dendro-dated to 1401, lies within a later structure, but the early roof is unusual in having king-posts (central supporting posts which run up to the roof apex) and a ridge. A similar roof survives in the Old Rectory at nearby Westwell.[58]

Timber was also used in conjunction with stone. A number of timber-framed houses on High Street have rear or gable walls of stone, while in other cases, most notably at Calendars on Sheep Street (Figure 33), both materials are used in the façade. This house has a number of unusual features, but recent dendrochronology (Panel 8) has shown that both the front range and the rear wing were built at the same time, around 1473. The decoration of the spandrels of the doorway is consistent with the date of the timber framing above. For this major construction project, timber was used on the façade for decorative purposes, as well as being the main structural material for the more utilitarian wing to the rear. Some 50 years later, stone and timber were again used together for the Tolsey, Burford's main civic building (Panel 6).[59]

Stone

But it is stone which gives Burford its special character (Panel 13). The local stone is from the Taynton Limestone Formation, a term which covers beds of varying character within the Jurassic limestones of the Great Oolite. As well as the tiny spherical ooliths (or grains) which characterise the stone, there are also beds containing shells and fossils. The stone from Upton, Windrush, Barrington and Sherborne is a fine-grained whitish freestone, and it is difficult to state with certainty the quarry from which a particular stone has come. On the other hand, the similar stone at Taynton has an orange hue, while brownish ironstone is also found to the south of Taynton. White Guiting stone has been used in a number of modern buildings in Burford. Some stones in 23 High Street (Lenthall House) and the rear ranges of Glenthorne (174 The Hill) show clear signs of reddening, characteristic of fire damage.[60]

Quarries at Burford are not mentioned in documentary records until 1435 and, of the three then operating, two produced mainly roofing slates. Nearby Taynton was producing stone much earlier. It was used at Merton College, Oxford, in 1310, and probably at Burford church. The quarry at Upton, later 'Kit's Quarry' after its owner Christopher Kempster (died 1715), was partly owned by the Hospital of St John at Burford, but probably produced ashlar for high-status buildings only. It provided stone for All Souls College, Oxford, in 1441. Roche House in Sheep Street, possibly

Figure 36 Good building stone was widely available from quarries in and around Burford. This quarry at Hanborough (photographed in 1890) lay a few miles further east, but like Burford's quarries had been worked since the Middle Ages.

built by Kempster, shows the use of this stone in the later 17th century. Some higher-status buildings used Bath stone, among them The Great House (of a similar date to Roche House) and the Methodist Church on High Street, built as a town house around 1725.[61]

Roofing Materials

Thatch was probably the commonest roofing material in the early Middle Ages, but in the 15th century (possibly following fires in thatched houses, or through greater affluence) stone slates were used. In Oxfordshire a steep roof-pitch often indicates a former thatched roof. This may be seen externally at 45 Witney Street and 80 High Street, and internal evidence at 82 High Street shows how adding timbers onto the 1430s structure flattened the roof pitch in the 17th century, probably when thatch was replaced by stone.

The stone slates which cover most roofs in Burford are called 'presents', and were quarried and split manually with picks: they are thicker than the mined and frost-split slates from Stonesfield (called 'pendles' locally). Welsh slate replaced some stone slates in the 19th or 20th centuries, and stands out now as an example of this phase of modernisation. More unfortunate was the replacement of stone slates with artificial tiles on council houses on Witney Street in the late 20th century, to prevent the hypothetical danger of falling slates.[62]

MEDIEVAL COMMERCIAL BUILDINGS

Burford's medieval economy rested largely on wool, farming, and associated trades and crafts (Chapter 3). The built evidence for such activities is fragmentary, however. No obvious examples are known of the buildings referred to as wool stores in probate inventories of the 16th and 17th centuries, but probably they were barn-like structures, and some may survive behind the buildings on the main streets. For example, to the rear of the old court house in Lavington Lane can be seen the gable end of a stone barn, which has a distinctive 'candle-flame' lancet window – fairly common in this part of the Cotswolds. Its internal cruck frame (mentioned above) has been tree-ring dated to 1571. On the opposite side of Sheep Street were a number of barns, now mostly converted into houses (the Barn House behind 27 Sheep Street as early as 1929). Others can be seen behind the *Lamb*, and in the Bay Tree car park behind Nos. 90-98 High Street. This latter building has a roof of some quality, with two rows of purlins and wind-braces.

Figure 37 The distinctive 'candle-flame' lancet window in a barn at Titcombs, on Sheep Street. The building, dendro-dated to 1571, could have been a wool store.

Medieval shops have left little trace because of constant rebuilding. The earliest recorded (in 1404) measured 17½ft by 7ft by 7ft high, and may have been a semi-permanent construction in front of a High Street building. Most cannot be located, although an example mentioned in 1580 adjoined the Tolsey or market house. Fragments of a medieval shopfront survive inside 111-113 High Street, and blocked 14th-century arches in the carriageway to the *George Inn* may have once opened to small lock-up shops or booths (Panel 3). The Tolsey itself, built in 1525, reflects the importance of Burford's market, and was strategically positioned at the junction of the main market areas in High Street and Sheep Street (Panel 6).[63]

Burford also has remains of medieval inns, where well-to-do travellers, among them the prosperous wool merchants known to have frequented the town, might spend the night (Panel 9). The earliest surviving inn building lies within 124 High Street, recently tree-ring dated to 1401. This probably resembled a large house of the period, an open hearth in the centre of the hall providing warmth to the travellers before they retired to their rooms. Little now remains of the original ground plan, but possibly it had a

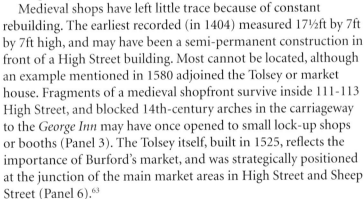

Urban Inns

As a place where the better-off traveller could spend the night, the medieval urban inn supplied accommodation of various grades, stabling, and food. Such inns were distinct from taverns, which were of no great size and were often housed in vaulted cellars such as that under 109 High Street (Figure 38). Further down the social scale were alehouses, distinguished from ordinary houses only by a sign outside (usually a bush).

Many larger inns were grouped around a courtyard entered from the street, with galleries at first-floor level giving access to the rooms: a good surviving example is the *New Inn* in Gloucester. Typically, the front range might have had dining rooms or a communal hall, with the kitchen and service rooms to the rear. Travellers' horses were stabled in the rear wings, with the sleeping accommodation in dormitories or private chambers above. As a centre of the town's social life, the inn courtyard was also a place where travelling performers could entertain the locals. On such occasions the galleries would have been packed with spectators.

Burford's earliest surviving inn building is the front part of the *New Inn* at 124 High Street (built *c*.1401). More extensive traces of courtyard layouts survive at the *George Inn*, the former *Bear Inn*, and within the later structure of the *Bull*. The best preserved is the *George*, where the gateway leads to two parallel courtyard ranges converted into cottages in the 19th century (Figure 91). A covered way linking the two wings was added about 1608: possibly it served as a viewing gallery, like that at the 14th-century *New Inn* in Oxford

Figure A *The front of the medieval George Inn. The carriageway to the courtyard dates partly from c.1300, but was heightened in the 17th century. The timber-framed range is 15th-century.*

Figure B *Part of the former courtyard gallery at the Bull Inn, now enclosed inside the building. Though the Bull is not known to have been an inn before the early 17th century, the arrangement is typical of courtyard inns generally.*

Figure C *The George, Dorchester-on-Thames: here a medieval-style open gallery still survives, giving access to upper rooms.*

(Figure D). A description in 1634 listed 25 rooms, of which at least 10 were heated and 10 were furnished with beds. Chambers with names such as the Star, the Cross Keys and the Lyon were probably on the upper floor, with the ostler's (or stableman's) chamber and storage rooms below. The *George* also has a cellar, lit by a window (now at ground level), and reached by a stone newel stairway. Though probably used for storage, it could also have been used for eating and drinking. Inns were also used for business transactions: the *Bull*, for instance, retains a large 16th- or 17th-century 'market room' at the rear.

In the 18th and early 19th centuries competition for the coaching trade affected the inns' architecture. The *Bull*'s new brick and stone façade (probably added c.1715) was no doubt aimed at making it unmistakable to the visitor arriving by coach, and the rebuilding also enabled the heights of the rooms in the street range to be increased. At the *George*, tall sash windows with thick glazing bars replaced the original windows of the jettied wing in the 18th century. But competition from railways killed coaching almost overnight, and by the later 19th century many Burford inns had closed or catered for other trades.

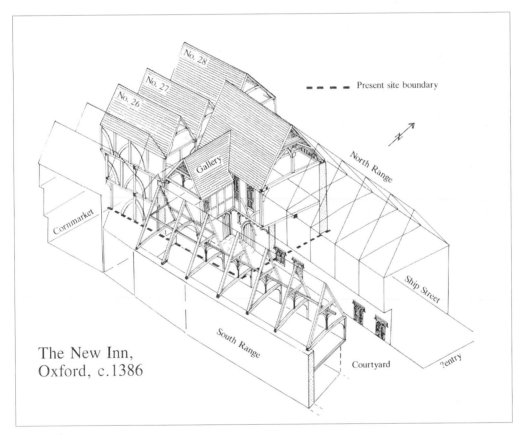

The New Inn,
Oxford, c.1386

Figure D *The New Inn in Oxford, a medieval courtyard inn built around 1386. Here the street frontage was fringed by a row of shops. In Burford, the George may have had small lock-up shops on the ground floor, marked by blocked medieval arches in the carriageway.*

Further Reading: Pantin, W A, 'Medieval Inns', in Jope E M (ed.), *Studies in Building History* (1961); Munby, J, 'Zacharias's: a 14th-Century Oxford New Inn', *Oxoniensia*, 57 (1992), 245-309 (from which Figure D is taken); Everitt, A, 'The English Urban Inn, 1560-1760', in Everitt (ed.), *Perspectives in English Urban History* (1973), 91-137.

small courtyard to the rear around which there would have been sleeping quarters, the kitchen and service rooms. Rather more survives at the *George*, a courtyard inn first mentioned in 1485. The building contains much earlier remains, however, and may have been an inn by the late 14th century, a period which seems to have witnessed a proliferation of urban inns.[64]

In some towns, meals and wine could also be obtained at a tavern. These were usually well-appointed stone vaulted undercrofts. The importance of cellars and undercrofts in the life of medieval towns can be seen in ports such as Southampton and New Winchelsea, where many were used for the storage of wine and other goods, and in Oxford where most were taverns. Of over 40 recorded cellars in Burford only one, under 109 High Street, has the architectural quality associated with tavern use, and can be dated stylistically to the last quarter of the 15th century, contemporary with the timber-framed house above. It is in two

Figure 38 The 15th-century undercroft of 109 High Street, contemporary with the timber-framed house above it. Like similar examples elsewhere, it may have been let for use as a tavern.

parts, that nearer the street comprising four bays created by arched stone vaulting springing from a central octagonal pier. Behind this is a further two-bay section, from which stone steps lead to the ground floor. In the bays are aumbries or recesses, presumably for lamps. The undercroft has been subject to a number of alterations over the years, with some of the bays partially blocked in, but seems always to have been accessible from both the street and the interior.[65]

Most of the cellars are found in the central part of the town, and as most of the properties have contained shops or inns at one time or another their presence is not unexpected. Many cellars, though lit by what seem to be 16th-century stone-mullioned windows (e.g. 112 High Street), are simple stone or brick-lined structures with a purely utilitarian aspect, and are likely to have been used for storage of goods. Some, however, have stone newel stairways, and in one case (*Antiques at the George*, 100 High Street) there is a fireplace set in the rear wall at an intermediate level, suggesting an earlier semi-basement used as a drinking room for the inn.

CONCLUSION

Some of Burford's medieval buildings remain visible for all to see, as a stroll along High Street makes clear. Closer investigation, however, has shown that far more survives in fragmentary form behind later fronts, or embedded in later buildings. Together, these structures allow us to paint a fairly broad picture of the medieval town, and to put the standing buildings in some sort of context. Examples of high-quality building in stone fit the popular conception of this as a stone-built area; yet equally striking is the amount of high-quality timber construction, some of it in oak. Wychwood Forest, like the numerous quarries, was only a few miles away, and clearly both building traditions co-existed in Burford, often within the same building. Surviving remains have also allowed us to glimpse a broad range of houses, from modest cruck cottages largely rebuilt later (as at 94 High Street) through to imposing stone or timber-framed houses built by prominent merchants. Most were arranged lengthways along the street, heated by open hearths or early fireplaces, and often had a two-storeyed cross-wing, though at least one major house (at 115 High Street) was arranged around a courtyard. The town's commercial activity is reflected not only in its surviving inns, but in the more fragmentary evidence for shops, taverns, cellars and wool stores.

The one medieval building not yet discussed, however, is to many visitors the most obvious of all, and is certainly the oldest and largest. It is to this – the parish church – that we now turn.

Chapter 5

Medieval Church and Religion

Figure 39 Burford church
from the south-east.
The tower's lower part,
with its round-headed
Norman openings, is part
of a mid-12th-century
rebuilding. Most other
visible features (including
the spire) are from
later additions and
remodellings, particularly
in the 15th century. The
former guild chapel, once
freestanding, is on the
far left.

So far we have looked exclusively at Burford's secular buildings and at the history behind them. But as with most towns or villages, by far the oldest, largest and most complex building is the parish church, its elegant 15th-century spire visible for miles around. The church's origins almost certainly pre-date the beginnings of the planned medieval town, while the building itself reflects not only changing religious practices but, as with any church, the social and economic life of the community. As with the town's secular buildings, therefore, this chapter aims to set the church in context, looking at its Anglo-Saxon origins, the religious life and organisation of the medieval town, and finally at the building itself.

BEGINNINGS: AN ANGLO-SAXON MINSTER?

The church as it exists today is predominantly a late medieval building, a series of piecemeal additions grouped around a 12th- and 13th-century core. But despite the absence of clear built evidence there was, as indicated in Chapter 2, almost certainly a church at Burford on or near the same site in the late Anglo-Saxon period. If so, it fell probably into the broad range of pre-Conquest churches called minsters, which until the 10th or 11th century were the main focus for religious organisation across much of England. Unlike later parish churches these institutions were collegiate, served by communities of priests living a semi-monastic existence. They also served large areas, sometimes covering up to 10 or more modern parishes. Some excavated minster sites comprised extensive complexes of buildings, which included at least two churches as well as associated domestic ranges.[66]

Evidence for a small and probably quite late minster at Burford is circumstantial but suggestive. Analysis of the town's layout has shown that the medieval town was apparently preceded by a late Saxon settlement by the river, set within a circular enclosure which contained the site of the existing church (Chapter 2). The settlement's location by the river may be significant: many known minsters stood by rivers, and the church's medieval dedication to St John the Baptist may reflect its early role as a local centre of baptism, covering a wide area. In the later Middle Ages Burford church was also unusually well endowed, another common

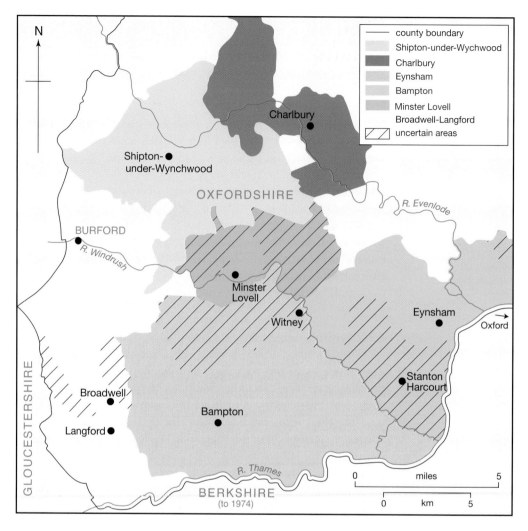

Map 14 Conjectural reconstruction of late Anglo-Saxon minster parishes in west Oxfordshire, drawing on work by John Blair. Burford lay outside the known minster parishes, and may have had mother-church status over the 'blank' area between them.

indicator of early origins. In 1291 its land and tithes were worth over £40, far more than most ordinary parish churches, and in the early 17th century its glebe (the land belonging to the church) seems to have included 200 acres or more (six yardlands), with meadow and sheep pastures. The apparently early development of a market at Burford may be further evidence, since many known minsters stimulated the growth of markets and sometimes of small proto-towns in the late Saxon period.[67]

Moreover, the existence of a minster at Burford would fit the local context. The areas dependent on other local minsters – at Charlbury, Shipton-under-Wychwood, Langford, Bampton, Minster Lovell, and Eynsham – have been partially reconstructed from a variety of sources, as shown on Map 14. This leaves a large 'blank' area around Burford, whose ecclesiastical status in the late

Saxon period is currently unknown, but which could have been subject to a church at Burford. Fulbrook, just north of the river, was certainly a chapelry of Burford in the Middle Ages, while the nearby hamlets of Upton and Signet remained part of Burford parish into modern times.[68]

Nothing is known of any minster buildings at Burford, although the church itself was apparently rebuilt in the 11th or 12th century, and was certainly replaced by a substantial Norman building in the mid-12th century. By then the earliest stages of the planned Norman town had been laid out, giving the church a new urban status. Its ecclesiastical status, however, had almost certainly dwindled to that of an ordinary parish church, with only an average sized parish and a single priest. The same fate was shared by many late Saxon minsters in the early Norman period, as the foundation of small local chapels in surrounding rural settlements slowly eroded their former jurisdiction.

VICARS AND CLERGY

Soon after 1167 the earl of Gloucester, as lord of Burford, gave the church's endowment and advowson (the right to nominate clergy) to Keynsham abbey in Somerset, which he founded and endowed around that time. Such gifts were common, both as expressions of personal piety and to augment the income of a particular religious house, which received the bulk of the church's annual income from land and tithes. As always in such circumstances, Burford was served thereafter by a vicar – a priest who, instead of receiving the church's whole income as a rector did, received only a small proportion as laid down by the bishop. All of Burford's medieval vicars were nominated by the abbey, subject (as always) to the bishop's approval.

In Burford's case the vicar's share was valued in 1291 at only £6 13s. 4d. a year, less than a fifth of the church's total income, but fairly average for most parish clergy in the area. The vicar's portion seems, however, to have been substantially increased in the later Middle Ages. By 1535 it was worth over £30, more than twice Keynsham abbey's share, and in the early 17th century it apparently included significant amounts of land: far more than that enjoyed by most rectors, and certainly more than most vicars. The vicar's portion also included a house, which was mentioned from the 13th century and stood probably on the west side of High Street, on the site of the Old Vicarage and Cobb House. Keynsham abbey retained a house nearby, which was let to tenants.[69]

Despite being served only by vicars, Burford attracted some ecclesiastical high-flyers. Among the most notable was Richard

Figure 40 A late medieval requiem mass, from a Book of Hours dated *c*.1470-80. The priest raises the consecrated host, while additional clergy (both tonsured) look on, and hooded mourners with long tapers attend the coffin. The funerals of some of Burford's wealthier inhabitants may have looked similar, with mourners thronging the church and the poor awaiting alms outside.

Chauncellor (vicar 1480-1515), who held six churches besides Burford, spread across England from the City of London to Malmesbury and Hertfordshire. Clearly such men are unlikely to have spent much, if any, time at Burford, and day-to-day care was presumably provided by assistant clergy, possibly including chantry priests and priests from the Hospital of St John (below). Little is known of them, though Chauncellor had a curate in 1512, and in the 1520s there were at least five resident clergy besides the vicar – among them curates for Burford and Fulbrook, and a chaplain paid an annual wage or stipend. In addition to this large clerical

establishment, some of the more obscure medieval vicars may have
actually lived in Burford.[70]

Vicars' relations with townspeople were not always good. In
1344 Henry Dawes of Burford took legal action against the vicar
Robert of Thornham and his chaplain, who together with other
local men had allegedly assaulted him 'so that his life was despaired
of'. Conversely, at the end of the 14th century several armed local
men set upon the vicar Walter Eymer, destroying his goods and
property in an attempt to drive him from the living and secure
the institution of their favoured candidate. Such instances, though
colourful, were nevertheless unusual, and there is no reason to
consider them typical.[71]

POPULAR RELIGION

The religious attitudes of medieval townspeople are partially
recoverable through wills leaving bequests to the church, and
through the building itself. From the late 14th century in particular,
prominent townsmen made numerous gifts for the maintenance
of side altars and of priests to serve at them, for candles or tapers,
for fittings and furnishings, and for the general beautification or
enlargement of the church – a significant indication both of the
town's wealth, based on the growing prosperity of the Cotswold
wool trade, and of the popular piety and civic pride of leading
merchants (Panel 10). Local wills mentioned no fewer than 10
side altars, dedicated to the Holy Cross, Holy Trinity, All Souls, St
Clement, St John, St Katherine, Sts Mary and Ann, St Roch (patron

Figure 41 A medieval
Candlemas procession.
The festival (on 2
February, the Purification
of the Virgin) involved
the symbolic kindling
and blessing of candles
in church, sometimes
preceded by a procession
and followed by civic
festivities.

Chantries, Obits and Altars

To medieval parishioners heaven and hell were not abstract ideas but reality, reinforced by the wall paintings which adorned most parish churches. Wealth and prestige were no safeguard against damnation: artists frequently delighted in showing merchants, kings, bishops, and even popes among the tormented souls in Hell.

Such a fate might be avoided through good works and adherence to Christian doctrine and ritual. But even so, the deceased might be condemned to centuries in Purgatory, where tainted souls were purged of their accumulated sins. Consequently, much medieval religious practice revolved around the idea of intercession. For those locked in Purgatory, masses or prayers offered on their behalf by priests or pious relatives could reduce their sentence – much as a petitioner in the living world might intercede before a judge, lord or ruler. In a debased form such beliefs led to trafficking in indulgences (respites of time in Purgatory), sold by dubious characters such as Chaucer's Pardoner.

Against this background, it was common for well-to-do parishioners to endow side altars, obits, and chantries. The 'obit' paid for a mass to be celebrated on the anniversary of a person's death, interceding for his soul. Chantry priests were paid to say regular (often daily) masses for the departed and their families over several years, and sometimes for ever; indeed some bequests financed construction of specially built altars or side chapels for this purpose, occasionally even providing a priest's house.

In Burford, as in most places, evidence for such practices takes many forms: bequests in wills, surviving brasses and inscriptions in the church, and physical

Figure A *A 15th-century soul-weighing in South Leigh church, not far from Burford. The Virgin intercedes on behalf of the souls in St Michael's scales, while the mouth of Hell gapes open.*

evidence of former chapels or altars. The primary motivation was undoubtedly religious, but social prestige played a part. Social precedence in church was as much a part of medieval life as religious ritual, and the wealthy townsmen who paid for new fittings or glass were deliberately displaying their wealth in the town's largest communal building, just as they did through their houses, furnishings, and dress.

Figure B *Part of a damaged 15th-century inscription around Burford church's south transept window, exhorting people to 'pray for the souls of the father and mother of John Leggare of Burford, by whom this window is ornamented'. Presumably Leggare paid for the window's tracery or for its glass.*

Figure C *The south-east chapel was built and endowed by John Pinnock (died c.1486), who in his will asked to be buried 'in the chapel of St Trinity, newly built at my own expense'. Pinnock left a further bequest for the chapel's upkeep, and 20d. to maintain a lighted taper in honour of the Virgin. The Pinnock family arms and a brass to an earlier John Pinnock were still in the chapel in 1574.*

From the will of Richard Bishop of Burford (1508):

To be buried by my wyf before thymage of Our Lady in the burgeyssis chappel. To ... the said chapell where my wif lyeth 20s; to the Trynitie chapell in the same church 20s.; to Seynt Kateryne chapell beyng there 6s 8d ...

I will that all my hole londes and tenementes ... be sold ... And yerely while the same money shall or may dure and contynewe, the ... corporate body of the burgeys [burgesses] to finde an honest preeste to syng at the aulter where my wif lyethe ...

Provided alway that myne executours or burgeys doo kepe myne yerely obite to the valour of 20s. as long as my preeste shall or may continewe

Figure D *Memorial brass to John (died 1437) and Alice Spicer, under the tower. The English inscription requests that the onlooker 'for charity ... pray for me to our Lord that sitteth on high, full of grace and of mercy.' The scrolls unrolling from their praying hands ask mercy from 'Mary mother maid', a common medieval invocation of the Virgin. The main inscription goes on to record the building of a new rood-loft at John's expense, 'With a lamp burning bright/To worship God both day and night'. John had also paid for a 'gabul wyndow' – possibly the existing west window, although that may be earlier in date.*

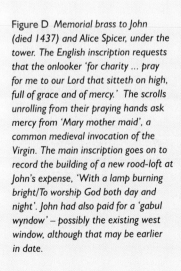

of the plague-stricken), St Stephen, and St Thomas of Canterbury. Lights or tapers were kept burning on most of them, and several included an image or statue of the saint. Eight altar locations can still be identified in the church, several of them with damaged brackets and canopy work for votive figures (small statues left as an offering to the saint). Bequests were also made for upkeep of the rood (a large image of the crucifixion suspended over the chancel arch in all medieval churches), whilst a bequest to 'the altar of Thomas Spicer' suggests a strong personal identification with the parish church.[72]

Other bequests included sums for repair of windows, bells, books and vestments, and for a chalice, in almost all cases in return for masses for the soul of the deceased. The south transept window contains an undated inscription naming its donor as John Leggare, while a merchant's mark, possibly of one of the Wisdom family, survives in re-set glass in the east window. The wholesale enlargement and partial rebuilding of the church in the 15th century must also reflect the support of wealthy townsmen. The grand south porch features the arms of the Nevilles, lords of the manor from 1449, while John Pinnock built the south-east chapel around 1485 (Panel 10). John Cakebread left 10s. in 1396 towards 'repair or improvement of the tower', probably one of a series of gifts by parishioners which allowed addition of a spire some decades later.[73]

The merchant guild's involvement in religious life was reflected in the erection of a freestanding guild chapel in the churchyard in the mid-13th century. It remained a separate building until the late 15th century when it was extended eastwards into the church, perhaps indicating a growing identification of the civic life of the town with the church. At the same time it was re-dedicated to St Mary and St Ann, to whom there had previously been an altar in the chapel. Within the church itself, a small enclosed chapel, later dedicated to St Peter, was created in connection with the building of new nave arcades. It has been suggested that enlargement of the nave and aisles may have partially blocked the view of the high altar, and that the new chapel served as a people's altar, visible from the largest possible area.[74]

Popular religious processions are unrecorded, though one was perhaps preserved in the annual parading of the 'Burford dragon' on the feast of St John the Baptist (24 June). The tradition continued into the late 18th century, and has recently been revived (Figure 26). The dragon has traditionally been associated with an apocryphal Anglo-Saxon battle near Burford, but seems more likely to have been an emblem of the town guild paraded at ceremonies (such as Whitsuntide processions) in which the guild played a role.[75]

THE MEDIEVAL PARISH CHURCH

Tucked away in what still feels like a secluded religious precinct, Burford church exerts a striking visual impact, its pinnacles, Norman tower, and slender spire towering above the flat riverside landscape. At its core is a large Norman church built for the recently established town in the mid-12th century, embedded within a variety of additions from the later Middle Ages. In both size and complexity this is clearly an urban church, its profusion of side chapels and surviving medieval decoration, even after the iconoclasm of the Reformation, evoking the wealth and popular religious piety of the medieval town.

No trace of the Anglo-Saxon church has been discovered. Inside, however, the stair turret to the existing central tower may

Figure 42 The nave of Burford church, looking east. The stair turret (on the right), with its small round-headed doorway, may survive from a late 11th- or early 12th-century building. Mid-12th-century features include round-headed Norman arches under the tower, the scars of a contemporary low-pitched roof in the wall above, and higher up a blocked Norman window, originally external. The nave arcades and upper windows (or clerestory) are 15th-century.

Figure 43 The church's west door, with its typically Norman zig-zag decoration, is from a mid-12th-century rebuilding. The window above is much later (15th-century).

Figure 44 The blocked south doorway of the former guild chapel, one of several features which confirm the chapel's 13th-century origins. The niche above contains a crucifixion.

be left over from a late 11th- or early 12th-century rebuilding, roughly contemporary with the town's creation. By the mid-12th century the town's growing success was perhaps already making the church inadequate, and the building was replaced by an impressive Norman church with a large central tower and great west door. Possibly the work was done soon after the church revenues were given to Keynsham abbey, which may have contributed to the cost. Remains of this building include the west doorway and the tower's lower part, with its Norman detailing inside and out (Figures 39 and 42). Comparison with other churches shows that the east end could have been a rounded apse, although no evidence survives either way. There may, however, have been a chamber above, since a blocked doorway in the chancel arch leads from a former wall passage in the tower.

The church was again considerably enlarged between 1200 and 1240, which roughly coincides with extensions to the planned town (Chapter 2). The chancel (beyond the tower) was extended, north and south transepts were added, and aisles were built north of the chancel and south of the nave. Dating evidence includes several distinctive 'lancet' windows (now blocked), and carved 'stiff-leaf' decoration in the south transept's west arch. A further addition was the freestanding chapel built south-west of the church by the merchant guild, the merchant body which represented Burford's wealthiest inhabitants and by then effectively ran the town (Chapter 3). Though later remodelled and brought into the church it, too, contains mid-13th-century features, including a now-blocked south doorway.

But it was during the 14th and particularly the 15th centuries, with the expansion of the Cotswold wool trade after the Black Death, that the existing church took shape, largely through addition of aisles and chapels. As a result the church's exterior is confusingly irregular, and now looks predominantly 15th-century. St Thomas's chapel was added in the late 13th or early 14th century, replacing an earlier aisle, and an altar recess in the south transept was inserted a little later. Subsequent additions were a small chapel north of the chancel, the large three-storey porch, John Pinnock's south-east chapel, and remodelling of the chancel's north aisle. The guild chapel was extended into the body of the church around 1500, when a parishioner requested burial 'in the new chapel of the Blessed Mary in the parish church of Burford': its window details are similar to those at St George's chapel, Windsor, which were probably erected by the Burford mason Robert Janyns in 1503-6. By far the greatest building campaigns, however, requiring considerable communal effort, were the heightening of the tower and addition of a spire

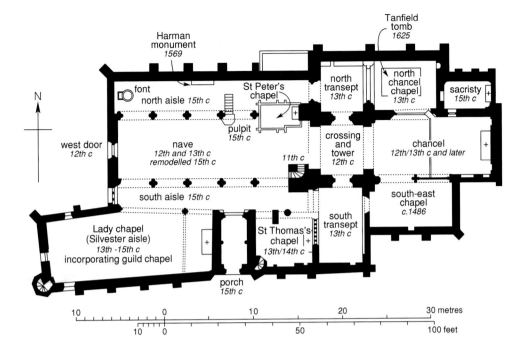

Figure 45 Ground plan of Burford church, showing its main parts with approximate dates.

in the early 15th century, and the addition around 1450 of nave arcades and a 'clerestory' of upper nave windows, bringing light flooding into the rebuilt interior. The vastly increased weight of the tower seems to have caused major structural problems, which the builders offset by partially infilling some of the arches and providing additional buttressing.[76]

Fragments of decorative painting are reminders that the whole church was probably painted with multi-coloured decorative designs and didactic images. These would have been supplemented by polychrome statues, altar lights, and above all by the great rood crucifixion over the chancel arch, to which John Spicer made bequests in 1437. All this was swept away at the Reformation, when medieval fixtures were ripped out to make way for the new Protestant religion – a story taken up in a later chapter.

THE HOSPITAL OF ST JOHN THE EVANGELIST

A final feature of Burford's medieval religious life was the Hospital of St John the Evangelist, situated on the outskirts of the town (Chapter 2). Medieval hospitals were small religious institutions catering for the poor, sick and destitute or for passing travellers, be they pilgrims, merchants, or migrants. That at Burford was most likely founded by the earl of Gloucester in the mid-12th century, and was endowed with lands in Rissington, Little Barrington (both

Figure 46 Almost the only remnant of the medieval hospital is this 13th-century arcade, embedded in the house (called The Priory) built on the site after the Dissolution. The arcade was discovered during building work in 1908, and reconstructed to form a screen; its original position within the hospital is not known.

in Gloucestershire), Asthall, and Widford. Though not particularly wealthy, it attracted some eminent clerics as master, among them the royal clerk William Doune (appointed 1389). Two other masters, William Creek and Thomas Cade, were also vicars of Burford (1453-7 and 1515-42).

How active a role the master and brethren took in the town's religious life is not clear, though some may certainly have found additional work as chantry priests, saying masses for the souls of deceased parishioners under the terms of their will. In 1322, in return for a gift of land, the hospital also undertook to find a priest to say daily masses in nearby Asthall church, for the souls of members of the Cornwall family. The foundation of the Warwick Almshouses in Burford in 1455-6 addressed many of the same charitable functions as the hospital, and perhaps hastened its decline; nevertheless it continued until the Dissolution of the monasteries under Henry VIII in 1538.[77]

Chapter 6

Burford in Transition 1500-1790

So far we have been concerned with the medieval town: its origins and planning, its economic functions, and its people and buildings. The 16th century marked something of a watershed. With the decline of the trade in raw wool, a main basis of Burford's medieval wealth was lost. Expanding cloth manufacture briefly filled the gap and generated some considerable wealth in the town, but the phase proved short-lived: by the late 16th and early 17th centuries Burford was already slipping into the role of an undistinguished market town serving its immediate locality. From the mid-17th century to the mid-18th a small malting industry flourished, and in the 18th and early 19th centuries the town became a stopping-point for coaches, reflecting the continuing importance of the east-west routes passing along Witney and Sheep Streets. But Burford failed to develop fully as a social centre, and during the 19th century the central elements of its economy were lost: the railways destroyed coaching, and agricultural depression helped undermine its market, fairs and craftworks. Only with the 20th-century development of tourism and services did it begin, in a small way, to recover and to find a new role.

As with the earlier period, the town's changing fortunes from the 16th century are a key to understanding its buildings and geography. This and the succeeding chapter explore the context in more detail, looking at Burford's changing economic role, its changing society, and the sorts of people who occupied, adapted or rebuilt the properties along its streets. The buildings themselves are explored in Chapter 8.

THE 16TH-CENTURY TOWN

From the early 16th century a variety of documents (wills, taxation records, town records, and deeds) allow us to draw a more detailed picture of Burford society than for the earlier period. Together they illustrate the continuing presence of a small, wealthy and influential minority at the top of Burford's social hierarchy, within what was still a small but growing town of perhaps 750 people. In 1523-5 five of the 10 wealthiest men in the taxation or subsidy list served as alderman, bailiff or steward in the town guild or corporation, and by 1544 this number had risen slightly to 13 of the top twenty. Burgesses (ordinary guild members) were still drawn largely from the wealthier inhabitants, though the source of their wealth was shifting. The 16th century saw a move from wool-trading to increased cloth manufacture, albeit one that proved short-lived, and by mid-century specialist wool-traders had disappeared from the governing élite. In 1566 this consisted (both officers and burgesses) of men of varied status and occupations: a gentleman, four major traders (mercer, two clothiers, a chandler), possibly three innkeepers, and a craftsman (tailor). The occupations of two burgesses are unknown.

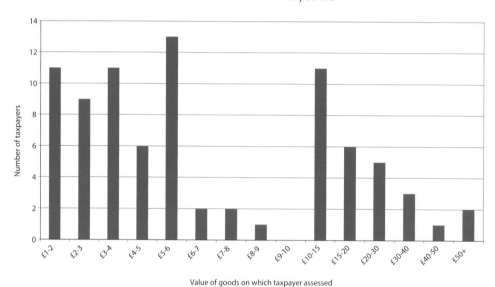

Taxable wealth in 16th-century Burford

Number of taxpayers

Value of goods on which taxpayer assessed

Figure 47 Taxable wealth in 16th-century Burford, based on the lay subsidy (or taxation list) of 1544. The two wealthiest taxpayers included the clothier John Jones.

Subsidy or taxation lists from 1523-5 and 1544 (Figure 47) indicate a modest overall increase in the proportion of wealthier inhabitants, a development which can be associated with evidence for greater comfort and literacy. In the 1520s the assessed wealth of over 85 per cent of those listed (69 names out of 81) was less than £10, with nine per cent valued at £20-£40 and one man, John Busby (died 1530), outstripping them all with possessions worth £200. Busby, about whom little is known, paid £10 in tax, almost one third of the town's total contribution. By 1544 Burford's wealthiest man was the clothier John Jones, with possessions valued at £90 – this at a time when 75 per cent of those listed had goods worth £10 or less, and only 13 per cent had £20 and more. However, as the tax was based on the value of a person's goods, the wealth of men like Robert Payne (ranked second at £50) or the mercer Simon Wisdom (ranked fourth at £35), who had invested heavily in land and property, may have been considerably underestimated.[78]

Townspeople's wills illustrate the range of living standards. The wealthy owned land and other property, bequeathed valuable household goods, and expected burial in church in the guild chapel or a side chapel. The 'middling sort' (artisans, craftsmen, husbandmen) were leaseholders, bequeathed fewer goods, and requested burial in the church. People low in the social scale left small sums of money and few household goods, and hoped for burial in the churchyard. The high living standards of the wealthy are particularly conspicuous in late 16th-century wills. Velvet, satin and fox fur were popular embellishments for clothing, while gold rings and other jewellery were frequently bequeathed. Sumptuous furnishings are also mentioned, such as silk cushions and Arras work coverlets. The clothier Edmund Silvester (died 1569) even had a spice mortar, suggestive of aristocratic trappings, while the vicar Richard Hopkins (died 1593) owned a cupboard for drinking glasses, 21 fruit dishes, a pair of virginals, and window glass. The

Figure 48 Part of the probate inventory of the vicar Richard Hopkins (died 1593), whose well-furnished house contained books, virginals, cushions and hangings, fruit dishes, and various cupboards.

modernisation of Burford's medieval building stock (Chapter 8) was no doubt led by such people, although many humbler buildings followed suit over the next century or so.[79]

The 16th century also saw rising literacy levels. Books had been available to the laity for some time: charges against local Lollard heretics in 1521, for instance, included the reading of forbidden

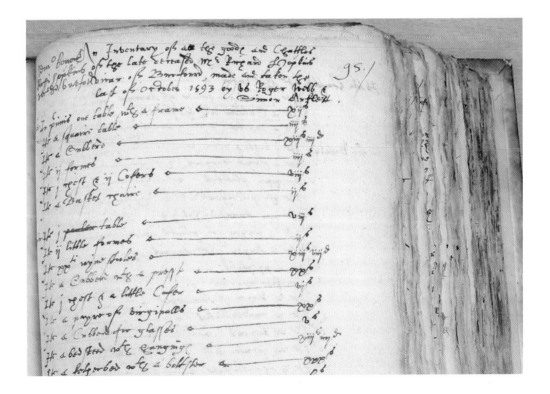

Map 15 Places from
which immigrants into
Burford are known to
have come in the 16th
century. As earlier many
were from the immediate
area, but increasing
numbers came from
further afield, particularly
Gloucestershire and the
west.

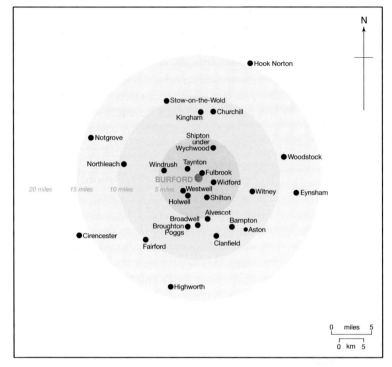

religious works. From the 1580s book ownership, as revealed by
wills, became increasingly frequent. Religious texts, especially
the Bible, were most commonly owned, but songbooks, works in
foreign languages and books on surgery also appear.[80]

Burford's population continued to include numerous
immigrants, hoping to better themselves through apprenticeship
and employment. Most migrants still came from within 10 miles
(Map 15), although the number from more distant places (such
as Solihull in Warwickshire, Cirencester in Gloucestershire, and
Wales) increased. Clearly the road from Gloucester and the
west was well used. People also left Burford, most moving short
distances while a few went to London. The main stimulus was
betterment, though some women moved upon marriage: the 1580
will of John Wilkins, for example, shows that his daughters had
married men in Clanfield and Northleach.[81]

REFORMATION AND REVOLUTION

The Reformation and Beyond

The religious impact of the Reformation, which in a few decades
swept away the elaborate paraphernalia of late medieval religious
life, is discussed in a later chapter. But in Burford, as in many

towns, the religious revolution had important social consequences too. The surrender of St John's Hospital to Crown Commissioners in 1538 opened a new chapter in Burford's history: its properties passed into secular ownership, and from 1543 belonged to Edmund Harman, barber-surgeon to Henry VIII. Harman lived chiefly at Taynton (where he was buried), but probably began conversion of the Hospital's buildings into a gentleman's residence known later as The Priory. From 1547 he was also lessee of Burford manor, thereby becoming the town's first resident lord. The immediate impact may have been limited, since Harman was already associated with Burford through his marriage to Edmund Silvester's daughter Agnes. In the succeeding century, however, the presence of a large gentry house on the town's western edge had important consequences.[82]

The Reformation affected Burford's secular life in other ways too, and in particular the guild, whose late medieval functions had included administration of lands and money given for maintenance of the guild chapel and prayers for souls. Under Edward VI (reigned 1547-53) such 'superstitions' and associated

Figure 49 Monument in Burford church to Edmund Harman (died 1577), courtier and barber-surgeon to Henry VIII, who acquired the site of the dissolved medieval hospital. The monument was erected in Harman's lifetime. The intriguing figures in the upper part were copied from pattern books, and in Harman's time may have been associated with the expanding New World (Peter Mason, *The Lives of Images* (2001), 91-100).

organisations were swept away. The Crown stripped the Burford guildsmen of many of their charity properties and rented or sold them, though the guild itself escaped dissolution; eventually the townspeople replaced many of their losses, and re-established considerable responsibility for charitable works. In 1571 the guild founded a Grammar School which it endowed partly with surviving guild properties, thereby defending them against any future appropriation. It also repurchased properties, a task largely achieved by 1599. Following these tribulations the guild reasserted its supposed position within the town by compiling (in 1605/6) the 'Ancient Ordinances … of the Corporation … of this Town and Borough of Burford'. The use of the term 'corporation' underlined that the burgesses claimed to be a lawfully constituted body, serving the town's administrative interests.[83]

Despite the Reformation's rejection of charitable works as a means to salvation, townspeople continued to make charitable provision in a humanistic spirit. The mercer Simon Wisdom endowed an almshouse on Church Lane in the 1580s, and money was bequeathed for roads, bridge and public buildings. Some individuals made direct bequests to deserving individuals: in 1586, for example, Benjamin Jones left money to 25 people including Ann Miller, the 'blind maid', 'Welsh Margaret', 'mad Joan' and 'lame Bess'. The main support for the poor, however, came from rates levied under national Poor Law legislation (from 1552), and administered by parish overseers.[84]

Burford people continued to participate in popular recreational activities, such as the annual Whitsun hunt in Wychwood and football: a presumably raucous match against Taynton in 1609 was

Figure 50 Burford Grammar School in Church Lane, founded by the guild in 1571 probably at Simon Wisdom's instigation. This drawing of 1821 pre-dates its enlargement in 1868. A plaque dated 1579 (now on the front wall) was moved here from Wisdom's almshouses nearby in the 19th century.

afterwards equated with the Trojan War. Horse racing (discussed more fully below) probably also started in the early 17th century: the earliest reference dates from 1620 when a man 'at the race' was murdered. The location of the racecourse is unknown, but was possibly on downland near Upton.[85]

Conflict and War

In the first half of the 17th century Burford became embroiled in both local and national conflict. On Edmund Harman's death in 1577 his Burford estate reverted to the Crown, and was bought in 1583 by the lawyer and politician Lawrence Tanfield (c.1551-1625). Tanfield rose to become chief baron of the Exchequer, and almost certainly undertook the rebuilding of The Priory, at which King James I was a guest in 1603. In 1617 he purchased Burford manor as well, and two years later seems to have initiated legal action against the burgesses for allegedly usurping manorial rights, namely the administration of the town, its markets and courts. The corporation lost (1621), but survived and redefined itself as administrator of the town's charities. Nonetheless in 1628 a Royal Commission, possibly influenced by Tanfield's widow, challenged the corporation's right to administer even those. The corporation successfully defended its position, though its role was initially diminished. New trustees were appointed drawn from county gentry, but they lost interest, and the corporation regained control.[86]

After Lady Tanfield's death in 1629 the Priory estate and Burford manor passed to the Tanfields' grandson Lucius Cary, Viscount Falkland. Needing money, he sold the estate and manor in 1637 to the lawyer and Parliamentarian William Lenthall, famous as

Figure 51 Burford Priory, the imposing Elizabethan mansion built probably in the 1580s by the lawyer and politician Lawrence Tanfield. The chapel (on the left) was added by William Lenthall in 1662. The house was halved in size in the 19th century (see Gazetteer).

Figure 52 Sir Lawrence Tanfield (died 1625) and his wife, depicted on a grandiose family monument in Burford church. The kneeling effigy in front depicts their grandson Lucius Cary, Lord Falkland (died 1643).

Figure 53 William Lenthall, Speaker of the House of Commons, who died at Burford Priory in 1662. The likeness is by the well known court miniaturist Samuel Cooper (died 1672).

Speaker of the House of Commons in the 1640s-50s. After the Restoration Lenthall retired to Burford, where he died in 1662.[87]

Despite Lenthall's connection, there is little evidence that the town took a Parliamentarian line in the Civil War: indeed three Burford men (David Hughes, Leonard Yates and Thomas Silvester) made loans to the Crown in 1648, possibly under duress. As elsewhere in west Oxfordshire, however, day-to-day disruption must have been considerable. Burford's location on important routes and its proximity to the royal court at Oxford gave it an unenviable strategic importance, and armies on both sides used it as a resting point. A skirmish occurred at the turn of 1642-3 when the Royalist Sir John Byron saw off a small troop of Parliamentary dragoons, and in 1644 King Charles was at Burford twice. The Parliamentarian Lord Essex also passed through the town, quartering his troops in the church. The church was again used to house troops in late 1644 and 1645, after which the churchwardens had to pay for 'making clean the church after the soldiers went away'. The most notorious incident came after the formal end of the War, with the crushing of the Leveller rising in 1649 (Panel 11).[88]

A MARKET AND COACHING TOWN, c.1630-1790

A Changing Economy

Following the decline of its wool and cloth trades Burford became primarily a centre serving its locality, providing a weekly market, annual fairs, and other retail and craft services. The only minor structural modifications to its economy arose from transport developments. In the 17th century improvements to

Burford and the Levellers

Fred Roe.

Figure A *Graffito carved into the font by Anthony Sedley,
one of the Leveller mutineers imprisoned in Burford church
in May 1649. Sedley was among those set free.*

By May 1649 the Parliamentarians had won the Civil War and Charles I had been executed, but political and religious debate continued. Most radical were the Levellers, a loose group of agitators advocating free speech, complete religious freedom, and the right of every free man to vote. They were particularly strong in Cromwell's army, where discontent was fuelled by mounting pay arrears, and by rumours that a regiment would be sent to Ireland without pay.

As the pay issue dragged on, three regiments in different places mutinied and set out to join together, quartering, by chance, at Burford on Sunday 13 May. Meanwhile Cromwell and Lord Fairfax had set out from Andover to intercept the rebels. Arriving at Burford in the middle of the night, the two commanders stormed the town. Many mutineers fled, a few tried to hold out in the *Crown* on High Street (where one man was killed), and the remainder, about 340 in total, were captured and imprisoned in the church. Four were condemned to death, and on Thursday 17th were brought from the church, one at a time, to be shot against the churchyard wall, as the remaining prisoners watched from the church roof. The parish register notes the burial of three of them; the fourth received a last-minute reprieve, and was forced to preach to his fellows and publish a pamphlet condemning the mutiny. Cromwell and his men departed, leaving the churchwardens to repair the leads of the roof, and to pay for the church to be cleansed.

The Levellers' radical agenda had far-reaching influence, still celebrated by those on the political Left. Since 1975 the mutineers have been commemorated at Burford Levellers Day, held on the Saturday nearest the day of the executions and marked by a procession through the town and topical speeches in the church.

Figure B *Levellers Day 2004: members
of the Workers' Educational Association
parade along Burford High Street, led
by marchers in 17th-century pikemen's
costume. (Courtesy of Newsquest
Oxfordshire).*

the River Thames apparently stimulated the development of a small malting industry, and in the 18th century the expansion of coaching services through the town helped stimulate victualling and innkeeping. It is difficult to trace short-term trends, but the continuation of most trades, together with a significant population increase to well over a thousand by 1800, suggests that Burford was modestly prosperous.[89]

Burford's long-established Saturday market remained a vigorous trading occasion, reinforcing the long-established relationships between town and hinterland, and agriculture and trade. The market was described in 1673 as well frequented, and over a century later, in 1805, as a large market. The principal traded commodity was corn, but livestock was also traded, notably sheep, cows, other cattle, and horses: in 1782 the market was said to be one of the best cattle-markets in Oxfordshire. Likewise Burford's two annual fairs, both of medieval origin, endured throughout the period, continuing to be held on 25 June and 14 September (changed to 5 July and 25 September in 1752-3 following Britain's

Figure 54 Burford's annual hiring fair, established by 1728, continued through the 19th century, as shown in this photograph of 1895 taken on Sheep Street outside Garne's Brewery and the *Lamb Inn*.

adoption of the Gregorian Calendar). Like the weekly market the fairs were trading centres for corn and livestock, though cheese and toys were also significant. By 1728 a separate hiring fair (for employment of agricultural workers) had been started, held close to the autumn fair, and from 1785 an extra fair was held on the last Saturday in April, its attractions including a public ox-roasting.[90]

Burford's working population included a few major traders (importers and retailers of goods), numerous craftsmen, and a few professional men. There must also have been labourers and agricultural workers, but they are largely undocumented. In the late 17th and 18th centuries the principal major traders were mercers (sellers of various goods unobtainable locally, such as cloth, thread, paper, spice and metal), with probably about four in business at any one time. Some businesses continued across extensive periods at the same premises, though under different operators: 115 High Street, for example (former home of Simon Wisdom) was occupied by the mercers Francis Keble in the mid-1680s, Richard Whitehall in the 1720s-30s, and John Patten in the 1750s-80s. No. 109 High Street (London House) was occupied by Timothy Abraham, probably a mercer, in the 1730s, and was still a mercer's shop in 1790. A similar number of traders were chandlers and tallow-chandlers (or candle-makers): the chandler Thomas Choules, for example, who left Burford in 1764, occupied premises south of the Tolsey in the heart of the town, at 128 or 128-132 High Street. From the mid-17th century until the 1770s a few other substantial Burford men were still designated as clothiers, including Paul Silvester (who occupied a substantial house in 1662), and John Payton (who leased 12 Witney Street in the 1660s-70s). By now, however, such clothiers were probably merely traders and retailers of cloth.[91]

Crafts included many practised from the Middle Ages, although there was no large-scale specialist industry. Craftsmen included bakers, clothworkers, tailors, leatherworkers, metalworkers, and building workers (e.g. masons). Leather working was prominent. The main source of leather probably remained the tannery by the town bridge, which members of the Silvester family ran until Paul Silvester went bankrupt in 1781. When the business was sold in 1811 its scale was considerable: there were 156 tan pits, a glue pit, bark house and bark mill. Leatherworkers included several shoemakers (called cordwainers), one or two saddlers, and collarmakers (makers of horse collars). In the late 17th century Burford was renowned for saddles, and examples were presented to Kings Charles II and William III. But in the 18th century only two saddlers are known: Solomon Jeffs (active 1730s-90s) and his son James. Other leatherworkers included at least two glovers, while

Figure 55 Trade tokens (substitute coinage) issued by the waggoner Leonard Mills and the clothier John Payton, both in 1669. Payton was lessee of Bull Cottage (then called The Talbot) on Witney Street, and Mills may have lived at 27 Sheep Street (Figure 83).

Edmund Waine, a breeches-maker and glovemaker, died around 1775. Textile craftsmen also appear to have been relatively few, possibly only two or three tailors at any time, and a similar number of weavers (most of them broadweavers). Only one dyer is recorded (Edward Warner, died 1773). One small-scale innovation was the start of paper-making at Upton mill, within Burford parish, which continued until the early 19th century.[92]

The 'professional' element in Burford's population remained small. In the late 17th and 18th centuries there were usually two or three apothecaries and two surgeons. The former included Nicholas Willett, who leased 124 High Street (the former *Crown Inn*) in 1734, and the property remained a pharmacy thereafter. A scrivener was mentioned in the late 17th century, and from the late 18th century onwards there were usually one or two resident lawyers.[93]

Malting and Coaching In 1635, following a period of works, the River Thames was re-opened to large barges below Oxford, thereby restoring direct access to the London market for places around the Upper Thames. By the early 18th century large quantities of malt were reportedly being made at Burford, carried to Radcot Bridge eight miles to the south, and conveyed by barge to London. The earliest known maltster in Burford was Lawrence Yeate, who leased

Figure 56 Maltings at the former Garne's Brewery on Sheep Street (left), photographed in 1994. Commercial malting was carried out at Burford from the 17th century, benefiting from the reopening of river transport on the middle Thames.

Figure 57 An omnibus outside the *Bull Inn* or *Hotel* in 1890. By then such services connected only with the railway; in the 18th century, however, the *Bull* was one of Burford's chief coaching inns.

47-49 High Street in 1658. In the late 17th century at least four more Burford men were maltsters, including Richard Cumberson (died 1684), whose goods were valued at £455. There continued to be a similar number of maltsters until the 1760s, and malthouses were built at 21 and 91 High Street, on the site of the 19th-century brewery in Sheep Street, and probably elsewhere. But after the 1760s there are few references to malting, and in the late 18th century a visitor to Burford observed decayed malthouses. The industry was ruined probably by competition from malting areas newly linked to London by canal.[94]

Burford also benefited from developments in road transport. From the early 18th century coach services linked Oxford with Gloucester, Bath and Bristol, while by the 1730s services between Gloucester and London passed through Burford as an alternative to their main route through Lechlade and Abingdon. Traffic growth was apparently stimulated by the turnpiking of the Gloucester-Oxford road from 1751, and of the Burford-Cirencester road from 1753. A coach service from Burford to London was established by 1761, and by the 1780s Gloucester-London coaches passed through Burford as their main route. Coaches travelling along the ridgeway road in west Oxfordshire (now the A40) descended into the Windrush valley and crossed Burford via Witney Street and Sheep Street, passengers usually taking meals at the town's inns.[95]

Coach traffic probably encouraged the opening of new inns and expansion of some existing ones. From the late 17th to the late 18th centuries 16 new inns and alehouses were opened in Burford, although 11 closed. The *Bull*, in the town centre, appears to have superseded the *George* as the leading inn, taking over the adjacent *Talbot Inn* (on Witney Street) in the early 18th century, and absorbing the neighbouring *Angel* in the late 18th. By then it was a prime venue for social events, auctions and business deals, and retains a large 'market room' at the back. In 1800 its lessee, Mr Stevens, appears to have taken over business from the *George*, which he used briefly as an annexe and then closed. Other new inns included the *Lamb Inn* and *Golden Ball* (later *Golden Fleece*) in Sheep Street (mid-18th century), and the *Red Lion* and *Bell* in High Street (late 18th century). When named public houses were first listed in 1774, there were 27 in Burford.[96]

The spread of new consumer goods and the development of social activities at Burford, particularly for the gentry, seem to have created few new occupations in the town. Possible exceptions were the bookseller Thomas Hughes (died 1683), the peruke- (or wig-) maker Francis Turner (died by 1739), the hatter Edward Chavasse (died by 1770), and the tea-dealers John Bateman and Henry Mander (died by 1807 and 1809). In the late 18th century there were also one or two clockmakers.[97]

Social Hierarchy

The first list of people who paid the hearth tax, introduced in 1662, makes it possible to study a broader range of Burford's society. In particular, the section of society from which the élite was drawn can be roughly determined. The list names 142 householders (mostly men) whose houses had between one and 15 hearths, a rough indicator of size and status and therefore, probably, of wealth. If the tax list is compared with the list of corporation bailiffs in the years around 1662 (taking bailiffs as representative corporation members), it emerges that these town officers were men taxed on three to 14 hearths. This suggests two features of Burford's society: first, a division between people with one or two hearths (i.e. those living in cottages and small houses) and an 'upper layer' with larger houses; second, that above that line men became bailiffs irrespective of wealth. This upper layer comprised 79 households, possibly about 40 per cent of the total after allowance for under-recording of the poor.[98]

Figure 58 Part of the
hearth tax returns for
Burford in 1662, listing
householders and the
number of hearths or
fireplaces on which they
were taxed. The extract
begins with Paul Silvester,
clothier (five hearths), and
ends with Mr John Jordan
(10 hearths, in a house on
the site of the Methodist
church).

The upper layer in 1662 consisted of innkeepers, traders
(especially major traders such as mercers and clothiers), craftsmen,
independent gentlemen, and probably professional men.
Innkeepers included Edmund Heming of the *Bull* (14 hearths)
and Thomas Matthews of the *Bear* (13 hearths), both of whom
served as bailiffs – though innkeepers are, of course, a special
case, since their large premises represented capital wrapped up in
their businesses rather than personal wealth. Nonetheless, in 1667
Richard Veysey of the *George* left possessions worth £409. Major
traders, all of whom served as bailiffs, included the mercer Francis
Keble (eight hearths, possibly at 115 High St), ironmonger Richard
Hayter (six hearths, probably at 41-45 High St), and clothier John
Payton (five hearths, 12 Witney St). Craftsmen included the saddler
Thomas Eve (six hearths) and freemason John Ward (five hearths),
both of whom were bailiffs, and shoemaker Richard Haynes
(three hearths at 69 High St), who made major bequests totalling
£240. Other hearth-tax payers who served as bailiffs included the
bookseller Thomas Hughes (died 1683), who left goods valued
at £179, and maltster Stephen Smith (died 1672), whose goods at
death were worth £90.[99]

The pre-eminent independent gentleman in 1662 was John
Jordan (died 1663), occupier of a large house on High Street
which had 10 fireplaces. He, too, served as bailiff, owned seven
houses in Burford and properties in four other places, and made
bequests to his daughters worth £330. A descendant who rebuilt
the house (now 75 High St) some 60 years later was clearly in
touch with sophisticated London fashions. Other independent
gentry included Walwin Hopton (taxed on six hearths at 26

Figure 59 Robert Aston's bale tomb in Burford churchyard. Aston (died 1698) was successively keeper of the *Bull* and *George* inns.

Witney St), who was owed over £500 at his death in 1685. Professional people included the vicar Christopher Glynn, who paid tax on 10 hearths.[100]

The composition of the town's upper layer as seen in 1662 remained similar in the 18th and early 19th centuries, comprising (as was usual in small towns) small numbers of innkeepers, major traders, craftsmen, independent gentry and professionals. In 1758 a list of 34 so-called 'principal persons' included two innholders and three other victuallers; a clothier, draper, grocer, and ironmonger; a brassworker, butcher, coachmaker, flax-dresser, glover, mason and tanner; and a surgeon, two apothecaries and a schoolmaster. In the 1790s the bailiffs included an innkeeper, two surgeons, a joiner and a turner. Prominent innkeepers in the late 17th and 18th centuries included Robert Aston (died 1698) of the *George* and the *Bull*, who is commemorated by a striking bale tomb in Burford churchyard. Prominent major traders included the mercer Richard Whitehall (1700s-30s), who probably refronted Simon Wisdom's former house at 115 High Street, while in the 1750s-70s the maltster William Upston (91 High St) was a prominent townsman. The pre-eminent gentry remained the Jordans and their successors the Chapmans. The leading professionals were surgeons. John Castle, who had formerly lived at Tewkesbury (Glos.), built The Great House on Witney Street around the 1690s. He served regularly as bailiff, and his active involvement in church and charitable affairs was reflected in the house's remarkable painted decoration, with its devotional scenes and symbolism. William Chavasse, another surgeon, was prominent in the 1770s-90s.[101]

Figure 60 The long gallery of The Great House on Witney Street, an imposing classical mansion built for the physician John Castle *c.*1700. By his will Castle gave his cousin Elizabeth 'liberty to walk in the gallery', which gives fine views from its oval windows.

Social Activities and Social Provision

Figure 61 One of the extraordinary panel paintings in The Great House, probably depicting its owner John Castle. The house can be seen behind.

Figure 62 Race meeting card for Burford races, September 1753.

During the 150 or so years after Charles II's Restoration, a variety of sporting and cultural activities are recorded. Most took place intermittently and at existing premises: unlike some small towns, Burford did not become a highly developed social centre with clubs, frequent events and coffee houses or theatres.[102]

The principal social and leisure activity was horse racing, which was resumed after the Civil War and continued until the 19th century. Meetings were possibly intermittent until the 1740s when they became an annual fixture, with sometimes two meetings a year in the 1750s-60s. Visitors included aristocracy and gentry from outside the town: in 1681 Charles II attended, probably with his mistress Nell Gwyn. By the 1780s the races had been moved to Aldsworth (Glos.) about five miles away, and were formally associated with Burford for the last time in 1802. Thereafter they were effectively replaced by races organised by the private Bibury Club, probably founded by 1792 and named after its headquarters at Bibury Court, also in Gloucestershire. The race meetings generated income for townspeople, especially innkeepers: their importance for Burford was demonstrated in 1780 when the town contributed £50 towards prize money to help reinvigorate the races. Townspeople took advantage by organising other social activities during the race meetings. Most took place at the *Bull*, and included cockfights, balls, and performances by actors and comedians.

Similar social events were held at the *Bull* at other times of the year. In the 1750s-90s there were assemblies and balls, an annual cockfight between birds belonging to Oxfordshire and Gloucestershire gentlemen, and performances by a fire-eater, comedians and players. Some events probably took place outside in the yard, though a heated function room at the rear has late 17th- or 18th-century features and perhaps housed some of the grander gatherings. The only building specially erected for social or sporting purposes was a cockpit on Priory Lane, opened in the 17th or 18th century and disused by the early 19th.[103]

This relatively low level of social activity, compared with other towns, is presumably explained by the smallness of Burford's resident gentry, though some inhabitants were in contact with a much wider world: in the late 1770s and 1780s, for example, Mrs Sophia Gast at The Great House corresponded with the novelist Fanny Burney. The same lack of resident or nearby gentry probably also explains the modest provision of private schooling in 18th- and early 19th-century Burford. A clergyman's widow briefly kept a school in the mid-18th century, and a boarding school for Young

Figure 63 Public cock-fighting (shown here at the Royal cockpit around 1800) was a popular entertainment. The Burford cockpit in Priory Lane would have been a much smaller building.

Ladies opened in 1773 and lasted until the 1830s. The most notable private school was a Quaker School, Hillside Academy, which flourished under Thomas Huntley in the later 18th century. By contrast Witney had five private 'academies' in 1823, while Banbury had no fewer than 12 private schools in 1832.[104]

One area of town life that remained fairly vigorous was the donation of funds for charitable purposes, usually to the corporation or churchwardens as trustees. Gifts were numerous in the 17th century, though less so in the 18th: major charity funds rose from about nine in 1600 to 28 in 1700, and to 35 in 1780. The most substantial gift was the foundation and endowment of Castle's Almshouses in Guildenford by the surgeon John Castle in 1726, to house four poor widows. Most gifts were more modest bequests of money for investment, mainly to assist the poor; such provision supplemented the parish's poor rates, and donors hedged bequests with requirements so as to target the 'deserving poor'. Both Elizabeth Tanfield (1629) and Robert Veysey (died 1666) provided gifts for widows, while Richard Hayter (1666) augmented payments to almspeople, and James Tretham endowed an annual payment to a maid servant (1666). In the 17th and early 18th centuries several charities were also founded to fund apprenticeships for poor boys. Bread charities, which usually provided a weekly distribution of loaves, were popular in the 18th century, and before 1702 Elizabeth Meady started a charity to provide clothing for poor people.[105]

Figure 64 John Castle's almshouses at Guildenford, founded in 1726 to house four poor widows. The building has been much altered.

CONCLUSION

The preceding pages have traced the stages by which a prosperous medieval wool centre with international trade links declined into an undistinguished 18th-century market town, buoyed only by its coaching, its small malting industry, and by the presence of a few resident gentry, professionals and wealthier tradesmen. But, if late 18th-century Burford was a very different place from its 15th-century predecessor, it had still not reached its nadir. That was to come during the 19th century, as the collapse of coaching, the failure to secure a railway, and national agricultural depression all took their toll. That story, together with the town's 20th-century reinvention as a picturesque tourist centre, forms the subject of the next chapter, before we return to Burford's buildings to see how these changes were reflected in the fabric of the town we see today.

Decline and Rebirth: Burford from 1790

Chapter 7

Figure 65 Burford High Street in 1890, looking south. On the right is the Tolsey or market house of 1525 (Panel 6), with, beyond, John Newman's drapers. On the left, part of Wiggins' (later Castle's) butchers and John Sharp's furniture and china shop. The street's width reflects its creation as a medieval market place.

The previous chapter traced Burford's transformation from prosperous medieval wool centre to undistinguished country town. During the 19th century, damaged by a universal decline in coaching, by its failure to secure a railway link, and from the 1870s by the loss of its market and through agricultural depression, the town entered on what must have seemed a period of terminal decline. Traditional craftsmen and retailers, some of them moderately prosperous, continued to serve the town and its agricultural hinterland, and a few prominent townsmen with professional backgrounds continued to give a lead in town affairs. But 19th-century Burford seems over all to have been a run-down and impoverished place, with significant numbers of labourers and small craftsmen crammed into subdivided cottages and cramped cottage yards.

Ironically, this very stagnation proved the key to the town's renaissance. By the early 20th century writers, artists and tourists, many of them inspired by Arts and Crafts ideals, were rediscovering Burford, which was no longer perceived as run-down but as an 'unspoilt' backwater. By the 1920s such incomers were transforming both the town's social tone and its physical appearance, a process which, with the development of modern tourism and of modern ideas about building conservation, continues in modified form to the present day. The next chapter explores the impact of these changes on Burford's buildings and visual appearance. The present chapter fills in the background, examining the town's changing social and economic character during these critical periods.

A TOWN IN DECLINE, 1790-1870

19th-Century Stagnation

In 1812 the ridgeway road south of Burford was turnpiked and improved, and coaches subsequently travelled that way rather than through the town centre. This probably damaged Burford's economy, although no inn is known to have closed immediately, and the *Bird-in-Hand* (which adjoined the new route) was rebuilt. Coach traffic declined probably when railways provided alternative routes, most notably when Gloucester was connected to London via Swindon in 1845. In 1847 only two coaches were reported to pass daily through Burford, and services evidently ceased in the period 1861-3. Burford reverted to being essentially a market, shopping and service centre for its locality.[106]

Occupations recorded in the 1841 census enable much of Burford's economy to be seen for the first time in a comprehensive way. Of Burford's male heads of households, 51 per cent (130 out of 256) were engaged in crafts and services (excepting publicans, major retailers and professionals). The next largest group, 30 per cent of male household heads (77 of 256), were agricultural workers, mostly labourers, who within the town were consumers rather than producers. There were also small groups of 'major' retailers such as grocers and an ironmonger (13 or 5 per cent), professionals (11 or 4 per cent), and publicans (9 or 4 per cent). The first two groups were similar in size to their 18th-century counterparts, while the number of publicans was smaller.[107]

Figure 66 Burford occupations in 1841, based on information in the 1841 census.

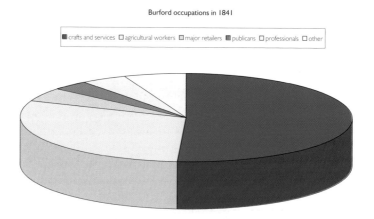

Burford occupations in 1841

■ crafts and services □ agricultural workers □ major retailers ■ publicans □ professionals □ other

Figure 67 (opposite) Wyatt's saddlery business, established in part of the former George Inn by 1881. Leather working was important in Burford from the Middle Ages, and remained significant in the 19th century.

The main groups of craft and service occupations in 1841 were the same as in the 18th century: victuallers, textile workers, tailors, leatherworkers, metalworkers, and building workers. The last were the largest group, about 35 men including masons (11), slaters and plasterers (six), and carpenters (five). Leather working remained prominent, employing 19 men who included cordwainers and shoemakers (13), saddlers (two) and glovers (two). There were also 19 victuallers (excepting publicans), including seven bakers and six butchers. Clothworkers were nearly extinct: only two dyers were recorded and no weavers, though there remained 10 tailors. Other craftsmen included four basket-makers, two papermakers, a straw-hat maker, a cabinet maker, a watchmaker, and a twine-maker.

By now financial services were developing. A savings bank started in 1826 continued until the 1860s, and in 1830 there was

a branch of a Cheltenham bank in Sheep Street. It was replaced before 1842 by a branch of the County of Gloucester Bank, which later operated probably from 51-53 Sheep Street, and erected a new building in Sheep Street in 1878. Insurance companies also appointed agents in Burford: one was recorded in 1823-4, four in 1847, and 14 in 1864. The number fell to five in 1887 and two in 1895.[108]

Between 1841 and 1871 there was little change in Burford's economy, the only innovation being the development of a small commercial brewery in Sheep Street from around 1840. From c.1855 it used a Burford-built steam engine for crushing malt.[109]

Outside Pressure and Social Reform

On Boxing Day 1792 Burford's leading inhabitants gathered to confront perceived threats to social stability following the French Revolution. Meeting in the 'town hall' (probably the Grammar School) they pledged loyalty to king and Constitution, and resolved to oppose disloyalty, dissent and disturbance. The surgeon William Chavasse chaired the meeting, and copies of its resolutions were placed for signing at the *George* and *Bull* inns, and with the mercer Charles Street at 115 High Street. Though such meetings were held in towns throughout England, Burford's response shows a capacity by the town's prominent inhabitants to exercise resolute leadership. But during the next 40 years this seemingly declined under economic pressure.[110]

In the late 1790s economic depression and high corn prices caused poor-relief costs to escalate rapidly throughout England: in Burford they rose from £853 in 1798 to £1,722 in 1801. The burden was substantial, in that Burford's poor rate in 1803, 15s. in the pound, was allegedly the second highest in Oxfordshire. Administration of the poor law was maintained with difficulty, but other responsibilities were neglected. Between 1805 and 1814 no charity accounts were prepared, and no property trustees appointed: by 1822 there was only one trustee, who died intestate in 1826. In 1822 the corporation was 'practically moribund', comprising only an alderman and three burgesses. Economically the town suffered not only from redirection of coaches away from the town centre but from the cessation of horse racing between 1827 and 1834 (below), which probably lost it a good deal of casual trade. Even the town's most prominent gentry were not exempt. In the early 19th century the Lenthall family, owners of The Priory and lords of the manor, fell into financial difficulties, probably through unsustainable expenditure on inclosure and family settlements. Around 1808 John Lenthall demolished half

Figure 68 The Priory, seat of the Lenthalls since the 17th century, was partly demolished in 1808 and later sold. As shown here it was derelict by the 1890s, and was restored in stages during the early 20th century.

of The Priory, and in the 1820s his son sold the estate piecemeal, culminating in 1828 with the sale of The Priory, remaining lands, and the lordship. Since the new owner, Charles Greenaway, lived elsewhere, Burford once again lacked a resident lord.[111]

The seeming lack of leadership and difficult conditions provided the opportunity for a newly arrived clergyman to alter social attitudes and behaviour. Similar developments occurred in other towns, but in Burford changes were particularly quick and thorough. In 1826-7 the curate Alexander Dallas, a veteran of the Peninsular War, mounted a military-like campaign to raise religious and moral standards. He re-emphasised Sunday as a day of religious observance by persuading shopkeepers to end Sunday opening, prevailing on farmers to pay labourers on Friday rather than Saturday, promoting church services, and establishing a regular Sunday school. Moral standards were tackled through 'district visiting' (division of the parish into districts, each visited by parishioners), through evening lectures (for example on the Lord's Prayer), by encouraging people to save with a new Savings Bank, and by establishing the Burford Friendly Association. Dallas also tried to increase the efficiency of poor relief, and to make the poor more 'disciplined'. He pressed parish officers to undertake their duties, provided allotments to promote self-sufficiency, instituted a soup kitchen and blanket distribution in winter, made rules for the Poor House, and started a Poor Improvement Society to reward the industrious poor. He also rebuilt the medieval Warwick Almshouses near the church. Perhaps more controversially he attacked the town's 'Whitsun revels', the traditional (and often raucous) Whit Sunday procession to Cap's Lodge in Wychwood Forest, where the town received a deer carcass. He apparently stopped the revels, though the annual venison feast continued.[112]

Figure 69 Alexander Dallas, the dynamic and evangelical curate of Burford 1826-7, who had a marked influence on the town.

Figure 70 The Great (or Warwick) Almshouses on Church Lane, originally founded in 1455-6 to house eight poor people. Though the building was altered in the 16th and 17th centuries and 'rebuilt' in 1828, some of the external fabric may be original.

Dallas's curacy happened to coincide with the cessation of horse racing near Burford by the Bibury Club. Racing was revived from 1835, with a one-day annual meeting, and ended in 1848 when it was allegedly suppressed by another reforming clergyman, the vicar of Aldsworth. The venison feast ended *c.*1854 when the gift of bucks was stopped in preparation for the inclosure of Wychwood.[113]

Social Structure and Authority

Despite the economic problems besetting the town, a wealthy and dignified section of Burford society can be distinguished in the 1841 national census by identifying households that employed resident servants. Excluding publicans, there were 33 such households (10 per cent of the total). Their heads were similar to the kinds of people who belonged to the upper layer of Burford society in the late 17th and 18th centuries: major traders, craftsmen, independent gentry, professionals and minor officials. This suggests continuity, though professionals were now slightly more prominent, and gentry less so.[114]

Major traders with resident servants in 1841 consisted of five grocers (e.g. Thomas Bowl at 117 High St), two drapers (e.g. Thomas Tanner at 128-132 High St), and the spirit merchant John Hunt (91 High St). Craftsmen with servants (as opposed to apprentices) included two tailors, four bakers and two butchers. In addition, nine publicans employed resident servants, though many presumably looked after guests. The inns with the largest numbers of servants were the *Red Lion*, *Lamb*, and *Bull*. Only three people were described as 'independent', of whom probably only James Chapman (at 75 High St) was prominent in town life. Known as 'Squire Chapman', he was allegedly an eccentric. The professional element now included several lawyers: two attorneys and two solicitors, including James Price in Sheep Street. The surgeons were

Thomas Cheatle at 7 High Street (Riverside House) and Robert Pytt at The Great House, and there was a bank agent, schoolteacher and the vicar. Other employers of resident servants included a relieving officer and an excise man.[115]

At the other end of the social spectrum, many of Burford's poorest people in the 19th century were accommodated in cramped and presumably insanitary cottage yards behind the main street frontage, whose development is described in the next chapter. In 1851 there were probably six such yards, accommodating a total of 32 households. The largest were the so-called 'College' behind Nos. 56 and 64, and George Yard at the rear of the former *George Inn*. The former contained 11 households, including six headed by male agricultural labourers and three headed by women (see Gazetteer).[116]

Figure 71 Dr T.H. Cheatle (died 1906), son of the surgeon Thomas Cheatle. Both were prominent in town affairs.

The smallness of Burford's wealthier class probably explains how strong-minded individuals of acknowledged high status were able to assert authority. From the late 1820s to *c.*1860 the surgeon Thomas Cheatle accumulated public offices, administered charity properties, and was prominent in social activities. He became alderman of the corporation in 1828, served as churchwarden, became registrar of births and deaths, and a magistrate. He was active in local Conservative politics, and president of the cricket club. Eventually, in 1858, complaints about his management of charities led to a public enquiry and abolition of the corporation by Act of Parliament (1861). From the early 1860s to late 1870s Edward Marriott, a retired India Army captain who lived at The Great House, assumed a similar role to Cheatle. He served as churchwarden, magistrate, trustee of Burford Grammar School, and treasurer for the church's restoration, and was involved in an attempt to obtain a railway line. In the mid-19th century the main town offices were held mostly by the same sort of people who had served as bailiff in the 17th century, though with a little more social stratification. Churchwardens tended to be landholders, professional men and major traders, whereas overseers of the poor tended to be innkeepers, major traders and craftsmen.[117]

Figure 72 The former cottage hospital on Church Lane, set up by T.H. Cheatle in two converted cottages in 1868 and extended in 1886. In 1902 it was replaced by a building at the end of Sheep Street.

By the 1860s Burford society was divided by religious denomination, with an estimated 200 nonconformists by the late 1860s (Chapter 9). Relations were usually peaceful. The only major dispute occurred in 1871, after a ratepayers' meeting voted to establish a school board under the 1870 Education Act. The town's High Church vicar, Revd J.H. Burgess, responded by obtaining a poll of ratepayers, the town's first. On voting day (22 July) parties fought and abused each other. The board was rejected, and the church bells were rung. A board was nonetheless accepted in 1873, following Burgess's departure.[118]

Figure 73 Part of the Elizabethan Revels held in August 1908, which included a recreation of Elizabeth I's arrival in 1574, a grand procession, and dancing, games and donkey races. In the background are Wisdom Cottages (1 High Street).

From the 1860s new organised leisure facilities and activities were introduced. Some were overtly intended to encourage 'improving' behaviour, such as a reading room in the Tolsey (1861) and a working men's reading room in Sheep Street (1864). Others probably had a similar intent, such as the annual fête (held from 1862), cricket matches, brass bands and musical societies. These latter activities continued into the 20th century, culminating in the foundation of the Burford Recreation Society in 1904, which was dominated by shopkeepers. In 1906 it bought Falkland Hall (42-44 High St) as a venue for meetings and entertainment, and in 1908 sponsored an Elizabethan pageant.[119]

A NEW WORLD: BURFORD SINCE 1870

Burford 1870-1945

In the late 19th and early 20th centuries Burford's 'traditional' economy weakened. Markets and trading fairs ceased, while the number and range of traditional craft occupations declined sharply. During the same period the town adapted to new markets created by social and technological developments. Its range of shops and services changed, and increasingly provision was made for tourists.

Burford's centuries-old role as a marketing centre declined suddenly in the 1870s. The weekly Saturday market seems to have contracted in 1873 or 1874, the July fair ended by 1876, and the April fair was said to be very small by 1877. Only the autumn hiring-fair remained lively, continuing until 1914. The decline in livestock trade was ascribed to stock sales held in the surrounding area, while Witney's flourishing livestock market may also have diverted trade. Burford's losses were made worse by the agricultural depression of the 1880s-90s, which pressed hard on local farming, and by the increasing penetration of factory-made goods. Burford failed to attract compensatory activity (in particular significant industry), and was disadvantaged by its failure to secure a railway.[120]

Between 1871 and 1901 two trends were especially notable. First, the number of agricultural workers declined, from 70 male household heads in 1871 to only 21 in 1901. This reduced a sector of demand within the town. Second, the number of leatherworkers fell from 19 male household heads in 1871 (including 10 cordwainers and shoemakers) to only four in 1901 (saddler, shoemaker, bootmaker, and boot- and shoemaker). In the following years the number of craftsmen in all sectors fell considerably. The 1901 census recorded 129 craftsmen, whereas in 1910 a trade directory listed only 39 craftsmen and small craft businesses. Though a few craftsmen remained in most sectors, by

Figure 74 By 1895 only the autumn hiring-fair continued, though stalls and attractions still spread along Burford High Street much as they probably did for the medieval fairs and market. The fair finally closed in 1914.

the Great War Burford's economic activity probably appeared to consist mainly of pubs and shops. In 1910 there were 10 public houses, while the town's shops included five drapers, five grocers, two booksellers, two china- and glass-dealers, and a wine and spirit merchant. Many of the drapers and grocers closed soon afterwards. Brewing continued at Garne's brewery, and in 1903 Jabez Wall expanded his rope-making business behind High Street by building a small factory (Gazetteer, 142 High St).[121]

Such changes eventually had profound social consequences, creating the conditions that attracted new kinds of people. In 1901 the town's wealthier section (as indicated by employment of resident servants) was little changed from 1841: it continued to comprise professional men, major retailers, a few craftsmen and other people. But the decline of Burford's market and fairs from the 1870s reduced the overt association with agriculture, while the decrease in agricultural labourers and craftsmen, caused by agricultural depression and other factors, changed the balance within Burford's society. In particular middle-class outsiders started to 'discover' Burford, and a remote, inert town gradually became appreciated as a haven for retreat and retirement. It particularly appealed to writers and academics. Among the first writers to visit Burford was the Revd H.C. Beeching (1859-1919), poet and later essayist and dean of Norwich, who took holidays in the Burford area from the 1880s and in 1907 acquired the Old Rectory. From the early 1890s the Revd W.H. Hutton (1860-1930), an Oxford don and prolific historian, lived partly at The Great

Figure 75 Two Burford writers.
R.H. Gretton (left), former London editor of the *Manchester Guardian* (1904-11), wrote the monumental *Burford Records* (1920) and restored 25 Sheep Street. W.J. Monk (right), shown here at one of Burford's early 20th-century pageants, was a former master at Ipswich grammar school, and author of several popular histories of Burford.

House. The young Compton Mackenzie (1883-1972) lived at Burford from 1904 to 1906, and from *c*.1911 Burford was the home of the historians R.H. and Mary Gretton, who published books on the town's history. The presence of such people brought outsiders to the town, as did enthusiasm for cycling and the new popular vogue for the Cotswolds. Burford's charm was publicised by newspaper articles, and in books by the local writer W.J. ('Toby') Monk, by W.H. Hutton and by H.A. Evans.[122]

A few minor artists also settled in Burford, such as H.E. Conway (at The Great House from 1912), while Miss Murdoch established the Burford Hand Weavers. Folk dancing took place in an old barn in Sheep Street. Such activities were undoubtedly influenced by the broader Arts and Crafts movement, which flourished in the Cotswolds around this period – indeed William Morris's widow Jane briefly leased the former Cottage Hospital on Church Lane, apparently for her daughter Jenny, while the Huttons became close friends of May Morris at Kelmscott Manor (Panel 12). Incomers also began restoring some of Burford's older houses in vaguely Arts and Crafts styles, fashioning semi-rural but comfortable homes while at the same time creating an idealised image of the past (Chapter 8). [123]

Signs of this new world, encompassing horse-less transport and tourism, were evident in new businesses opened in the town between 1890 and 1914. By 1891 there was a bicycle depot at 50 High Street, and William Holtom, stepson of an engineer, made bicycles at 49 Sheep Street. By 1899 Holtom had established a shop in the High Street (at No. 142), and by 1910 there were three cycle dealers and agents. The town also catered for touring cyclists. In 1895 the *Bull Inn* offered accommodation to them, and in 1910 there was a cyclists' restaurant at 35-39 High Street and probably a cyclists' café at 26 High Street. Soon afterwards R.G. Foster opened a car showroom at 64 High Street, and Gilbert Bowerman an antiques shop at No. 70.[124]

By the 1920s-30s Burford's economy stood between two worlds. The old world of craftsmen providing services for the town and its locality continued to ebb. By 1939 there were no leatherworkers, only one tailor, one blacksmith, and two builders, though the victualling, retail, and professional sectors continued much as before, Barclays Bank opening a branch in the 1930s at 118-122 High Street. New economic activities expanded slowly, and by 1939 there were three motor garages and seven hotels. Other inhabitants included an architect, forestry consultant, and accountant – the advent of motor transport having presumably made it easier for professional people with distant customers to work from the town.[125]

Burford and the Arts and Crafts Movement

By the 1860s a growing number of artists and designers were disenchanted by mass-production, and by what they saw as a corresponding decline in style, craftsmanship, and public taste. The Arts and Crafts movement was their aesthetic response, drawing on the idealisation of pre-industrial medieval society championed by figures such as A.W.N. Pugin (1812-52), and on a socialist rejection of the mindless repetition demanded of factory workers compared with traditional craftsmen.

Figure A *William Morris's daughter May: in later life a close friend of the Gretton family in Burford.*

Figure B *Cecil Sharp (1859-1924), folksong collector and revivalist, who paid several visits to Burford.*

Among its most famous proponents was William Morris (1834-96), who, with others in his circle, produced hand-crafted wallpapers, textiles, furniture and books aimed at recapturing the spirit and quality of medieval craftsmanship. The movement developed a strong architectural dimension, dedicated to reviving traditional vernacular architecture based on local materials, traditional local styles, and fine craftsmanship. Morris lived only a few miles from Burford at Kelmscott, and founded the Society for the Protection of Ancient Buildings (the 'Anti-Scrape Society') partly in response to the over-restoration of Burford church in the 1870s (Chapter 9).

In Burford, such ideas were shared by many of the artists, writers and intellectuals who moved into the town c.1900-30, and exerted a strong impact on the town's social tone and appearance. Morris's daughter, May, remained at Kelmscott Manor until her death in 1938, and became a close friend of Burford incomers such as the Grettons (at Calendars on Sheep Street). Among other interests they shared an enthusiasm for English folk dancing: the folksong revivalist Cecil Sharp was a visitor to both Kelmscott and Calendars. The theatricals, handicrafts, and traditional dancing promoted in both places was typical of the cultural development of Arts and Crafts ideas in the early 20th century, although Burford never developed into a major centre of artistic craftwork comparable with nearby Chipping Campden.

Figure C *E.J. Horniman of The Priory, who restored several Burford buildings in a Vernacular Revival style derived from Arts and Crafts principles (Chapter 8).*

Figure D *Handmade door-ironwork at 162 High Street, one of the buildings restored by Horniman.*

Figure 76 From the early 20th century Burford had several motor garages, catering partly for the burgeoning tourist trade. The central porch at 64 High Street was inserted for Foster's motor garage in the 1920s.

Figure 77 Charles East, council chairman for many years, and a devout Baptist.

Changes in town government completed the town's transformation. In 1894 a civil parish council was inaugurated under national legislation, making Burford's government non-denominational. Members were initially elected from all sections of society, including labourers, but inclusiveness was not sustained and government reverted to dependence on willing individuals. As before, particular people became pre-eminent. Charles East, for example, a water engineer and Baptist, served as council chairman from 1894-7 and 1899-1922. [126]

Modern Burford

By the late 1940s Burford's society consisted of three main groups: first, a comfortable group of middle-class people who worked in the town, such as shopkeepers and schoolteachers; second, retired incomers such as RAF officers; third, a small group of working-class people who increasingly lived in the newly built council houses. Writers and academics continued to live in Burford, among them the folklorist Katherine Briggs (1940s-70s), the historian David Ayerst (mid-1960s-1992), and the historian the Revd Dr V.H.H. Green of Lincoln College, Oxford (1960s-2003, at 25 Sheep St). From 1947 the national magazine *The Countryman* was edited in Burford.

This new mix of people provided a basis for new activity in the performing arts. During the War the Burford Orchestra was started, along with a dramatic society which lasted until the 1970s. The Briggs sisters organised Shakespeare productions in their garden and plays in the parish church, and in the late 20th century an annual festival brought professional musicians to the town. [127]

Figure 78 The former Garne's Brewery on Sheep Street, where brewing continued until 1969. The building is now a tourist information centre. The large central archway was inserted in the 1840s.

Burford's economy experienced mixed fortunes in the decades after the Second World War. Little craft activity survived, and relatively small industrial enterprises proved difficult to sustain. Rope-making ceased soon after the war, and brewing at Garne's was stopped in 1969 following sale of the business to Wadworths of Devizes (Wilts.). The rope factory was re-used from 1952 as a printing works by Watchdials, and employed about 50 people, but that too closed. The only continuing traditional occupation was building, three small building companies remaining in 2000. Car maintenance initially expanded, and at one point there were six garages, but contraction followed and only one garage (in Guildenford) survived in 2007.

By the late 20th century Burford was primarily a small retailing and service centre, providing for its own population, the surrounding area, and tourists, but also attracting customers from a wider radius. Shops offering basic provisions included the butcher Castle (111 High St), the baker Huffkins (98 High St), and from *c.*1970 a small supermarket at 74-76 High Street. Shops catering partly for tourists included antique shops and galleries. In the late 20th century there were about nine antique shops, including those of Roger Warner (1936-86, at 115 High St), Jonathan Fyson (from 1970, at 50 High St), and Manfred Schotten, specialist in sports equipment (established from *c.*1980 at 109 High St). Five or so galleries included the Brian Sinfield Gallery (from 1972, at 150 High St) and the Stone Gallery (from the 1980s, at 93 High St). Several other retail businesses sold high-quality, relatively expensive goods, and attracted shoppers from a considerable distance including Oxford. They included the Oxford Shirt Company (64-68 High St) and House of Simon (123 High St), while the Burford Garden Company, a garden centre just outside the town, was in 2006 Burford's largest business.

Only a few basic local services remained. Among them were two banks (of which Barclays moved to 95 High St in the 1970s), a firm of solicitors at 51-53 Sheep St, and a hairdresser, dry cleaner, taxi hire, and acupuncturist. Services aimed largely at visitors included some six hotels, four restaurants (including the *Dragon Inn* at 152 High St, serving Chinese food), and three tea rooms (at 35-39, 98 and 121 High St). A few professional firms and people also continued to provide services for more distant customers, including four estate-agencies, an architect, interior designer, and management consultant.

From the 1980s new economic pressures caused further social change. As house prices rose local people became unable to afford houses in Burford, and outsiders increasingly bought properties for investment. The stock of 'social housing' was considerably

Figure 79 Present-day Burford shops: Christmas Court, developed in the 1980s behind a 19th-century shopfront, with a gift shop to left and confectioner's to right. Parts of the building are medieval.

reduced by the sale of two thirds of the council houses. Burford's resident population shrank, and indeed children became so few that Burford was called 'a town without children' (the town's schools providing mainly for the surrounding area). New incomers included members of the House of Lords such as Lord Windlesham, and representatives of 'celebrity culture', including (at 29 Sheep St) Evelyn Kark (1928-97), who, as Lucie Clayton, had run a London model agency and grooming school. Yet, as before, some long-standing residents became closely identified with town life. In the late 20th century, when the council had been elevated to a town council with a mayor, the Revd Raymond Moody served as a town councillor for 22 years and as mayor for six, alongside his roles as a United Reformed Church minister, sometime chaplain of Burford School, and prolific historian of Burford.[128]

CONCLUSION

The last two chapters have traced Burford's evolution from medieval wool town to modern tourist, retail and service centre, exploring, for each period, how national and local conditions affected its economic life and functions, and how in turn these changes altered the town's social character.

Much of this story has been teased from documentary records. But as we saw for the medieval period, the town's history is also reflected in its townscape and buildings, which can be investigated to tell us more about the town's ups and downs and about the lives and aspirations of its inhabitants. It is to the physical fabric of the post-medieval town that we now turn.

Chapter 8

Town and Buildings from 1550

Figure 80 Burford High Street in 2006. The long 19th-century façade of Nos. 128-132 (left) rubs shoulders with the 16th-century Tolsey; across the road is the white gable end of the *Burford House Hotel*, remodelled in the 1920s.

Chapter 4 showed how Burford's medieval buildings can be used not only to help us understand the structures themselves, but to help illuminate the broader life of the medieval town. The same holds true of the town's later buildings, which grew out of the very different social and economic world explored in the previous two chapters. Few tell a straightforward story. Almost every building bears signs of alteration or modernisation by generations of Burford inhabitants, and, as in any town or village, buildings reflect changing national styles as well as local needs and individual preferences. Close investigation of a wide range of buildings shows the broad outlines of Burford's building history, however, which for this later period can also be amplified by more extensive written evidence. The town's wider history was also reflected in changes to its underlying layout, characterised above all by piecemeal development of back plots behind the street frontages. It is to the general shape of the town that we shall turn first, before looking at the chronological development of Burford's buildings and what we can learn from them.

TOWN DEVELOPMENT 1550-1850

Population and Layout

In the later Middle Ages, as we saw in Chapter 2, many of the plots laid out on Burford's outer fringes seem to have been abandoned. This was a fate shared by many small towns in the period, and reflected a general population decline in the wake of the Black Death and over the next 150 years. From the 16th century, however, slow but steady population growth prompted a gradual re-expansion of the settled area in Burford. Taxation lists for the early 16th century suggest that the town's population was already beginning to recover, with perhaps 750 people living there. By the mid-17th century the population could have exceeded 900, though the figures (as always with population statistics before the 19th century) are contradictory and difficult to interpret. By 1801, the date of the first national census, the town's population was certainly over 1,500, accommodated in well over 200 houses. Numbers fell a little in the 1810s, but by the 1840s the population was almost 1,650.

Such increases are typical of the period, and must have required a substantial increase in housing stock. Between the 17th and 19th centuries this was largely achieved through new building within the historic town: infilling of empty spaces along the main streets, re-colonisation of areas abandoned during the later Middle Ages, and, increasingly, redevelopment of the back yards of existing properties. Alongside such changes individuals continued to redevelop their plots and the houses upon them in a piecemeal way, subdividing or amalgamating according to wealth, inclination and opportunity, refronting and rebuilding, and introducing new, more up-to-date fashions. Only with a gradual fall in Burford's population from the mid-19th century was the pressure on space temporarily reduced. By 1931 the town again had barely 900 inhabitants, a reduction which, by the early 20th century, was prompting abandonment of cramped back-yard dwellings and a return of houses to single occupancy. The first significant expansions beyond the ancient urban area followed only in the mid- and late 20th century, as the town attracted a new breed of incomers, and even then expansion was on a modest scale.[129]

Despite this gradual re-expansion of the built-up area, Burford's shrinkage during the later Middle Ages was still discernible in

Map 16 Burford's town boundaries in 1876 (in red). The town itself was known as the 'Inward', and the parish's rural parts (i.e. the townships of Upton and Signet) as the 'Outward'. The town included riverside meadow, but excluded buildings at the top of The Hill.

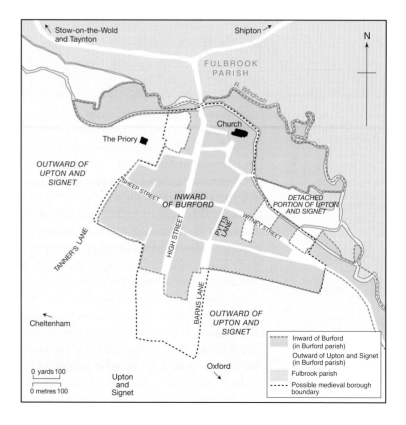

its 19th-century urban boundaries, when for the first time the division between the town (or 'Inward') and the parish's rural part (or 'Outward') was shown on large-scale maps (Map 16). Several areas laid out with burgages in the 12th or 13th century but later abandoned, among them the southern part of The Hill, were still excluded from the 19th-century town, despite having been redeveloped with continuous lines of buildings since at least the 17th century. The Priory was also excluded, presumably because (as the effective manor house) it was considered part of the rural manor. Witney Street mill and some plots on the street's south side also belonged to the Outward; the reason is unclear, but may relate to the mill's association with Burford's outlying agricultural settlements of Upton and Signet. The 19th-century town boundary did, however, include areas of riverside meadow, which had probably been taken into the town for the inhabitants' use at an early date.[130]

The only other significant change to the town's layout was a minor alteration around 1812 to the line of Sheep Street, which was straightened to follow its present course rather than passing through Priory Woods towards the river. The alteration had little impact on the town's geography, but gave the owner of The Priory greater privacy and more land for his gardens and woodland.[131]

Infilling and Back Plots

Infilling took several forms. On Sheep Street, agricultural closes at its west end were apparently built up between 1598 and 1652 (see Gazetteer). Elsewhere, plots were subdivided or amalgamated and their frontages redeveloped for new domestic or commercial premises, two of the most striking examples being John Castle's Great House on Witney Street (c.1700), and John Jordan's mansion on High Street (c.1725). There were, however, finite opportunities for the infilling of the main street frontages, and after the 18th century this ceased to be a major factor in the town's expansion.

Redevelopment of backs of plots offered far greater scope to increase the town's occupational density, without significantly expanding the urban area. This form of development also took place in the medieval period (Chapter 2), but became increasingly common in the 18th and 19th centuries. In some cases the burgage was divided to allow a second house to be built in what had been the rear garden, fronting onto a back lane or side street which gave access to the new property. Nonconformist chapels, as relatively late additions to the urban scene, were often built on such sites, sometimes because a member donated the back part of his own plot or because such sites were the only ones available: a notable Burford example is the Quaker Meeting House in Pytts

Lane (*c.*1709). More frequently back plots were built up with
outhouses, workshops and industrial premises, stretching back
from the main building which occupied the street frontage. Access
was via the back lane which marked the plot's rear boundary, or
through an archway from the main street, a common feature of
urban coaching inns.

As the town's working population increased, so, too, did the
need for cheap housing. Back plots started to be developed for
domestic use by creation of cottage rows (many of them converted
from earlier outbuildings), which fronted onto a footpath running
back from the main street. The decay of the inn trade in the 19th
century offered a further stimulus to this development, good
surviving examples being Bear Court (Panel 1) and George Yard
(Map 17 and Figure 91). Further up High Street, development
behind No. 134 shows how density of building on some plots
was gradually reduced from the later 19th century, as ownership
changed and urban housing conditions improved.[132]

Map 17 Back-plot
development at George
Yard, where buildings
belonging to the former
inn were converted into
cottage accommodation
after 1800 (*Figure 91*).

16TH- AND 17TH-CENTURY REBUILDINGS

Rebuilding of Burford's poky cruck cottages probably started in
the late 16th century. The most obvious change was the encasing
or rebuilding in stone of load-bearing walls, mostly with field
stones in mud mortar. The liberal use of timbers inserted into
the stonework of many of the 17th- and 18th-century cottages
prevented sagging, and wooden door and window lintels can be
seen all over the town. As Figure 81 demonstrates, the 17th century
saw a significant improvement in the housing stock, and many
buildings of this period survive today. Timber was often replaced
by stone, for example at the Burford Gallery (69 High Street) and
Hill House (139 The Hill). At the latter, what seem to be sawn-off
joists can be seen above the ground-floor stonework, suggesting that
part of the front was formerly timber-framed and possibly jettied.

Signs of Burford's rebuilding can also be seen in stones which
seem out of place. Moulded stones from older windows survive
in the south wall of Swan Lane, and a 16th-century stone mullion
seems to have been re-used as a window sill at the former brewery
in Sheep Street. Some other possible examples of re-use are more
difficult to interpret. The arched doorways at Nos. 78 and 69 High
Street (the Mermaid and the Burford Gallery) are probably 14th-
century, but do not sit comfortably with the rest of their frontages
and may have been reset. Some doorways are known to have been
moved, such as that at Hill House in the 1950s.[133]

There were probably two main phases of stone re-use. The
first followed the Dissolution of the monasteries in the mid-16th

Figure 81 Building activity in Burford, based on surviving examples. Dark blue bars show new building or rebuilding; pale blue bars show refrontings (excluding shopfronts).

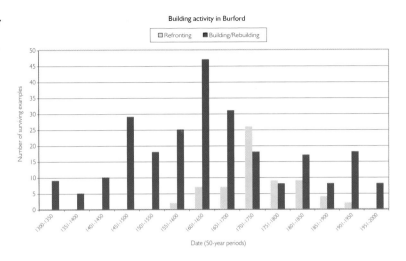

Building activity in Burford

□ Refronting   ■ Building/Rebuilding

Number of surviving examples

Date (50-year periods)

century, and it may be that the locals 'borrowed' building materials from the Hospital of St John the Evangelist before its rebuilding as The Priory in the 1580s. In the immediate post-Dissolution period such re-use of stone is most likely to have been for building rubble, with the carved work hidden, and as late as 1824 some of the stones in an outhouse near the church seem to have come from The Priory, where one of the Lenthall family offered stone for sale (including carvings of saints and martyrs). The setting of carved or moulded stones as decorative features seems, by contrast, to be a late 19th- or 20th-century fashion. A roundel at Shoo Cottage, for example, clearly the spandrel of a 15th-century arched opening, was apparently inserted after 1909, since it does not appear in a photograph of that date.[134]

Figure 82 Self-conscious re-use of old carvings or mouldings was a late 19th- and 20th-century fashion. This 15th-century spandrel at Shoo Cottage was apparently inserted after 1909.

The main change in the late 16th and 17th centuries, however, (as across much of England) was the flooring-over of medieval open halls, and the building of chimneys and fireplaces to contain the smoke in those houses which did not already have them. Evidence of such additions can be seen clearly inside 15-17 and 31 High Street, 91 High Street (the Golden Pheasant), and 139 The Hill (Hill House). External signs include the insertion of upper windows as at 188-192 High Street and Christmas Court (94 High Street), where the cruck frame restricted the height of the upper-floor rooms. Research on the reasons for this 'Great Rebuilding' dates back to W.G. Hoskins's pioneering work on rural houses in the 1940s. Among the factors at work were population growth, availability of cash from agricultural surpluses, and social changes including a greater emphasis on the individual rather than community. In towns the position was even more complex. There, prosperous entrepreneurs could afford luxuries

Building with Stone

The 'smartness' of a stone-fronted building reflects not only the quality of the stone, but the way it was quarried, cut and used. In Burford stone is laid in various ways, reflecting the status of the building and the owner's means. The extremes are semi-drystone walling (used between plots and roads), and the finely dressed ashlar (smoothed and square-cut blocks) which front some better-quality houses. In between are at least five clearly recognisable variants. Not all stone was meant to be seen, however. Keying marks and flecks of coloured lime show that the cruder stones in many buildings were covered with render and limewash, particularly in the 18th century when polite taste required constructional details to be obscured. Sometimes (as at 49-51 Witney Street) the render or buttered mortar was scored with a wooden tool, creating the illusion that the house was of best quality ashlar. Much of Burford's remaining render was removed in the 20th century, reflecting our modern penchant for bare stonework.

Another technique was to use roughly squared stones, taken perhaps where stone could be easily cut to shape with a hand-axe. Examples can be seen at 28 High Street and 2 Lawrence Lane. We do not know whether this was meant to be seen and taken for 'poor man's ashlar', or whether it was rendered to cover up the imperfections.

A Semi-drystone walling (Priory Lane): deep joints with no visible mortar, and a mud and clay mix holding the inner stones together.

B Uncoursed (randomly arranged) rubble with random-sized stones. (Witney Street)

C Coursed rubble with random-sized stones at 33 Witney Street: care has been taken to select similar-size stones and lay them in horizontal lines or courses.

D Coursed and squared rubble with courses of varying heights. This resembles C, but the stones have been squared up and laid in regular courses. (Swan Lane)

E Coursed, squared and dressed rubble with courses of varying heights; resembling D, but with tool-marks and squared stones in evidence. (Witney Street)

F Coursed and dressed stone of ashlar quality with courses of varying heights; resembling E but with sawn stones in evidence. Pointing may be crude. (Church Lane)

G Coursed and dressed ashlar with fine pointing. This stone is usually only a thin facing on the street front, with rubble behind and in the gable walls.

H Crude rubble walling marked by keying marks and traces of render or limewash. As with many Burford buildings, this stonework was not meant to be seen.

I Scoring in render at 53 Witney Street, creating the illusion of squared ashlar stone.

J Varied stonework along Witney Street.

and domestic comfort from an early date (Chapter 6), although there would have been little incentive to improve houses rented to poorer workers.[135]

One of the most prosperous Burford townsmen in the late 16th century was the merchant Simon Wisdom (died 1586 or 1587), who seems to have owned up to 18 houses in Burford at one time or another. The so-called Wisdom Cottages near the bridge have a plaque stating that he rebuilt them as an endowment to the school in 1576, and his building activities at House of Simon (123 High Street) and 96 High Street suggest that he preferred to renovate existing buildings to bring them up to date, rather than building new houses. Nonetheless, new houses also began to appear in the early 17th century (those on closes at the south-west end of Sheep Street, for instance), while remodelling continued. Much of the 'Cotswold' character of Burford derives from this period. Stone-mullioned windows with hoodmoulds or labels abound. Gabled dormers at the street frontage can be seen in a number of properties built or refronted in this period, such as Wisdom Cottages, 151 and 162 The Hill, and (in Sheep Street) Waynes Close (No. 27), Culverclose (No. 39) and the *Bay Tree Hotel*. The *George Inn* underwent a major refronting around 1608 when John Collier incorporated the building to the south, and added a stone gable to the gateway (see Gazetteer).[136]

Window fashions and technology changed continually, and types and styles can often be dated quite closely. Thus the

Figure 83 Much of Burford's 'Cotswold' character derives from early 17th-century rebuilding. Though partly remodelled in the 20th century, No. 27 Sheep Street is typical, with its gabled dormers, stone-mullioned windows, and hoodmoulds.

Figure 84 Stone window-mullions with ovolo- (or convex) mouldings, shown in this cutaway drawing, are typical of Burford buildings in the earlier 17th century.

distinctive ovolo-moulded mullion which can be seen at 13 High Street, in part of the *Lamb Inn*, and in a fragmentary form at 21 Witney Street appears in the first half of the 17th century. The frame of one timber version in the gable of 127 High Street (*The Swan Gallery*) has a scalloped edge with ball decoration (Figure 85) – somewhat similar to a timber lintel above the larger first-floor window at 96 High Street, which, in turn, bears a resemblance to some lintels in Woodstock. Other mullion shapes are less easy to date, and the medieval appearance of some two-light stone windows with pointed heads (as at 67 High Street) may be misleading. In the Banbury region such types are considered to be 17th-century, although some Cotswold examples could be earlier.[137]

Great fun can be had trying to identify the traces of earlier windows in the frontages of Burford houses. The upper storey of the *Cotswold Arms* (46 High Street) shows the position of

Figure 85 Some Burford windows. Left: ovolo-moulded mullion-windows were sometimes built in timber, as at 127 High Street. The top has a scalloped edge with ball decoration, similar to some Woodstock examples. Right: medieval-style windows at 67 High Street, which could actually be as late as the 17th century.

the mullioned casements which preceded the present sash windows, while at 98 High Street the earlier windows had long timber lintels. Their size may indicate a former weaving shop, which would have needed good natural light, though there is no documentary evidence for this and the lintels may simply have been to spread the load.

Rebuilding probably ceased during the Civil War, but had certainly restarted by 1672 when the vicarage received a facelift: the present front most likely conceals an earlier building at ground-floor level, although the elegant first-floor rooms were part of the rebuild. Roche House (29 Sheep Street) was refronted in 1696, possibly by the mason-architect Christopher Kempster, who built his own house at his quarry at nearby Upton two years later. Another possible design by Kempster about the same time was the Old Rectory in Priory Lane. Here, an earlier house was extended to form a five-bay Queen Anne frontage with a central pedimented doorway. Around the same time the *Black Boy* inn in Witney Street

Figure 86 The Old Rectory on Priory Lane, built for an unknown owner. Its elegant Queen Anne front, possibly designed by Wren's master-mason Christopher Kempster (who owned quarries near Burford), hides an earlier building. Despite the name this was never a clergyman's house: the 'rectory estate' to which it belonged, though originally church land, was by this time owned by the Lenthalls.

was replaced by Burford's first major new house: The Great House (Figures 60 and 90), built for the surgeon John Castle.[138]

From the 16th century Burford householders also made internal improvements in comfort and decoration. In some cases fragments of wall-paintings have survived, sometimes within the roof-space as at 113 High Street. Other traces survive in main rooms, as with the chevron pattern on the beams of a house in Swan Lane (p. 182), or a floral scheme in rooms at 115 High Street (Simon Wisdom's house). Wisdom also had good panelling of the 1550s (with his initials and mark) in his parlour, and samples of mid-17th-century wallpaper from 115 High Street can be seen in the Tolsey Museum.

Sixteenth- and 17th-century fireplaces have flatter arches than earlier, with the mouldings of the jambs terminating higher up. Thus the front fireplace in the Wren Gallery (Bear Court, 34-42 High Street) could be 16th- or 17th-century, while three-quarter mouldings survive in two of the original fireplaces of 1649 in the *Bay Tree Hotel* on Sheep Street. In addition a large number of more kitchen-type or poorer domestic fireplaces survive from the 16th and 17th centuries, with timber lintels or plain stone surrounds. Amongst the former are those at Hill House, *Wren Gallery* and The Great House.

THE 18TH CENTURY:
REMODELLING AND REFRONTING

The most notable phase of redevelopment began in the early 18th century. Many old-fashioned timber-framed houses were given rendered façades, some with stone-like detailing as at 111-113 High Street. More striking was the brick façade of the *Bull* (Figure 87 and Gazetteer). This was part of a major upgrading of the inn around 1715, the extent of which can be seen in the changes of floor level inside. The use of this alien material must have been a calculated judgement by the innkeeper William Tash to ensure that his hostelry was noticed and remembered by visitors to Burford, who were now increasingly arriving by coach, and who were used to London and Bath fashions (Chapter 6). The rebuilding also enabled the heights of the rooms in the street range to be increased. The Tash family further extended the inn to the rear by acquiring the *Talbot Inn* (the 14th-century Bull Cottage), which later housed the *Bull*'s ostler (or stableman). The stables, one of which had four loose boxes for hunters, can still be seen in the yard.[139]

Figure 87 The *Bull Inn*'s brick façade, unique in Burford, made the inn instantly recognisable to travellers arriving by coach and used to London and Bath fashions.

An even more striking addition to Burford was made around 1725 when John Jordan, one of Burford's resident gentry, commissioned a new town house on High Street (now the Methodist church, Figure 114 and Gazetteer). Modelled on the influential Powis House in Bloomsbury (*c.* 1714), its grand classical frontage is unique in Burford, rivalled only by John Castle's Great House of a few years earlier. Its ironwork gates front a small forecourt or cour d'honneur, the only example in Burford, from which an imposing flight of steps leads to the central doorway. A recent book has speculated that the architect may have been Francis Smith of Warwick, though this remains unproven.[140]

In the mid-18th century, the well-off townsman wanted his house to have a fashionable smooth ashlar façade and rectangular sash-window openings, with freestone dressings and prominent keystones. As an important staging point on the coach route between Oxford and Bath, Burford clearly wanted to reassure its visitors that it was no provincial backwater. Glenthorne (174 The Hill) is a good example of the style, which is, however, best expressed in 66-68 High Street. There the windows are of Georgian proportions, with moulded architraves and accentuated moulded keystones. They are grouped together in pairs and triplets, a statement of prosperity if judged by the quantity of glass – although in each group the windows are cannily set less than a foot apart, so that they could count as one under the amended window-tax regulations of 1747. The doorway has a fashionable pulvinated frieze (or convex moulding) topped by a pediment.

Figure 88 In the 18th century many older buildings were given new sash windows. Those at 66-68 High Street (left), with their smart surrounds, are what fashionable townspeople aspired to. Horizontal sliding (or Yorkshire) sash windows (right) were a poorer man's version, since they fitted into existing window openings and did not require pulleys, cords and boxes.

This was not a completely new house, however, as indicated by the asymmetrical façade (see Gazetteer). In general, 18th-century sash windows can be identified by their thick glazing bars, which are now rare in Burford, though an example can be seen at Titcombs on Sheep Street. Poorer householders made do with horizontal sliding or Yorkshire sash windows (Figure 88), as at 61 and 154 High Street, 182 The Hill, and 21 and 41 Witney Street.[141]

Building activity was not confined to grander houses. Towards the end of Witney Street, Nos. 51 and 53 survive as separate cottages behind an elegant 18th-century frontage. In High Street, the handsome late 18th-century façade of Nos. 53-59 hides what seems to have been a purpose-built complex of dwellings with workplaces, which was occupied by five households in 1841. These examples, and the apparently deliberate creation of groups of cottages for rent (e.g. the pairs at 23 and 25 Witney Street), suggest the presence of developer-landlords in the late 17th and 18th centuries: John Jordan was apparently such a 'rentier', as indicated by the 1662 Hearth Tax return. In contrast, at the edge of the town two small, poor-quality dwellings were erected at what is now 57-59 Witney Street (on part of the plot of No. 55), while purpose-built cottage rows can be seen behind some High Street houses. That behind 56 High Street was popularly known as 'The College', probably an ironic comment on its communal life; it was recorded in 1793, and in the 19th century housed 11 families (see Gazetteer).

Inside the 18th-century house, those who could afford it installed panelling. Some fine raised and fielded panelling from the period survives in a rear room of 69 High Street. Some earlier fireplaces were replaced in the 18th century, but most surrounds are fairly plain; an exception is a remarkable Baroque fireplace in the rear wing of 128 High Street, probably from the early 18th century.

Figure 89 The 18th century saw much internal as well as external remodelling, including insertion of this Baroque fireplace in the rear wing of 128 High Street.

Few 18th-century shopfronts survive. The most important is the frontage at 124 High Street, converted from an inn to a shop for the apothecary Nicholas Willett around 1734 (Panel 14). A few shop fronts from the late 18th century are identifiable by their thick glazing bars and small panes of crown glass, for example at 121 High Street.

Figure 90 The panelled
staircase of The Great
House on Witney Street,
built for the physician
John Castle *c.*1695-1720.
Few Burford houses
are of such pretension,
though fashionable
panelling was introduced
into several lesser
buildings.

19TH-CENTURY BUILDING:
STAGNATION AND REVIVAL

Burford's prosperity was damaged in 1812 by the opening of a new
stretch of turnpike road on the ridge above the town, and suffered
further blows from its lack of a railway and loss of its market in
the 1870s (Chapter 7). There was little new domestic building in
these years, but behind the façades traces survive of the dwellings
of a growing population of labourers and tradesmen, who lived in
cramped conditions in subdivided houses and rows of backland
cottages. Many of these were labourers from surrounding farms,
displaced by machinery and later by the agricultural depression,
and coming into town where lodging was cheap. Cottage pairs and
rows had been built in the 18th century, but later developments
included Holland's Yard (behind 144 High Street), Bowl's (later
Godfrey's) Yard behind 156 The Hill, and a group on the opposite
side of the road including Wiggins' Yard (behind 135 The Hill),

Burford's Shopfronts

Figure A *The 18th-century apothecary's shopfront at 124 High Street, still a chemist's shop. The large sash windows are typical of the period.*

Figure B *The bow shop-window at 93 High Street was installed in the early 19th century, probably for a bakery. The relatively thin glazing bars are typical of this later period.*

Shopfronts have always been one of the most frequently replaced parts of town buildings, as on any modern High Street. Like many towns, therefore, Burford has few early examples despite its rich variety of domestic fronts. The earliest to survive, other than the fragments of a medieval shopfront inside 111 High Street (Panel 3), is the important 18th-century front at 124 High Street, converted from an inn to an apothecary's shop c.1734. Inside are drawers and fitments of the period.

A shop window at 121 High Street is late 18th-century, but most others are from the 19th and 20th centuries. Generally, those with thicker glazing bars are early (e.g. at 123 High Street). These became thinner in the early 19th century, for example in the bow-fronted window at 93 High Street (*Stone Gallery*). From the mid-19th century are the tripartite sash windows such as at 48 High Street (*Elm of Burford*). After the abolition of the glass tax in 1857, large sheets of plate glass replaced some earlier windows. Burford's economic stagnation kept their installation small-scale, however, and many earlier examples survive.

This gradual increase in window size allowed increased views of shop interiors as the century progressed. Some tradesmen and retailers never had purpose-built shop windows, however. In the side streets front rooms were often used, with goods displayed behind ordinary domestic windows.

Figure C *Some specialist shopfronts survive in Burford. At 49 High Street (formerly a butcher's), the wide sash would have opened completely to allow the meat to be seen in fresh air. Above can be seen the iron bars from which carcasses were hung. In the pavement outside are blue industrial paviors with a diamond pattern, provided so that passers-by did not slip when the counters were washed down.*

Further Reading: Morrison, Kathryn, *English Shops and Shopping: an Architectural History* (2003).

White Horse Mews (141 The Hill) and Perrin's Yard (behind 153 The Hill). At Wiggins' Yard there seem to have been six cottages occupied by labourers and hawkers, with some tradesmen and craftsmen, too. White Horse Mews had nine cottages in 1841, occupied by 17 people, and Perrin's Yard six cottages with 27 people in 1891 (see Gazetteer).

Figure 91 By the 19th century many poorer inhabitants were housed in cramped cottage yards behind the street frontage. George Yard, converted from former inn buildings after 1800, housed nine families (46 people) in 1841; this early 20th-century view looks back to the inn's former carriageway and High Street (Map 17).

Some of these cottages survive as rear wings or outbuildings of the front houses, their presence hinted at by side doorways. One group, Leather Alley (behind 47 Witney Street), housed a concentration of leather workers, but the other rows housed a diverse range of tradespeople. George Yard (Figures 91 and Gazetteer), which survives as a group of cottages, was a conversion of the stables and outbuildings of the former inn, while there were five families at Falkland Hall after the sale of the *Bear Inn* in 1830 (Panel 1). In the 19th century, more workers' cottages were added in Priory Lane to those formerly attached to Falkland Hall.

A number of the larger houses from earlier periods were also subdivided. Some survive as separate cottages, such as the three at 188-192 The Hill which were originally the services, hall and high end of a medieval hall-house, and the pair nearby at 184-186 The Hill, again probably carved from a medieval house. In other cases, the subdivision has now been reversed. At 147 The Hill the right-hand doorway was inserted in the early 19th century to allow access to a cottage in that half of the house, while the blocked doorway under the left-hand window led to a passage giving access to a third cottage at the rear. Other examples can be seen at 43 and 45 Sheep Street, and at 19, 23, 25 and 35 Witney Street.

Figure 92 Nos. 188-192 The Hill, a medieval hall house which, like many Burford buildings, was subdivided into cottage accommodation in the 19th century.

Despite the general loss of prosperity, many Burford householders in the 19th century continued to improve their properties. Around 1870 T.H. Cheatle, one of a dynasty of Burford doctors, extended his own house at 7 High Street (Riverside) with a two-storey Gothic extension to the east, placing his initials alongside foliage in the spandrels of the east lancet window. Lesser residents made do with improving their windows. Burford has many surviving early 19th-century sash windows, which are recognisable by their lack of 'horns': in the latter half of the century such horns were needed to strengthen the sash, after larger heavier glass panes became available.

19th-Century Commercial Buildings

Burford saw a certain amount of light industrial activity in the 19th century. Because it was small-scale and carried out in association with domestic accommodation it has, however, left few architectural remains. The buildings of Garne's Brewery in Sheep Street (Figure 78 and Gazetteer) have survived better than most. In the 18th century the site contained a farmhouse, four barns and an orchard, but by 1774 there was a malthouse which survives in converted form behind the *Lamb Inn* on Priory Lane. A perforated tile from the malting kiln has been built into the external wall. In the early 19th century the malthouse belonged to the Tuckwells, a farming family from nearby Signet, whose enlightened and innovative farming methods were praised by Arthur Young when he reported on Oxfordshire's agriculture in 1813. The brewery dates from the 1840s when the present archway was inserted into the front. It is now (2007) a Tourist Information Centre, but some features of the brewery survive within, such as the sloping cobbled floor down which barrels could be rolled.[142]

Also visible from Sheep Street is the former rope-works. Now converted into a house, this imposing structure with industrial blue-brick window dressings and banding lies to the rear of 136-142 High Street, and was built in 1903 (see Gazetteer for illustration). The High Street building had been an inn, the *Three Goats Heads*, but the Daniel family who ran it also wove hemp and made sacks as a sideline. Rope-making began after Abiah Daniel, the innkeeper's daughter, married James Wall in 1811, and the Wall family ran the business until it closed in the 1940s. The wide doorway to High Street is a reminder of the days when the ropewalk (the long straight area where strands of hemp were laid out to be twisted into rope) extended along the plot and out into the street.[143]

Further down High Street at No. 23 was the entrance and manager's house for the works of the Burford Gaslight and Coke Co. (formed 1864). Traces of the former entrance for loaded coal trucks can be seen on the façade. After the gasworks closed in 1914 it became part of the school premises.

Figure 93 The inside of the malthouse at the former Garne's Brewery on Sheep Street, photographed in 1994. Malting prepares cereal grain (usually barley) for brewing through controlled germination, followed by quick drying in a kiln. Perforated tiles (such as that reset in the Brewery's external wall) allow a flow of warm air which helps control the process.

Figure 94 Iron rings in the wall at 20 High Street, probably for tethering horses when a blacksmith worked here c.1900. Several other smithies operated on High Street.

Blacksmiths were important from the Middle Ages onwards, and in the 19th century shod horses and made iron fittings for houses. Ten metalworkers were listed in 1841, but only two smithies were shown on the 1921 Ordnance Survey map, at 24 and 74 High Street. The Hall family at 24 High Street had a forge in what is now the front room (see Gazetteer), and there is architectural evidence of others. The Barneses at 50 High Street had an outbuilding with a stack, possibly for a forge, while iron rings at the front of 20 High Street were probably fastenings for tethering horses. At No. 18 the name 'Richards Cottage' commemorates Bertram Richards, a tinsmith who lived and worked here from the 1920s.

As the 19th century drew to a close, Burford started to be discovered by cyclists and other tourists (Chapter 7). Tea rooms and antique dealers began to colonise the earlier shops, and new shop-fronts proliferated in High Street and Witney Street (Panel

Figure 95 This bow-fronted shop window at 103 High Street looks late 19th-century, but was actually inserted in the 20th. For more on shopfronts, see Panel 14.

Figure 96 Many of Burford's long burgage plots contained outbuildings connected with the occupier's trade. Pigsties survived behind Castle's butchers on High Street until 2003.

Figure 97 The Greek inspired entrance to the courthouse on Lavington Lane, built in 1844: one of several new Victorian public buildings in Burford.

14). In the late 19th century large sheets of plate glass replaced the earlier windows in some shops, though we should not forget that a number of premises did not have shop windows. In the side streets the front rooms of houses were used as shops, and leave no architectural trace. There is nothing now to suggest that 2 Priory Lane was a fish-and-chip shop, for example.

Behind the house or shop on the street, many of Burford's long burgage plots contain signs of structures for activities ancillary to the main retail range. Inn properties had courtyard access to stables and residential wings, while butchers kept animals and slaughtered them on the premises. Behind Castle's butcher's shop at 111 High Street was an abattoir, and at its far end near Pytt's Lane pigsties survived until 2003. Over time, the buildings nearest the shop were converted into meat stores, while those further away were rented out to other local businesses. There are former furniture workshops behind 115 High Street, while the various rear outbuildings of ironmonger Thomas Holland's property (134 High Street) in the 1890s can still be identified today in a row of shops and a cottage.

19th-Century Public Buildings

The high Victorian period also saw the construction of a number of public buildings in Burford, in a variety of contemporary revivalist styles. In 1844 a new courthouse was built in Lavington Lane in a Greek Revival style. In 1863 a Gothic style was chosen for the Church Schools (now the Warwick Hall), no doubt in deference to their position near the churchyard. In 1869 William Wilkinson (a prolific architect from Witney but by then based in Oxford) used

a rather more subtle Tudor style for the new Police Station at 164 The Hill. With its stone mullions and central, plain Tudor-arched doorway, it seems intended to blend with its older neighbours, for example the 'Gabled House'. Wilkinson's Elementary School of 1875-7 is more Jacobean than Gothic, and the new cottage-hospital extension of 1886 in Church Lane (Figure 72) took its cue from the Georgian townhouses of the town. The County of Gloucester Bank of 1878 is firmly Gothic, however, with two-centred arched doorways and an asymmetric elevation. The architect is unknown, but the building has style and assurance, and may possibly be by Medland and Maberly of Gloucester. By 1889 the Devon tin-magnate who built Tiverton Villa (in Guildenford) was already moving towards an eclectic Edwardian style.

By the end of the 19th century, Burford thus had a number of modern buildings of which it could be proud. But its popularity was based on its picturesque older houses, and in the new century these attracted the attention of restorers.

THE PRESENT IN THE PAST: BURFORD'S BUILDINGS IN THE 20TH CENTURY

Early 20th-Century Restoration

The Arts and Crafts movement, which throve for a glorious but brief period in the Cotswolds around the turn of the century, also left its mark on Burford (Panel 12). Its most devoted disciple in the town was Emslie J. Horniman, who was responsible for the restoration of a number of properties including his own house (The Priory), The Gabled House (162 The Hill), the roof of the Staffordshire Pottery (33 High Street), and parts of the *Highway Hotel* (117 High Street). On some jobs he employed Alfred Groves, builders based at Milton-under-Wychwood, whose workmanship cannot be faulted. Even doorway ironwork was hand-made to suit. Long Wivets on The Hill (No. 170) was remodelled around 1910 in a Cotswold style, most likely by Charles Pether, the local builder whose house this was, while three cottages on The Hill were remodelled to form the present Pytts Piece (No. 157).[144]

In the spirit of the times, this early restoration work was often aimed at re-creating what the building might have looked like when newly built. With the passage of time it is now sometimes quite difficult to distinguish between work of different periods, but clues to the 20th-century work include lack of weathering, and anachronisms such as over-sized mullioned windows – for example those at Culverclose on Sheep Street, which date from the 1930s. Careful examination of some buildings can show where modern

Figure 98 17th-
century-style mullion
windows and doorway
at 39-43 Sheep Street
(Culverclose), dating
from the 1930s. Early
20th-century restoration
work in Burford rarely
strove for scientific
accuracy or followed
traditional building
techniques; nevertheless,
it gave Burford much of
its present-day character.

materials and techniques have been used. The close-studding and
jetty bressumer of the *Burford House Hotel*, for example, restored
by Horniman in the 1920s, have been secured to the façade with
nails rather than the traditional wooden pegs (see Gazetteer). This
approach to the restoration of historic buildings would not be
acceptable today, but it was a key feature of the town's revival in the
early 20th century, and can now be appreciated in that context.

Modern Expansion

Further infilling of back plots took place through the 20th century,
with new houses built behind properties on High Street and
Sheep Street. Some were provided with new access ways such as
Sylvester Close or White Horse Mews, while others made use of
existing alleys and back lanes, as at Castles Yard off Pytts Lane.
This demand for space for development has resulted in a general
disappearance of garages and barns throughout the town, as well
as the loss of many gardens. Infilling is an ongoing process, and

Map 18 (opposite) Post-
medieval and modern
alterations to Burford's
town plan. Features
constraining growth are
shown in red; infill in
blue; and 20th-century
expansion in green. Based
on Ordnance Survey ©
Crown Copyright. All
rights reserved. Licence
number 100020457.

is still taking place: Cheatle Close at the top of The Hill, laid out
in the mid-20th century, is an imposition of new properties into
an existing residential layout, while Windrush Court has replaced
Windrush School, itself an early 20th-century infill development in
an unoccupied area of the medieval town.

The laying out of entirely new areas of settlement is a
relatively recent phenomenon at Burford, beginning in the early
20th century, and subject to a variety of modern and historical
constraints. The site of The Priory and its associated lands still

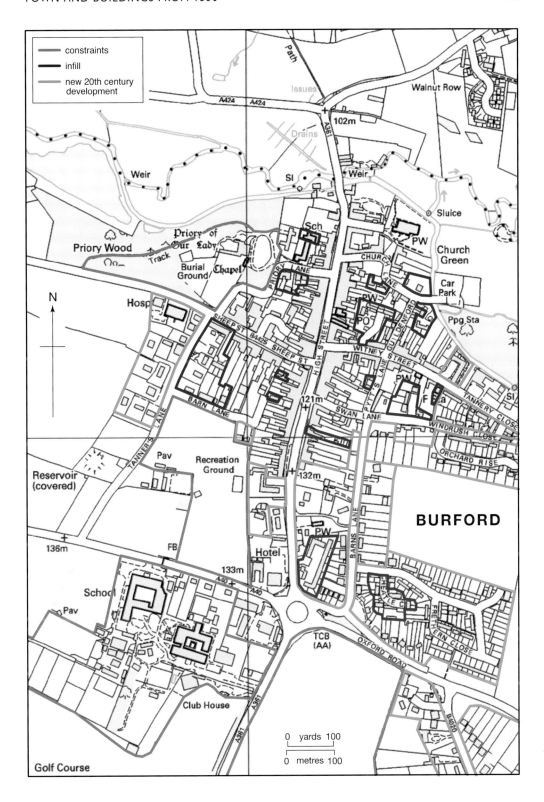

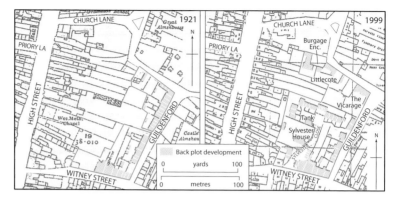

Map 19 Ongoing development along Witney Street and Guildenford. The building plots outlined on the 1921 plan were carved from the long medieval burgage plots running back from High Street, probably at an early date. The late 20th-century development of Sylvester Close is a continuation of the same process.

restrict expansion north-west of the urban core, much as the Hospital of St John did in the medieval period. Similarly, the designation of a new recreation ground west of The Hill in 1932 prevented domestic occupation extending there, while expansion south of the A40 was hampered by creation of a golf course in 1936, and construction of new school buildings from 1958. New development was thus confined to the south-east of the town and a small area west of Tanner's Lane, while along Barns Lane development took place on land which had remained unoccupied since the later Middle Ages. Elsewhere development took place on surrounding fields and orchards, based for the most part on existing roads and field boundaries – although new internal roads give access to individual properties, the most extensive example being Fretherne Close and Wisdom Way.

But physical constraints are only part of the picture. As in the Middle Ages, Burford's recent development has been conditioned above all by centralised planning, which in a modern context reflects current ideas about conservation. Burford was one of the

Map 20 Like much modern development in Burford, houses at the top of The Hill were laid out within established field-boundaries, preserving older elements of the town's geography.

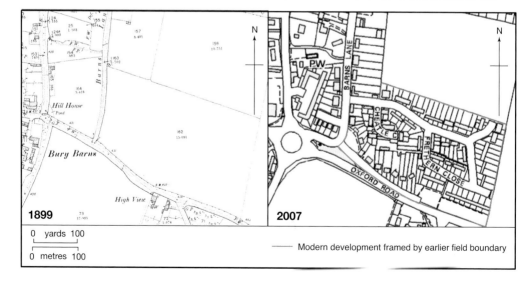

1899

0 yards 100

0 metres 100

2007

——— Modern development framed by earlier field boundary

first conservation areas in West Oxfordshire District, and lies within the Cotswold Area of Outstanding Natural Beauty. Local-authority decisions to target housing development in other Oxfordshire towns, combined with restrictions over alterations to shopfronts and to listed and unlisted buildings, have further preserved its appearance: indeed there is even a specific colour, 'Burford green', recommended for doors and other external woodwork. Whether such policies truly benefit the town and its inhabitants is outside the scope of this book, but certainly they explain its modern character. Burford's history emphatically marks it as a town, not a village; yet measured by its current size and amenities it sits uneasily on the cusp, frozen (at least for now) as a 'historic Cotswold town' largely untouched by modern building development.[145]

Figure 99 An unusual example of modern infill: public conveniences on High Street, inserted into a gap in the building line and carefully fronted to look in keeping with adjoining buildings.

New Domestic Building

Few houses were built in Burford between the wars, but what building there was continued to respect traditional local materials and features. The Vicarage in Church Lane, by the architect Russell Cox (1937), is a good example. Church Cottage on Lawrence Lane,

Figure 100 The Vicarage in Church Lane (1937), designed by the local architect Russell Cox: a good example of sympathetic 20th-century building in traditional styles and materials.

built in the same year by the same architect for C.T. Cheatle, of the Burford medical family, replaced a barn and outbuildings on the edge of their property, based on Riverside House. Cox also carried out conversions, for example the barn behind Titcombs (his own house in Sheep Street), and the former butcher's shop at 122 High Street. On Guildenford, the group at No. 3 has a 'rock face' aspect typical of the Cotswold vernacular revival. The detailed working of the quoins is typical of the period around 1900, but the building does not feature on a photograph of *c.*1900 and may also have been built in the 1930s. A little earlier, in 1925, the Grettons completed their restoration programme at Calendars on Sheep Street (Figure 33 and Gazetteer), which involved incorporating the small cottage next door and rebuilding the rear gable.[146]

One of the first post-war rebuildings (also by Cox) was for Nelson Garne, of the Sheep Street brewery. Dated 1946 with his initials in the gable, the Malthouse is a somewhat mannered version of the local vernacular style (see Gazetteer). White Oaks, on the upper part of The Hill, was one of the first grander new houses to be built in Burford (around 1960), in a standard Arts and Crafts style. Briggs' Almshouses in Sweeps Lane (1966) were endowed by Katherine M. Briggs, who lived in the Barn House to the rear of Calendars (27 Sheep Street), and followed the Cotswold vernacular with uncoursed rubblestone and a stone slate roof. Features include a pair of three-light stone-mullioned windows under a drip moulding, and doorways with plain Tudor arches. The council houses on Witney Street were designed in the wake of Sir Stafford Cripps's efforts in nearby Filkins to require the local authority to respect the local vernacular.[147]

By contrast New Stone House on Priory Lane, which replaced an earlier cottage in 1971, shows some of the unattractive features of its time: inappropriate aluminium window frames, and a bland unbroken exterior without a chimney. Also from the 1970s is a group of houses near the top of Barns Lane, built to a standard design then common across Britain, with no attempt to adopt local features.

During the last quarter of the 20th century, three main strands emerged: the infill developments discussed above, extensions to existing houses, and conversions of buildings to domestic use. In the central part of the town, Sylvester Close (1981) is particularly successful infill in planning terms, but spoilt by the architectural detailing such as the flimsy timber door-heads. Towards the end of the century, planning guidance tried to ensure that any new buildings fitted in better with the older ones, and houses to the rear of the Old Ropery on Sweeps Lane (1998) show the results of this guidance. Construction is of regularly coursed rubblestone, and Poundbury-influenced designs create the illusion of accretive development, such as the extension of a small house with a one-and-a-half storey range. There are also some good single houses, often architect-designed. That at 9 Sheep Street mirrors the enigmatic timber framing of Calendars further up, while Burford House and Peach Cottage (2000) in Church Lane, the white Guiting limestone bright and new-looking at the time of writing, reflect the various choices of neo-vernacular styles available in Burford. Architects can select features such as hoodmoulds and keystoned windows almost at random, as precedents for all can be found elsewhere in the town.

Figure 101 New Stone House on Priory Lane, built 1971. Here, little attempt was made to reflect local vernacular styles.

Figure 102 No. 9 Sheep Street reflects various aspects of the local vernacular, with its dormers and stone mullions. In particular it echoes the 15th-century timber framing of Calendars, further along the street.

Conversions to domestic use have mostly involved backland buildings, such as a barn behind Titcombs in Sheep Street (now linked to the house), and the Barn House mentioned earlier. Among former industrial buildings Island House, part of the mill complex near the bridge, has been converted to offices, and the Old Ropery became a house in the late 20th century.

Commercial Premises

In the town centre, changes of ownership and alterations to business premises accelerated during the 20th century. Blacksmiths were among the first to disappear. The smith's most common option was to repair the motor vehicles which had replaced the horses he once shod, and in the mid-to-late 20th century Burford had a number of such premises. Holloway's at 28 High Street retains a number of features including the base for the petrol pumps and the cash kiosk, while at Keylock's (125 High Street) the pumps were within the present shop, the pipes held on a gantry

Figure 103 Keylock's motor garage at 125 High Street, one of several buildings ingeniously adapted for such use. Petrol pipes were held on a gantry fixed to the wooden bracket to the right of the window, and were swung out over the pavement when a car drew up for fuel.

(Figure 103). The Priory Garage in Priory Lane repaired vehicles and sold fuel until April 2003, but at the time of writing only Byways Garage in Guildenford survived as a local garage.

Among new commercial buildings Barclays Bank, built on an empty High Street site in the 1970s, is not unsuccessful (Gazetteer, 95 High St). The architect has adopted a simplified form of the Georgian window-surround at the first floor, and the roof has stone slates laid in the traditional diminishing courses. The façade clearly masks a modern concrete or steel- framed building, however, while the signage is undisguisedly modern. Further down High Street, the insertion of a modern public convenience into a gap in the building line (Figure 99) was a brave move. The façade, using local materials, was a later addition to soften its impact.[148]

The Brewery site, which became vacant in 1995, presented some conservation challenges. The surviving structures have been sensitively adapted to office use, and the original layout can be understood both from the courtyard to the rear and from within the complex, where the Tourist Information Office occupies the office accommodation, re-using part of the main desk and allowing the sloping floor to be seen. On the site of the former tannery in Witney Street are the unassuming Burford Laundry near the river (weatherboarded and functional), and a modernist office block nearer the street. Although the stone could be said to be local in tradition, the roof is certainly not: almost mono-pitch, both slopes have Welsh slate coverings.

CONCLUSION

Burford is often portrayed as a quintessential 'Cotswold town', which has become a modern shorthand for photogenic streetscapes of gabled and stone-mullioned limestone buildings. Though Burford has plenty of genuine examples, closer investigation has shown that part of its Cotswold character is artificial: a modern pastiche reflecting the romanticised, loosely Arts and Crafts principles behind much of the early 20th-century restoration work.

Burford's authentic historic buildings display considerable variety, however, reflecting the town's shifting fortunes and changing character. Nearly all show signs of constant remodelling: one of the town's chief characteristics is the extent to which older (often medieval) buildings survive behind later façades or inserted doorways and windows. Some of those refrontings incorporated fashionable and sophisticated styles (classical doorways or sash windows, for instance), though the amount of remodelling compared with rebuilding reflects the limited means of many Burford inhabitants, as the town continued its slow decline. The main exceptions are Burford's three gentry houses, the only secular buildings to display any architectural pretension, and all reflecting landed or professional rather than commercial wealth. Nineteenth-century decline found expression in subdivision and cottage-yard development, of which clues remain all over the town. Yet 19th-century shopfronts and several new public buildings show the other side of the coin: that of a small market town which still retained some civic pride, and had enough professional or moderately prosperous inhabitants to give a lead in civic affairs. Commercial activity, too, is reflected in a myriad of small details, alongside more obvious monuments such as Garne's Brewery or the 1903 rope factory.

All these buildings reflect Burford's social and economic life. But alongside them sit a number of religious buildings: not only the parish church, but a variety of small Dissenting chapels built since the 17th century, as the laws governing religious nonconformity were relaxed. The next chapter completes our survey of Burford's post-medieval buildings by looking at these structures, and at the religious movements behind them.

The Ship of the Romish Church.

Burning of images.

Ship over your trinkets & be packing you papists.

The Temple well purged.

The Papists packing away their Paltry.

The Cōmunion Table.

Church and Chapel since the Reformation

Figure 104 A woodcut from John Foxe's Acts and Monuments, depicting (from a Protestant perspective) the destruction of traditional religion under Edward VI. At the top, 'superstitious' images and other furnishings are ripped from a church and burnt or carried off. Below, the king presents the revised English Bible, while Protestant worshippers hear a sermon before a simple communion table.

The Reformation of the mid-16th century marked a decisive break in English religious life, as great or greater than any of the purely secular changes described in previous chapters. In Burford, as elsewhere, these changes found expression in the town's religious buildings. The parish church, stripped of the trappings of late medieval religion, entered a new phase, its furnishings replaced and its interior reorganised. From the 1660s, with the legalisation of organised nonconformity, the town also acquired some small Dissenting chapels, which together make an important contribution to Burford's townscape and visual appeal. This chapter completes our survey of the post-medieval town by setting these buildings in context. The first part examines Burford's religious life since the Reformation and the impact of these changes on the parish church. The second explores the growth of nonconformity and the buildings which this produced.

REFORMATION TO RESTORATION 1538-1660

The Protestant Reformation – begun under Henry VIII and Edward VI, briefly reversed under Mary (reigned 1553-8), and consolidated under Elizabeth I – had a profound impact on Burford as on all towns and villages. The medieval paraphernalia of chantries, side altars, and images was swept away, while the Hospital of St John was suppressed and its property given to new owners. The Hospital site itself was acquired by the king's barber and courtier Edmund Harman, who may have begun its conversion into a country house now known as The Priory; Harman also obtained the glebe and tithes of Burford church, excepting only the income set aside for the vicar. The church lands were exchanged with Fotheringhay College, and eventually passed back to the Crown, which leased them to Harman's successors the Lenthalls. The advowson was aquired before 1611 by the bishop of Oxford.[149]

The attitude of most townspeople to such changes is unrecorded, though there is evidence for Protestant Dissent in Burford by the early 16th century, when England was still firmly Catholic. In 1521 charges of heresy were brought against 15 inhabitants said to attend meetings at the house of a local tailor, which attracted adherents from as far as Asthall, Witney, Lechlade, Wantage, and Steventon. Offences included supplying and reading prohibited books, reciting the scriptures in English, and speaking against pilgrimages and the cult of saints. The group appears to have formed part of an established Lollard (or heretic) network with London connections, and the fact that Burford was chosen as one of the places of public penance for those who recanted suggests that it was perceived as a hotbed of Dissent, and a suitable venue at which to set an example. Other inhabitants, given the scale of pious bequests to the church in the later Middle Ages, may have resented the suppression of traditional rituals, though Protestant sympathies certainly penetrated to the highest levels. Simon Wisdom, one of the town's most prominent merchants, was charged in 1530 with possessing three books in English, among them a copy of William Tyndale's New Testament. This, published abroad in 1526, was the first complete translation into modern English, and was banned by the Church authorities. Whatever the overall balance of views in Burford, within a few generations the changes must have become entrenched. All Burford's vicars formally subscribed to the Elizabethan religious settlement as required by law, and from the later 16th century very few inhabitants were fined for continuing adherence to Catholicism.[150]

The period following the Reformation saw a rapid turnover of vicars, with 15 recorded over 130 years. Many in the 16th century held several churches and quickly moved on to greater things, so that once again pastoral care fell largely to wage-earning curates. Curates rather than vicars witnessed many Burford wills, though two vicars in the 1580s and 1590s, Richard Hopkins and Bernard Robinson, witnessed some, and evidently spent some time in the town. During the 17th century the pattern changed, with many vicars staying for 10 years or more and apparently living locally. One reason may have been the relative impoverishment of the living through the machinations of Sir Lawrence Tanfield, who, as lord of the manor, collided with the town in several acrimonious disputes. Tanfield seems to have persuaded the vicar Philip Hill (1611-35) to part with much of the glebe and tithes in return for an annual life 'pension' of £80 and the living of Eaton Hastings in Berkshire. By the later 17th century the pension was only £40, and when John Thorpe became vicar in 1668 he found the vicar's endowment seriously depleted. What remained (still far more than most vicars enjoyed) were some 65 acres in Fulbrook, and tithes from two Burford mills, coppices and inclosures. Much of the vicar's land in Burford itself had been lost, however, and Thorpe's stylish rebuilding of the vicarage house in 1672, to the latest fashions, drew probably on his private means rather than those of the church.[151]

The Civil War and its aftermath brought considerable disruption to Burford, culminating in the notorious capture of rebel Levellers

Figure 105 The imposing classical frontage of the former vicarage house (now Cobb House) on High Street, rebuilt by the vicar John Thorpe in 1672.

there in 1649 (Panel 11). The vicar throughout this turbulent period was Christopher Glynn (1637-68), evidently an astute political operator since, unlike many contemporaries, he managed to retain his living from the final years of Charles I's reign, through the Civil War and Commonwealth, and into the early years of the Restoration. Presumably he avoided the extreme stances of both the Puritans and conservatives, bending to circumstance, and it may well be that many townspeople did the same. Nevertheless, Burford glimpsed religious controversy. The 'Ranter' Abiezer Coppe preached there in 1649, and in 1651 two outside radical ministers held a public conference there on the resurrection of the body. References in some early 17th-century Burford wills to Christ's 'elect and chosen servants' also suggest Puritan tendencies among some at least in the town.[152]

The main impact on the church building from the 1540s was the stripping out of side altars and 'idolatrous' images (including the rood and private memorial brasses), and the destruction of stained glass and wall paintings. The latter were replaced by whitewashed walls and, in the south-east chapel, by extracts from William Tyndale's and Miles Coverdale's English translation of the scriptures. Not all the destruction was necessarily immediate. The rood must certainly have gone under Elizabeth I if not under Edward VI, and an altar tomb in the south transept was 'defaced' by 1574; nevertheless, some other lost brasses were still in place in 1660. Further damage followed during the Civil War, when soldiers were twice quartered in the church (during 1644-5), and the captured Levellers were imprisoned there.[153]

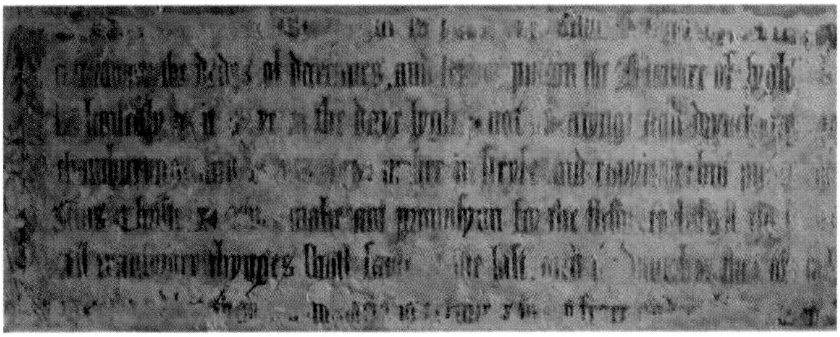

Figure 106 Extracts from William Tyndale's and Miles Coverdale's English translations of the scriptures, painted onto a wall in the south-east chapel after the Reformation. Probably they replaced medieval paintings or other 'idolatrous' images.

Meanwhile the building's various parts were adapted to new religious uses (Figure 45). St Peter's chapel in the nave (whose original dedication is unknown) became a private family pew for owners of The Priory, necessitating the cutting back of its medieval stone screens. St Thomas's chapel (known later as the Burgess Aisle) was fitted up with pews for the town corporation, and probably in the 16th or 17th century a row of low, square-headed windows was cut through its east wall to allow occupants to see

Figure 107 Silvester family monuments in the south-west chapel (formerly the guild chapel), which from the 1560s became effectively a Silvester mortuary chapel. Several other chapels were associated with particular families after the Reformation.

the high altar. Other chapels were named after local families who adopted them for burial or memorial. From 1568 the Lady chapel (the former guild chapel) became effectively a mortuary chapel for the Silvester family, whose imposing memorials line the south wall. The south-east chapel became the Bartholomew aisle, from the numerous family monuments installed there from the late 17th century. Most striking of all, the north chancel chapel became the burial place of Sir Lawrence Tanfield of The Priory (died 1625), whose widow took over the chapel with typical high-handedness to erect a grandiose Italianate monument, complete with recumbent effigies (Figure 52).[154]

ANGLICANISM 1660-1900

Vicars and their Flocks

Following the religious upheavals of the previous 130 years, with the Restoration of Charles II in 1660 the Anglican Church in Burford entered a period of relative stability, notwithstanding the gradual emergence in the town of organised religious nonconformity. The period 1660-1826 saw only five vicars, mostly resident in Burford, while the last two 18th-century incumbents (Charles and Francis Knollys) were father and son, who between them served the parish for over 80 years. The slackness of many 18th-century Anglican clergy has become notorious, and a 19th-century successor at Burford was unimpressed by Francis Knollys's performance:

> [He] was no example to his flock either in morals or religion. He never visited the parishioners except on secular business … gave them one sermon on Sunday, and did as little beside as ecclesiastical law allowed him.

Nonetheless, at a time when most parishes were lucky to see communion celebrated four times a year there was a monthly celebration during Knollys's incumbency. Knollys also appointed a curate, albeit one who was criticised locally for his lavish lifestyle and mounting debts.[155]

The 19th century, as so often, saw reinvigoration of Church life under energetic resident clergymen, although at Burford two of the most active represented polar opposites in terms of contemporary theological attitudes. Alexander Dallas, who served as curate for 21 months under the non-resident vicar William Birch (1826-36), was a member of the Clapham Sect, evangelical Christians devoted to social issues at home and abroad. On his

Figure 108 The private chapel built at The Priory by William Lenthall, then lord of Burford, in 1662 (Chapter 6 and Gazetteer). Despite his career as a Parliamentarian, the chapel's style suggests a degree of High Church religious conservatism on Lenthall's part by the end of his life.

first Sunday in post (Whit Sunday) he found only two persons in church beside himself and the clerk, and was shocked to learn that his parishioners were all at Cap's Lodge in Wychwood Forest, enjoying the traditional (and often raucous) Whitsuntide festivities. Dallas duly set forth to reform the town (Chapter 7). Reflecting his Low Church evangelical views he also re-arranged the layout of the church to focus on the pulpit, which was moved to the west end in the centre of the nave (Figure 109).[156]

By contrast John Burgess, vicar 1860-71, was a proponent of the Oxford Movement, an affiliation of High Church Anglican clergy which saw strong affinities between the Anglican and Catholic churches, and which favoured greater ritual in Christian worship. Burgess made significant changes, introducing a robed choir and giving considerable attention to the religious calendar and to

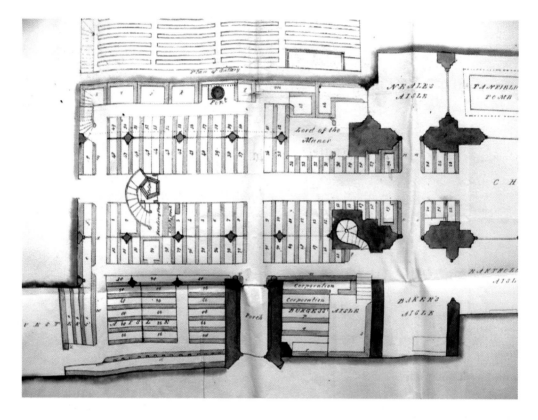

Figure 109 The church interior as re-arranged *c*.1827, reflecting Dallas's evangelical Low Church views. Seating was focused on the pulpit, which was moved to the west end in the centre of the nave. The arrangement was reversed by Dallas's High Church successors, and the galleries and private pews were swept away during the church's restoration from 1870.

correct religious observance, all promulgated through the church magazine. The number of services increased significantly, to two Sunday services with a weekly communion, prayers twice every weekday, and additional Friday sermons. The trend continued under his successor William Cass (1871-1907), who added a third Sunday service and, from his appointment until 1887, oversaw a major restoration of the parish church, begun under Burgess. Completion of the first phase of the church restoration in 1872 was marked by processions, special services, and town festivities:

> at 11 o'clock the Bishop, about forty clergy, and the choir, robed in their surplices, proceeded from the Vicarage to the Church, singing … from *Hymns Ancient and Modern* … . At two o'clock, upwards of 300 of the parishioners and friends sat down to a luncheon, provided by Mrs Porter, of the Bull hotel, in a large barn belonging to Mr Allen-Faulkner, situated at the upper end of the town.

Toasts and speeches followed, and the celebrations ended with music and dancing in the Priory grounds, evensong in the church, and a peal of bells.[157]

Completion of the restoration work was made possible through the support of prominent townsmen and landowners, among them Edward Marriott, JP, of The Great House, who matched pound for pound what Burgess raised from other sources. Not all parishioners were impressed by Burgess's and Cass's reforms, however. Dallas and his successors seem to have commanded considerable popular support, but from the late 19th century there was increasing polarisation between the Established Church and the town's nonconformist denominations, which prompted a general swing to Methodism (below). Burgess acknowledged the gradual decline in his congregation, attributing it to his own deficiencies, to the support given to nonconformist groups by many influential people in the town, and to 'the number of public houses', which he viewed as a further distraction.[158]

The Church Restoration

· WILLIAM · MORRIS ·

Figure 110 William Morris, father of the Arts and Crafts movement, who in 1876 was involved in a celebrated altercation with the vicar over the restoration of Burford church. The experience contributed to Morris's decision to found the Society for the Protection of Ancient Buildings (the 'Anti-Scrape Society').

In the 18th century the church was often neglected; the churchwardens were frequently in debt, and in 1703 and 1707 the spire suffered partial collapse. Dallas's rearrangements in 1826-7, though theologically significant, were largely cosmetic, the only structural changes being the raising of the floor to prevent flooding, and the salvaging of fragments of medieval glass and woodwork. The Victorian restoration of 1870-87, mostly superintended by the diocesan architect G.E. Street (died 1882), was urgently needed, therefore. Work began with the nave and aisles in 1870-2, and included, as well as structural repairs, removal of galleries, replacement of pews, re-roofing, removal of plaster, and removal of bones from a charnel house under St Thomas's chapel. A new arcade was built across the northern part of the chapel, and St Peter's chapel was re-created from the Priory pew.[159]

An indirect result of the restoration was the founding by William Morris of the Society for the Protection of Ancient Buildings. Passing through the town in 1876, Morris was shocked by what he felt was the insensitivity of the work that had been done, and proceeded to remonstrate with Cass for 'completely spoiling' a 'beautiful old church'. Street, he proclaimed, 'should be ashamed of himself, and I shall tell him so when I see him.' Shortly afterwards Morris drafted a letter 'urging the formation of a Society which might deal with such cases', and a few months later – following proposals for the restoration of Tewkesbury Abbey – launched the Society with a letter to the *Athenaeum*. Cass, though affronted at the time, subsequently regretted some of the restoration work, putting it down to his own inexperience.[160]

DISSENT AND MEETING HOUSES

Though subject to numerous restrictions and legal handicaps, from the reign of Charles II organised religious Dissent was legalised. Burford had a continuous nonconformist presence from the 1660s, though never on a particularly large scale compared with some towns: an Anglican enquiry in 1676 reported 21 nonconformists in Burford, compared with 77 at Chipping Norton and 76 at Henley. There were, however, several excommunications for non-attendance at the parish church in the later 17th century, and in the 1680s the bishop made specific enquiries about one Samuel Pack of Burford, 'preacher to dissenters', so that he might be 'proceeded against according to law'.[161]

One of the earliest Dissenting groups in Burford were the Friends or Quakers. As early as 1662 a meeting was broken up, and seven men imprisoned. Prominent in the movement was Thomas Minchin, a Burford mercer who was repeatedly excommunicated and imprisoned, and had his goods confiscated. In 1688 he bought land in Witney Street for a permanent meeting house, giving £383 towards its construction; the existing building, however, now entered from Pytts Lane, was not erected until 1708-9, as recalled in the date displayed on the modern gateway. The Minchins remained important figures in the local Quaker community, and as late as 1800 an obituary of Mrs Elizabeth Minchin called her a 'faithful and indefatigable preacher amongst the Quakers'.[162]

The Pytts Lane meeting house, with its rubble-stone walls and stone-slate hipped roof, is a simple expression of vernacular construction. As such it epitomises Quaker principles, which not

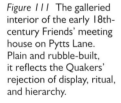

Figure 111　The galleried interior of the early 18th-century Friends' meeting house on Pytts Lane. Plain and rubble-built, it reflects the Quakers' rejection of display, ritual, and hierarchy.

only eschewed all ritual and hierarchy but rejected indulgence in dress, language, and daily life. Its front elevation has a central doorway with tall sash windows to either side. Inside is a gallery to south and west, altered in the 1730s perhaps for women Friends: in the 18th century the movement recognised the role of women, and separate spaces were created for their meetings. Sometimes these were in upstairs rooms separated by shutters from the main space, so that women could choose whether to be private or to participate in the main meeting. The elders' stand or bench was removed in 1947, when the movement adopted a more egalitarian layout for its meetings.[163]

Burford also saw an early Baptist presence. In 1660 Joseph Davis, a Baptist mercer of Chipping Norton and a 'zealous and pious preacher', was imprisoned at Burford, while the Samuel Pack harassed in the 1680s by Bishop Fell may also have been an Anabaptist. By 1700, meetings were held in an upper room of a house in the town, and in 1728 the Burford Baptists acquired a house in Witney Street, probably on the site of the modern chapel yard. The present building, on the site of the 18th-century graveyard, dates from 1803-4, and is a plain rectangular construction with four round-arched windows to the street. A gallery inside incorporates re-used 18th-century panelling. The pulpit was probably installed during a major programme of works in 1884-6, which included construction of a schoolroom.[164]

As elsewhere, 'old' Dissent was challenged in the 18th century by new sects established by John Wesley and others. Wesley preached at Burford several times in 1739 and 1740, on one occasion to

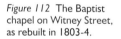
Figure 112 The Baptist chapel on Witney Street, as rebuilt in 1803-4.

Figure 113 Thomas Buswell, miller and corndealer, was one of the chief promoters of the Wesleyan Methodist meeting in Burford in the early 19th century.

an assembly estimated at 1,200-1,500 people. There is, however, no record of a Wesleyan Methodist meeting in Burford between Wesley's visits and the early 19th century, when the miller and corndealer Thomas Buswell invited Methodists from Witney to meet at his house – on the advice, according to a memorial in the present chapel, of a former 'vicar'. Possibly this was the former Anglican curate John Missing, who replaced Dallas in 1827 but may have shared his evangelical views. Despite some persecution (a visiting preacher's gig was pushed into the river during one service) the congregation grew, and a house on Priory Lane was converted to serve as a chapel. In 1849, however, a building of an altogether different class was bought for conversion: the Baroque former Chapman mansion on High Street, whose grand façade proclaimed the dominance achieved by the Burford Wesleyans in a very short time. The entire domestic interior was removed, the sash windows replaced, and ornaments on the parapet and gateway transferred to Cornbury Park, although part of the staircase balustrade survives in the altar rail. The interior was again remodelled in 1949 by Thomas Rayson of Oxford, taking cues from Sir Christopher Wren's church of St Stephen, Walbrook. Rayson also removed the inscription which had adorned the façade for its first hundred years as a place of worship.[165]

During the 19th century the Quakers in particular suffered mixed fortunes. In 1851 only five people attended their weekly meetings, while the Wesleyans attracted 250 and the Baptists around a hundred. There was also by then a small Plymouth Brethren meeting, attracting 20 people on average: meetings were in a converted soap and candle loft in College Yard, replaced before

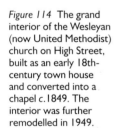

Figure 114 The grand interior of the Wesleyan (now United Methodist) church on High Street, built as an early 18th-century town house and converted into a chapel *c*.1849. The interior was further remodelled in 1949.

1877 by a meeting house in Witney Street. Combined attendance at the meeting houses very nearly equalled that at the parish church, and by the 1860s there were reckoned to be at least 200 nonconformists in the town, a level of Dissent which probably reflected antipathy to Burgess's new High Church innovations. Nevertheless, many members of the Anglican congregation seem to have absented themselves without becoming adherents of any particular nonconformist group. In 1866 Burgess noted 'a great number of people who go sometime to the meeting house and sometime to the church', and there appears not to have been any great animosity between Anglican and nonconformist townspeople – in the words of an earlier vicar, 'pure indifference and gross drunkenness are greater impediments here than any sectarian opposition'. The Temperance movement was, in fact, one thing which brought Anglicans and nonconformists together. In 1817 the Baptist meeting condemned 'all singing of songs, gambling, and frequenting of ale houses for the purpose of drinking and wasting time', while in 1893 the Quaker Quarterly Meeting noted that 'temperance work was needed' in Burford.[166]

Figure 115 The former Plymouth Brethren chapel on Witney Street, built *c*.1877. It became a private house in 1965.

20TH-CENTURY RELIGION

During the 20th century all denominations in Burford experienced predictably mixed fortunes, accompanied by a strong drive towards cooperation and ecumenism. The Quaker meeting enjoyed a modest revival from the 1890s, but by 1932 attendance had slumped, and a suggestion was tabled for renting the meeting house to the Youth Hostel Association. Fortunately the building was retained, and by 1955 a revived meeting attracted 10 or more members, increasing to 41 six years later. By contrast the Plymouth Brethren meeting closed in 1965, its meeting house converted into a private residence.

Roman Catholics, previously recorded only in very small numbers, became established in the 1930s, when a small congregation met in a wooden building in the grounds of Windrush School. In 1953 Irish construction workers employed at Brize Norton airbase attended mass there, and offered to build a larger church in their spare time. Working at weekends they made good progress on the walls, the work being completed by a contractor after their local employment ended. The new church, dedicated to St John Fisher and St Thomas More, was eventually opened in 1955. Transepts were added in 2002, their striking curved roofs supported on slender posts.[167]

Amongst the Anglican community, William Charles Emeris (vicar 1907-1937) managed to create greater cohesion, living

Figure 116 The Roman
Catholic church at the
top of The Hill, begun by
Irish labourers from Brize
Norton airbase in 1953.
The transepts, added in
2002, were designed by
Daniel Hurd Associates of
Birmingham, and are the
only significant examples
of 'modern' architecture
in Burford.

constantly at Burford with his two unmarried sisters, and turning
his house into a social focus for the town. His successor Reginald
Tucker remained for over 30 years. In 1941, at the height of the
Second World War, a Council of Christian Churches was formed
at Burford by members of the Church of England and of the
Methodist, Baptist and Roman Catholic Churches as part of a
spontaneous movement for the renewal of Christian life in the
town. This the Council hoped to achieve through lectures and
meetings and the development of a community centre, the lectures
to cover themes such as peace, religion and work, education and
citizenship, family, and the problems of evil, fatalism, war, and
materialism. Also in 1941, the Anglican Priory of Our Lady was
established in The Priory west of the town, restoring the site to its
original religious function. It was originally for women only, but
later accepted brothers as well, and was recognised as a Benedictine
community in 1952.

The church benefice, united with Fulbrook and Taynton in 1980,
was merged in 1994 with that of Asthall, Swinbrook, and Widford,
although the parishes themselves continued as distinct entities. As a
result, one man's cure of souls extended from the county boundary
along the Windrush valley, encompassing six churches – a partial
return to the extensive 'minster' parishes of the late Saxon period.[168]

Afterword

The pioneering historian W.G. Hoskins once famously remarked that we 'cannot understand the English landscape and enjoy it to the full … without going back to the history that lies behind it.' At the time he was thinking of rural England, but, as Hoskins himself recognised, the same holds true of towns. In the course of this book we have ranged from the Anglo-Saxon period to the early 21st century, combining documentary evidence with buildings and layout to explain how this small market town evolved, what factors moulded its character, and how the needs of its inhabitants shaped its development. In the process we have tried to look at Burford anew, digging behind the simplified image presented by the tourist books and turning instead to the hidden details: a blocked doorway here, a piece of re-used stone there, an odd-shaped plot boundary behind. If just a few of Burford's visitors, having read this book, turn their attention for a moment from the window displays to the intriguing details of the town and its buildings, then the book will have met one of its aims.

Much that has been uncovered during the work towards this book is new. That Burford is a typical medieval planned town has long been known, but only painstaking analysis of plot boundaries has revealed the likely stages of its early development, and the probable shape of the Anglo-Saxon settlement which preceded it. The comprehensive examination of so many buildings has similarly allowed some broad conclusions. Burford boasts several striking medieval houses, but the discovery of so many medieval remains behind later façades has allowed more to be said about the character of the medieval town and about its subsequent decline, which seems to have prevented a more complete rebuilding of its houses. In particular, we now know that medieval Burford was never a predominantly stone-built town, but that stone and timber building traditions co-existed, often in the same structure. Combining building investigation with documentary work has similarly helped make sense of particular buildings and cast light on some general themes. Among these is the subdivision of houses so prevalent in 19th-century Burford, as it became in part a town of cramped labourers' cottages and cottage yards, while aspects of the town's commercial life have been traced in its shopfronts, inns and outbuildings. More generally, the tree-ring dating described in Panel 8 provides a scientific framework for building investigation in the future, by assigning firm dates to particular building techniques. This applies not only to Burford itself but to the surrounding countryside, since medieval carpentry techniques tend to be broadly similar within a given area.

But perhaps the greatest surprise to readers familiar with Burford and the Cotswolds will have been how much of the town's modern image is a recent confection. Although perched on the edge of Oxfordshire only just within the Cotswolds, Burford is frequently presented as a quintessential 'Cotswold town' – heritage-industry shorthand for a photogenic streetscape of limestone-built houses, 17th-century-style gables and stone-mullioned windows. Burford has plenty of authentic examples, but, as Chapter 8 has made clear, part of its built character derives from early 20th-century remodellings, influenced by Arts and Crafts ideals and by romanticised views of what a medieval Cotswold wool town should look like. Modern planning restrictions, and the pressure for new buildings to copy 'appropriate' vernacular styles, have perpetuated the image, creating a townscape which is at least in part pastiche. To an extent this applies to other Cotswold towns as well. Chipping Campden, for instance, is also in part an early 20th-century invention. Looked at in detail, Burford's authentic historic buildings show a much greater diversity than the standard view of the 'Cotswold wool town', whether in style, building materials, or occupation and use.

Broad conclusions are valuable only if based on detailed research, which has underpinned the Burford EPE project as it does all VCH work. The examples cited in earlier chapters come from a much larger body of building evidence, which could not have been assembled without the close collaboration of VCH historians, architectural experts, and volunteers drawn mostly from the Oxfordshire Buildings Record. The remainder of this book presents the outcome of that collaboration, in the form of a historical gazetteer of buildings along Burford's main streets: a distillation of building and occupation histories designed to make sense of how and why Burford's houses, shops, and other structures have evolved in the way they have. This is the basic data on which previous chapters have drawn. More than that, it is the history of the ordinary and often anonymous people who have lived and worked in Burford over the centuries, and who in a piecemeal way shaped the town we see today.

Burford's Buildings: A Historical Gazetteer

The bulk of this book has concentrated on Burford's chronological development, showing how its townscape and buildings were moulded by deliberate planning and by the needs and aspirations of its inhabitants. This final section provides short individual histories, topographically arranged, of the houses, shops, and other buildings along Burford's principal streets. While the Gazetteer can be used independently it is best read in conjunction with the foregoing chapters, which discuss broad patterns of development, provide an overall context, and explain methods of construction, house layout, and other architectural themes.

Like earlier chapters, the Gazetteer combines detailed fieldwork with documentary research. Where possible each building's evolution is related to the people who lived and worked there, to changing uses, and to shifts in fashion and economic circumstance, whether in Burford or beyond. The survey divides High Street into three parts, lower (near the bridge), central (near the crossroads) and upper (running up the hill), each of which has a distinct character. Within those sections it runs separately along both sides of High Street, following the modern numbering sequence from north to south. Each section is characterised in a short introductory paragraph. The survey concludes with similar treatments of Sheep Street and Witney Street, and with brief accounts of Guildenford and The Priory.

Creating the Gazetteer

Though the Gazetteer draws on as wide a range of evidence as possible, it is important to recognise the difficulties faced in this sort of exercise. The vernacular buildings which characterise Burford are not generally of one date and are not architect-designed, but have evolved piecemeal over centuries (Chapters 4 and 8). The only way to reconstruct their development is through detailed examination of building styles and datable architectural details, combined with documentary evidence where this exists. Between 2003 and 2006, every building was studied in detail from the street with the help of volunteers from the Oxfordshire Buildings Record, who produced copious notes, drawings, and photographs to an agreed agenda. Several houses have been more fully investigated from inside, culminating, in a few cases, in dendrochronological or tree-ring dating. Not all buildings have been fully investigated, however, and new discoveries undoubtedly wait to be made. Even where buildings have been looked at in detail, it can often be difficult to know exactly how they were once used, since many of the changes introduced by past occupiers were transitory rather than structural.

Documentary evidence for particular buildings varies enormously. Unlike some small towns Burford has no comprehensive or continuous rentals, no early maps or surveys, and no 19th-century tithe survey. Leases and deeds for a handful of charity properties granted to the church, grammar school, or corporation survive in some instances from the Middle Ages, and there are burgage rent-rolls for 1652 and 1685. All those documents were printed in R.H. Gretton's monumental *Burford Records* (1920), although identifying properties within them still requires painstaking detective work. Deeds for other properties survive in private hands or with solicitors, and were studied through the notes and transcripts compiled over many years by the Revd Raymond Moody of

Burford. In addition, several hundred wills and inventories have been transcribed by the Burford Probate Group, in some cases allowing properties to be identified and their rooms and contents recorded.

Only from the 1840s does a single source detail the occupancy of every house in Burford. These are the enumerators' books compiled for the national census, which survive at ten-yearly intervals from 1841 and are currently available up to 1901. Enumerators were required to record every single household, listing all the occupants together with their trades and other information. Even so, houses are often difficult to identify, since house numbers were not introduced until much later and many 19th-century buildings were subdivided. Census evidence can be supplemented from 19th- and 20th-century trades directories (periodic publications listing the principal tradesmen and residents in individual towns and villages), and for 1912-15 by District Valuation records. These were compiled under the 1910 Finance Act, and for most places in the country include comprehensive lists of houses with their owners, occupiers and rateable values, all linked to an accompanying map. In Burford's case, this is the first comprehensive survey of the town in which properties are clearly identified, although the more detailed Valuation field books for Burford (which often contained building descriptions) are sadly lost. All these sources were used in compiling the Gazetteer, and were amplified by local knowledge. Even so, there are many buildings about which little or nothing is known before the 19th century.

Old photographs and drawings form the final type of evidence. Some show buildings which have changed beyond recognition, and can help to date both major and minor alterations (below, 20-26 High Street). Others show buildings which have gone altogether (below, 7 High Street), or help to tie documentary information to particular buildings, for example where an old shop-sign gives the name of a business (Figure 67, below, 109-113 High Street). Drawings pre-dating the age of photography can be even more useful, but require extreme caution, since artists did not always show exactly what they saw (Panel 1 and below, 25 Sheep Street).

Source Abbreviations used in Gazetteer

Citation of sources in the Gazetteer has been kept to a minimum. All entries draw on the ten-yearly censuses for 1841-1901, on printed trades directories, and on the District Valuation records in Oxfordshire Record Office. Other sources are given in abbreviated form where appropriate, and are listed below.

This printed Gazetteer draws on much more detailed information compiled during the research, which includes (for example) the names of all heads of households extracted from the censuses, and, where known, the names of other householders (with references). Those fuller versions are being made available on the England's Past For Everyone website, and will be deposited in paper form in the Oxfordshire Buildings Record archive.

BR: Gretton, R.H., *The Burford Records: A Study in Minor Town Government* (1920)
Inns: Moody, R., *The Inns of Burford* (Hindsight publications, Burford, revised edn 2007)
Jewell: Jewell, A., *Burford in Old Photographs* (1985)
Laithwaite: Laithwaite, M., 'The Buildings of Burford', in Everitt, A. (ed.), *Perspectives in English Urban History* (1973)
List: Listed Buildings Description
Pevsner: Pevsner, N. and Sherwood, J., *Buildings of England: Oxfordshire* (1974)
RM: Information from the Revd Raymond Moody, based partly on notes from title deeds in private hands

LOWER HIGH STREET

East Side: The Bridge to Church Lane

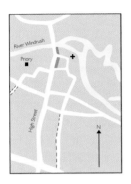

The miscellaneous buildings in this stretch of lower High Street reflect its varied social character, which included gentry and professionals alongside shopkeepers, tradesmen and craftsmen. Cottage accommodation survives at No. 1 (16th-century) and No. 23, and smart 18th-century façades at No. 2 (1790s) and 25 (1730s). Nos. 13 and 19 were inns, the latter sharing part of a long and elegant Georgian frontage which dominates this part of the street. Several other house-fronts conceal earlier buildings, which have been remodelled and in many cases sub-divided. The most notable are two medieval hall-houses, at Nos. 15-17 and 31.

The view north from Church Lane towards the bridge: No. 31 in the foreground and No. 7 (Riverside House) in the distance.

No. 1

In 1571 the Burford merchant Simon Wisdom granted a small cottage here to trustees for Burford Grammar School, rebuilding it as three cottages in 1576 (see plaque). The dormer gables and mullion windows are from this period, and a blocked window and former roof-line in the west (end) gable show how it was altered and increased in height. The school owned it until 1862 and let it to tenants, including successive members of the Silvester family (c.1628-after 1717). Paul Silvester converted it into a single house in 1693, and probably built the east wing for his tannery business. In the 1840s and 1850s it was a currier's house, yard and shop let to Edward Ansell, and after the Second World War became a doctor's surgery. In 2007 it was a private house. The ground-floor sash windows are late 18th- or 19th-century insertions. [BR 328, 331-2, 346, 458, 518-19, 553; Laithwaite 114]

No. 7 (Riverside)

Although there is a 17th-century rear range, this stylish house was probably built in the 1790s (owner unknown). By the 1840s the surgeon Thomas Cheatle lived here with his family and servants, and around 1869 demolished the neighbouring house (below) and built a Gothic extension on the east. The family, which included several prominent Burford doctors, remained here throughout the 20th century, C.T. Cheatle adding a further extension in the 1930s. The surgery entrance was via the archway to the right.

The small two-bay house demolished c.1869 stood behind the current gatepiers, and dated from the early 17th century (see photograph). Possibly it formed part of the Silvesters' property (see No. 1), and in the 1850s-60s was probably occupied with a timber yard by the carpenter William East. [Laithwaite 114; BR 519]

An early photograph of No. 7
High Street, showing the small
gabled house next door which
was demolished c.1869.

No. 13

Nos. 15 and 17

Nos. 19-21

Though ownership is unknown before the 1820s, this prominent building may have been an inn, as suggested by the wide entrance under an elliptical hood-mould, and a mounting block (to help in mounting a horse) outside. Its courtyard includes 17th-century timber framing, and an ovolo-moulded mullion window at first-floor level is early 17th-century. The 19th-century ground-floor window seems to have been set into an earlier doorway. Nineteenth-century occupiers included plumbers and painters (?1820s-60s), and a cooper and parish clerk (1870s-90s). [Laithwaite 85; *Inns* 55]

These houses began as a medieval hall-house (history unknown). No. 15 (left) comprised the service end, and No. 17 the cross-passage, hall, and upper end. The fragment of a south cross-wing remains at the rear. Seventeenth-century modernisation included inserting a kitchen fireplace (in No. 15), inserting a chimney stack into the passage to create a lobby entry, and raising the roof. Like many Burford buildings this was cottage accommodation by the early 19th century, and was progressively subdivided. No. 15 was separated probably in the early 19th century, and No. 17 became two cottages c.1870, one of them entered from a doorway (now blocked) in Lawrence Lane. Nineteenth-century occupants included a horse-breaker, coopers, bakers, and gardeners, and (at No. 17) the stonemason John Perrin (1840s-80s).

This long pair of 18th-century façades hides remains of two 17th-century houses. The left-hand or northern one (No. 19) was probably rebuilt when it became the *King's Arms Inn* before 1773. A former doorway is visible in newer stonework under the central window. The right-hand façade is slightly earlier, as can be seen at the eaves where they meet. The two were linked in 1933, when the whole building became the girls' school for Burford Grammar School. The doorway in No. 21 was probably created then.

Earlier houses here are documented from the late Middle Ages. In 1493 Robert Coke or Moke of Chilson granted a predecessor of No. 19 to Thomas Everard and his wife, and around 1526 it was given to Brasenose College, Oxford. The college's tenants included a

19-21 High Street, with (right) a
fire insurance plaque at No. 21,
dating from c.1739. The insurance
policy survives and gives various
details about the building.

shoemaker, Simon Perks (1620s-30s). The *King's Arms* continued here until the 1870s, under a fast-changing succession of innkeepers; of those John Richards (1850s) was also a farmer and ironmonger, while his daughter was a coal merchant. Occupants from the 1880s were corn merchants, members of the Potter family. A predecessor of No. 21 was occupied in 1526 by a mason, William Este, and in 1739 by the fellmonger John Smith, whose fire insurance mark survives on the façade. His premises included a malthouse and stable and were insured for £400.

By 1841, like many Burford houses, No. 21 had been subdivided, its northern part successively occupied by a millwright (1840s-50s), a general dealer and lodgers (1860s), and carpenter (1870s-90s). The southern part housed a mason (1840s) and shoemakers or cordwainers (1850s-80s). [Pevsner 518; *Inns* 54-5; *BR* 458, 672-3; ORO QSD V/1-4; Guildhall, Sun policy 82516]

No. 23

This small cottage with its rubblestone front is of 17th-century origin, but has been increased in height. Nineteenth-century occupants included agricultural labourers and probably, in 1851, a sawyer. In the 1860s it became the entrance and manager's house for the Burford Gas Light and Coke Company (formed 1864): the straight joint to the right, and the long timber lintel over the door, show where trucks entered, loaded with coal. After the gasworks closed in 1914, it became part of the school premises. The fanciful name Lenthall House is modern.[*Oxford Chronicle* 19 Nov. 1864]

No. 25

This smart façade hides an earlier house, owned in 1685 by Richard Bartholomew. The earliest datable feature is a rebuilt 16th-century stair turret to the rear, and a steeply pitched 17th-century roof can be seen through the quatrefoil openings in the sides of the parapet. In 1729 William Bartholomew of Turkdean (Glos.), gent, sold it to his lessee Thomas Smallbones, a victualler. Smallbones probably remodelled it, since the façade is typical of Burford in the 1730s. The ground-floor window pair on the right shows one typical response to the window tax, since it counted as a single window. The blocked attic window may also reflect the tax, but was more likely included to complete the unity of the symmetrical façade. The flat door hood conceals remains of an earlier pedimented one.

In 1778 Richard Smallbones sold the house to the carpenter John Arkell (d.1807), whose daughter leased it. In 1820 it was probably occupied by William Brookes, gent, and in the 1840s by a lady of independent income, Ann Osman. Later occupiers included a tailor and tanner, the Baptist minister William Piggott (1880s), and the doctor Frederick Lane (1890s). The shop window may have lit the tailor's workroom, and also served a 1930s shop. The name Warwick House is modern. [*BR* 454, 457; RM]

Nos. 27 and 29

These two small adjoining cottages, though of different date, were both altered in the 19th century, and their low ground-floor ceilings remain visible below the tops of the front windows. No. 27's 19th-century ashlar front hides an 18th-century cottage, owned in 1723 by an edge-tool maker, in 1756 by a lifeguardsman, and from 1759 by a joiner. Later occupants included a straw bonnet maker (1840s), grocers (1860s-80s), and a butcher (1890s). It ceased to be a shop *c*.1900, when the existing sash windows probably replaced a shop window. The wide opening below lights a cellar.

No. 29 (right) may be late 16th-century, and in the 1830s-40s it was owned by Chipping Norton tradesmen. Occupants included a sawyer, a grocer and tea dealer (1850s), a plumber and glazier, and a groom (1870s-90s). The roof was raised in the mid-19th century, as shown by the smoother stone of the uppermost courses, while a blocked doorway to the left suggests that it was once divided into two. Though now a shop it retains its cottage frontage.

No. 31

This 19th-century rendered shopfront conceals a medieval house (history unknown), which was mostly timber-framed and had an open hall. A blocked window high in the gable wall has 14th-century trefoil tracery. A fireplace and first floor were inserted in the 17th century, and probably around the same period a timber-framed rear wing with boxed oriel windows was added over a stone ground floor: the roof line is slightly above that of the original building. Eighteenth-century owners, who let the house to tenants, included one of the prominent Jordan family, and from 1775 to 1807 John Arkell, carpenter, who also owned Nos. 25, 27, and 29.

By the 1840s it had been divided, the northern part occupied successively by a widow, grocer, labourer, and iron tinplate worker, and the southern part as a tailor's and draper's shop. Richard Forest had a shop in the northern half by 1881 and subsequently acquired the whole building, continuing until the 1920s as a hawker, china dealer, and specialist in boots and shoes. The entire front was reconstructed in timber and render perhaps by Forest, forming two shop-fronts and a smooth façade in front of the earlier building line. Some good 19th-century shop fittings survive at the rear. Blocked windows and doorways in the Church Lane elevation relate presumably to the building's division or to earlier usage. It remained a shop in 2007.

West Side: The Bridge to Priory Lane

Two important buildings dominate this side of lower High Street. Cobb House near the bridge, with its prominent Dutch gables, incorporates part of the former vicarage, while Falkland Hall on the corner of Priory Lane became associated with the neighbouring *Bear Inn*. Most other buildings are 17th-century houses or cottages, many of them occupied in the 19th century by tradesmen or labourers. A few, such as the former smithy at No. 24, show signs of their earlier use.

Lying back from the road near the river are the surviving buildings of the former town mill. Island House (the early 19th-century mill building) has been converted to offices, and nearby is a small pump-house which supplied Burford with water. Other buildings there were millworkers' houses and cart sheds.

Looking south towards Bear Court and Falkland Hall; No. 18 (Richards Cottage) in the foreground.

Cobb House and The Old Vicarage

A vicarage house stood on part of this site from the Middle Ages, and a surviving medieval range at the rear may be part of it. The main street-front range, recognisable by its imposing three-bay façade with a datestone of 1672, is from a rebuilding of the vicarage probably by the vicar John Thorpe (Chapter 9). The range may have been built on the foundations of an earlier structure, but its shaped gables and symmetrical front, with a first-floor *piano nobile*, were clearly designed to signal a new age of gentility and fashion in Burford. Towards the bridge, the large double gateway from the street and a small adjoining structure to its left are the last remnants of Cobb Hall, a quite separate late medieval courtyard house which was demolished *c*.1870. Its site now forms part of Cobb House's garden.

Most 18th- and early 19th-century vicars or curates lived here at least occasionally, but in 1836 the house was said to be dilapidated. A new block, possibly by the architect Henry Underwood (1787-1868), was built at the rear for the incoming vicar, Edward

The street front.

Left: the addition of 1836 at the rear, which since 1958 has formed a separate house. Right: Cobb House's gateway, which originally belonged to a neighbouring medieval house (Cobb Hall) demolished c.1870.

Philip Cooper (a relative of Jane Austen), and a coach-house to the left was built at the same date. Later vicars lived here with their families and servants until c.1937. During the Second World War the premises were used by the armed forces, and were later divided into flats for families awaiting council housing.

The Church sold the property in 1955, and in 1958 it was divided. The front part was bought in 1960 by Raymond and Joan Moody, who named it Cobb House; that and the 1836 block (now known as the Old Vicarage) remained separate houses in 2007. [Pevsner 518; information from Raymond Moody; Images of England nos. 420234, 420235, 420236 and 420237]

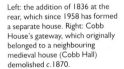

No. 18 (Richards Cottage)

An earlier house here is documented from 1435. In 1492 it was given to the churchwardens, and from c.1571 to c.1958 belonged to the trustees of Burford Grammar School. The coursed and squared front is 17th-century, and the stone-mullioned casement windows with drip-moulds are high-quality features of the period, possibly paid for by the trustees. Blacksmiths lived here as tenants from the 1650s to at least the 1730s, followed in the 19th century by plumbers, glaziers, and another blacksmith. The doorway goes with the 17th-century front; its lintel had cracked before the tinsmith Bertram Richards had his name carved on it in the 1920s, when he lived and worked here. In the 1950s the school headmaster lived here. [BR 328-9, 331-2, 346, 422, 424, 426-7, 449, 458; RM]

Nos. 20-26

The three rubblestone cottages numbered 20, 22 and 24 are probably all of 17th-century origin, and may have once formed a single property: the front of No. 22 extends under the eaves of No. 20, and has a jagged join with No. 24. As with many Burford buildings, the façade of No. 20 includes some ashlar blocks which have been 'pecked' to hold a covering of render. Fragments of limewash are visible both here and at No. 22, though there the front was rebuilt in the 19th century. A predecessor of No. 20 is documented from the 1430s, when it belonged to Keynsham abbey in Somerset, and in 1571 the site was occupied by a barn.

The Hall family's smithy at No. 24 Hight Street, c.1900. The building still shows signs of its former use (below).

No. 26 (Providence Cottage).

From the 1840s, and probably much earlier, all three cottages were occupied by craftsmen or tradesmen, including bakers, wheelwrights, tailors, slaters, and blacksmiths. Iron rings in the front of No. 20 were probably for tethering horses when a blacksmith worked here c.1900 (Figure 94). From the 1830s to 1970s No. 24 was a smithy run by the Hall family, and the segmental-headed openings in the ground floor date from that period. Until 1970 two of them were stable doors, but the central one has been filled in to make a window. An iron hook and bracket on the wall were also for the smithy. The significance of the date 1827 (scratched over the door) is unclear, while the Sun fire insurance plaque at No. 20 came from a house in London.

No. 26 is of similar date but higher quality, with its stone-mullioned windows and upstairs flat-arched fireplace. The off-centre doorway opens to a through-passage. The casement windows are 18th-century in style, but may date from a 20th-century restoration. The house was at one point divided into two cottages, and 19th-century occupants were labourers of probably lesser status than their neighbours. In the early 20th century it was briefly a cyclists' café. [BR 322, 328-9, 331-2, 422, 424, 426-7 (No. 20); Jewell 23; RM]

Nos. 28 and 32

This smart 17th-century façade of neatly squared limestone blocks, with characteristic drip-moulds over the first-floor windows, probably unites two separate 16th-century houses. A small diamond-mullion window from one of them is still visible off the large (20th-century) central passageway. A watercolour of 1821 by J.C. Buckler shows two large gabled dormers (now gone) and two plain central doorways, perhaps inserted as part of a recent re-division into two cottages. The house remained divided

throughout the 19th century, occupied by labourers and tradespeople including an earthenware dealer, butchers, grocers, a cordwainer, and a hairdresser.

The present wide opening dates from the building's use as a garage in the 20th century. The canopy roof covered petrol pumps on the plinth beneath, and the small front window opened to the pay-kiosk. The shopfronts were inserted in 1960, probably around the time that Welsh slates were laid on the roof. The garage closed in the 1970s and the site was redeveloped, with two shops in the front part and domestic premises behind. [Laithwaite 4; RM]

Nos. 34-42 (former *Bear Inn*)

The *Bear Inn* was established here probably in the late 1640s by Thomas Matthews (died 1680). Parts of this complex series of buildings are earlier, however: 16th-century features include a Tudor-arched fire surround, and in a ground-floor room a large kitchen fireplace with a former bread oven. When the inn was opened, existing buildings were probably remodelled. Many of the surviving timbers are re-used, and the gateway and street-front are probably 17th-century, while the neighbouring Falkland Hall seems to have been adapted as a lodging range soon after (Panel 1). An external stairway behind the gateway led to the inn's upper storey. To the rear, there was a through-route to Priory Lane until blocked by a garage in the 1980s. Two fashionable Georgian windows shown in J.C. Buckler's drawing of 1821 were inserted in the 18th century, though only the first-floor one now survives.

The original inn closed between 1760 and 1774, and in the early 19th century the stables in the courtyard (now shops and showrooms) seem to have been converted into cottages, as evidenced by the chimney stacks. John Jones, a carpenter who bought this building and Falkland Hall in 1830, re-opened the inn some 10 years later. By the 1910s it was owned by Clinch & Co. of Witney, and continued as an inn until the 1960s. Thereafter it was remodelled as shops and renamed Bear Court. [Laithwaite 4; *Inns* 34-6]

Nos. 42-44 (Falkland Hall)

The building's alleged but unproven connection with the clothier Edmund Silvester (died 1569) is discussed in Panel 1. Sixteenth-century features include part of a window surround at the back (now out of sight in a new development), and a doorway and window behind 4 Priory Lane, while the symmetrical High Street front, with its distinctive central oriel window, shows Renaissance taste. The fabric has been much altered, however. No trace remains of the former central chimney-stacks, the roof has been completely renewed, and a stair turret at the rear has been removed.

In the mid-17th century the building was remodelled, probably as a lodging block for the adjoining *Bear Inn*. This included linking it with abutting cottages on Priory Lane: restoration at 2-4 Priory Lane in 2005-6 showed that No. 2 connected with Falkland Hall at all three levels, although there was a noticeable gap between the buildings, covered by the present outer wall. The cottage's first floor has been tree-ring dated to 1650. Outside, a moulded string-course above Falkland Hall's ground-floor windows carries on round the building into Priory Lane, also linking it with the first cottage. The general configuration (stair turret at the rear to allow more space in the main building, large central stack to heat at least two rooms at each level, and links to the Priory Lane range) all strongly suggest its use as inn accommodation (Panel 1). Georgian-type windows were inserted at ground- and first-floor level in the 18th century.

After the *Bear* closed Falkland Hall was apparently divided into cottages, and up to five households were recorded here in 19th-century censuses. In 1890, after some time vacant, it became a Salvation Army citadel. The large first-floor opening in the Priory Lane elevation replaced a window during the 19th century, and was used for taking in goods. In 1900 there was a platform below it.

Burford Recreation Society bought the building in 1906 and renamed it Falkland Hall, in a fanciful reference to Laurence Tanfield's grandson Lucius Cary, Viscount Falkland (who had no connection with the building). In 1920 the War Memorial Committee bought it for the town and vested it in trustees, who let it for meetings and community activities, including a brief stint as a cinema. From 1962 it was let as commercial premises. As a result of such changes the interior has been virtually gutted, though in 2000 the town council proudly placed a sculpted lion on the oriel, designed by local architect John Melvin. [Above, Panel 1; Laithwaite 4; RM]

CENTRAL HIGH STREET

This central area of High Street, focused on the main crossroads and market area, was the commercial heart of the town, and contains some of Burford's most striking buildings. Many are of medieval origin, and include former inns and prominent merchants' houses as well as shops and other commercial premises. A variety of mostly 19th- and 20th-century shopfronts reflects more recent commercial activity. The following account divides this central area into four discrete blocks (two on each side), each punctuated by side streets.

East Side: Church Lane to Witney Street

The imposing former mansion house at No. 75 dominates this stretch of High Street, which rises gently to the central crossroads. There are, however, some other striking buildings among this run of smallish cottages and shops, most notably the long 16th-century frontage of No. 33, the tall three-storeyed front of Nos. 53-9, and the long Georgian façade of No. 91. Medieval houses survive behind several later façades, and a 14th-century archway (possibly reset) at No. 69. *The Burford House Hotel* (No. 99) is one of several buildings remodelled in a 'Cotswold Vernacular' style in the 1920s, which together lend Burford part of its distinctive character.

Looking south from the Jordan family's 18th-century mansion to Witney Street and beyond. In the foreground is No. 69 with its 14th-century stone archway.

No. 33

The long, early 16th-century frontage of No. 33, with (right) the whitesmith and musical wind-instrument maker Henry Titcomb (died 1882), who lived in the building's left-hand part in the 1840s-60s. Some of his clarinets and a serpent still survive.

Built probably around 1500 for an unknown owner, this must have been quite a grand house, its long rubblestone façade straddling two medieval plots. The earliest feature is the damaged Tudor-arched blocked doorway to the left of the present (1980s) front door. The large stone-mullioned windows are 17th-century insertions. By the 1840s it had been subdivided like so many Burford houses, the northern part occupied by the whitesmith, spring-maker and musical-instrument maker Henry Titcomb (1840s-60s), and the other part by a greengrocer. A rear wing was probably added soon after it was reunited c.1880, perhaps for the furniture dealer Bartholomew Fisher (occupant 1890s-1910s).

Around 1920 E.J. Horniman of The Priory acquired the building and heavily restored it, in line with his Arts and Crafts leanings (cf. 99 and 117 High Street). The restored roof with two rows of purlins can be seen inside the current shop. The building was vested in the Horniman Trust, and used first as a gymnasium for Burford Grammar School, and by the 1950s as a metalwork shop. In 2007 it was the Staffordshire Pottery shop.

A neighbouring house, probably occupied by a basket maker in the 1840s-70s, was demolished after Horniman acquired the site, to be replaced in the late 20th century by public conveniences. [RM]

Nos. 35-39

In 1652 a house here was owned by William Elston and held by William Haynes; by 1685 the owner was William Lenthall esquire (of The Priory), and the tenant Richard George. The front of the 17th-century building was probably extended forwards in the 18th century, but there are few external clues. In the 1840s the occupier was a baker (hence the outline of a large bread-oven in the passageway to the side), and in the 1860s-80s the grocer, coal- and corn dealer Richard Hemming, who in 1881 farmed 25 acres. In 1901 it was a baker's and confectioner's, and in 1910 a cyclists' restaurant. Bordered sash windows were inserted in the late 19th century, and the modern symmetrical shopfront (on the left) was perhaps made for the post office which was here in 1938. By then the house had probably been divided: its right-hand part was fronted by a small garden, and had a sash window with glazing bars, whose location is marked by irregular stonework and cement mortar. That was replaced by a separate shop window in the mid-20th century. In 2007 the building remained divided between the *Priory Tea Rooms* (left) and a gift shop (right). [BR 448, 457; Jewell 124]

Nos. 41-45 and Nos. 47-49

Like the neighbouring property this house belonged to the Elstons (by 1598) and later to the Lenthalls, who let it. Heavy beams with joists laid flat suggest 16th-century origins, and wide first-floor windows were reduced in size in the late 18th or early 19th century, replaced by the present square ones with small panes. Nineteenth-century occupants probably included a cordwainer (1840s), a plasterer (1850s), a baker (1870s-80s), and a plumber, glazier and painter (1890s). Before *c.*1960 the building became part of Forest's clothing business, and remained a shop in 2007. The projecting shopfronts are 20th-century. [BR 340, 347, 436, 448, 457; RM]

The double-gabled smooth stone frontage of *c.*1903 conceals remains of another medieval house. A pair of wide ogee-arched door-heads of *c.*1340 survive set into the south wall of the present stairway, apparently in their original position; presumably the doorways led to or from an important reception hall or solar, suggesting that the house extended some way towards the south. The rear of the building is timber-framed, and there is a later fireplace with a heavy timber lintel. The front rooms have wooden panelling and a Victorian grate. The entrance door on the left (No. 47) opens onto a passageway to the rear of the plot, where a range of timber-framed and stone-clad outbuildings of the 17th and 18th centuries, once used for the trades carried on here, has been converted to domestic use.

By 1598 the house belonged to charity trustees for supporting the church, and was occupied by Thomas Heming (died 1628), barber-surgeon. Later lessees included Lawrence Yeate, maltster (1658), William Bowles, collarmaker (1684), and John Tomlin, woolcomber (1730). By 1787 it was the *Bell Inn*, last mentioned in 1854 and latterly doubling as a grocer's and post office. Sold in 1860, it became a tailor's and cabinet maker's (1860s), a tailor's and draper's (1870s-1900s), and butcher's (1900s-10s). The wide butcher's shop window is typical (Panel 14). The front part became a fish-and-chip shop in the late 20th century, and in 2007 was an estate agent's. [BR 340, 347, 434-6, 519; ORO QSD V/3-4; RM]

No. 51

This rubblestone façade would once have been rendered: most of the window surrounds have been pecked to allow render to adhere properly, in an 18th-century attempt to create a 'polite' frontage matching that to the right (Nos. 53-9). In 1851 the occupier was a carrier, and in 1861 Robert Woods, 'lessor of houses'. From 1891 to 1915 it was George W. Matthews, 'insurance agent, assistant overseer, and collector of gas and water rates', who probably inserted the present late 19th-century windows and perhaps removed the render. By 1941 it included a fish, fruit and vegetable shop; the current shopfront has plate-glass windows, that to the right installed for a jeweller in 1953 (local inf.). In 2007 the building contained a gift shop.

Nos. 53-59

The builder of this impressive, late 18th-century three-storey frontage, with its symmetrical façade of ashlar limestone, is unknown. A central doorway leads to a through-passage and rear courtyard, with a collection of much-altered earlier buildings. Each side of the building has a separate entrance, wide 18th-century fireplaces, and coal cellars. The intention may have been to create a high-class lodging house or a mixed domestic/working complex, but nothing is known before 1841 when there were five separate households, headed by a basket-maker, milliner, agricultural labourer, horse-keeper, and painter. Between four and six households were recorded throughout the 19th century, but in 1910 the property was apparently vacant. For much of the 20th century a shop on the south side of the entrance was the collection and delivery office of the Burford Laundry (local inf.): graffiti on the façade may date from that period. A bookshop occupied the north side from 1971-93. In 2007 the front still contained two shops behind domestic window openings, with domestic properties at the rear.

No. 61

The building retains a Tudor-arched fireplace and probably the roof from an earlier structure: the roof's 'waney' ridge suggests pre-17th-century timbers. From the mid-17th century to the early 20th the premises were frequently let to bakers: in 1652 the clothier Thomas Silvester was leasing it to Thomas Jordan, baker, and others were recorded in the 1680s, 1770s, and 1840s-1900s, with an ironmonger in the 1860s. The façade is early 19th-century, built of coursed and dressed limestone of sub-ashlar quality, and with sliding or 'Yorkshire' sash windows to the first floor. The shopfront was there by 1902 but has since been remodelled, as has the dormer.

By 1841 there was a separate house at the rear, occupied successively by a basket-maker, baker (1850s), and bootmaker (1860s-70s, with two governesses as boarders). [*BR* 451, 459; RM; Jewell 35]

No. 65

This narrow cottage (now a shop) occupies a small plot probably severed from No. 67 next door. The rough rubble, probably collected from fields in the 17th century, is strengthened by larger stone quoins. The change in the stonework above the first-floor window shows that the front has been raised to form a low parapet, probably *c.*1735 to link it with the *Dolphin Inn* next door. The façade was rendered to create a smooth surface, but this was removed in the 20th century. The large-paned first-floor sash-window is 19th-century, and the shopfront 20th-century. [Jewell 55]

No. 65

No. 67 (former *Dolphin* or *Plough Inn*)

The Dutton family owned this property from the 1650s to 1777, and the Chapmans from then until 1826. By 1735 it was the *Dolphin Inn*, renamed the *Plough c.*1819 and closed *c.*1868-71; from the building evidence, however, it was never remotely comparable with Burford's major coaching inns. The 18th-century façade is of coursed and squared limestone; a horizontal string-course protects a wooden 'spreader' which extends across the whole front, giving added structural support. The first floor has two large three-light mullion-and-transom windows, which may have lit an upper function room.

In the 1870s the occupant was a cordwainer, and in the 1880s-90s a 'dealer' or general shopkeeper. The present bay shop-window, with its Cotswold stone slates, replaced a smaller 19th-century version. The alley door to the right, of four vertical planks with strap hinges and a Suffolk latch, is 20th-century, and gives access to Shoo Cottage at the rear; two 15th-century quatrefoils over the doorway were also inserted in the 20th century. In 2007 the premises formed part of a shop with No. 65. [*BR* 452, 462; RM; *Inns* 60; ORO QSD V/4]

No. 69

The stone archway to the street is late 14th-century and, though it may have been reset, parts of the house are medieval. Just above the arch are the ends of floor-joists possibly from a former jetty; the joists can be seen in the alley, laid flat in medieval style. The quality of the stonework changes above the line of timbers, suggesting that the upper storey has been rebuilt, probably in the 17th century.

Seventeenth-century owners (the earliest for which there is evidence) included John Templer (died 1626), his son-in-law the Revd Edward Davis of Shilton (fl. 1652), Edward

The 14th-century archway at 69 High Street. The sawn-off floor joists of a former jetty can be seen above it and in the passageway.

An 18th-century shell-hooded alcove cupboard in 69 High Street, part of a refurbishing by one of the Glyn family.

No. 75 (now Methodist church)

No. 81

No. 83

Davis of London, goldsmith (died 1680), and the Revd Robert Glyn of Little Rissington (recorded 1680-99). Glyn's son Robert, a presumably wealthy London salter, may have installed the fine raised and fielded panelling and shell-hooded alcove cupboard in one of the rooms to the rear, which extends some way down its plot. Throughout that period the house seems, however, to have been mostly let to the Haynes family, shoemakers and shopkeepers, who bought it in 1742. Later owners included Henry Mander (1806), shopkeeper, whose family remained here in 1841, and from 1846 George Hambidge, grocer, draper, and wine and tea merchant, whose family remained until the early 20th century. In the passage are some metal rails, chains, and hooks dating from the building's use as a grocer's.

The roof-line was lowered in the 20th century to link it with No. 67 next door, and the first-floor windows were moved at the same time. The boxed shop window on a stone plinth is mid-20th-century. In the late 20th century the building was a dress shop, and in 2007 the *Burford Gallery*. [Pevsner 517; *BR* 448; RM; Jewell 55]

A substantial house occupied this large site by 1665, when it had at least 10 fireplaces. In 1609 Robert Veysey settled it on his sister Ann on her marriage to Richard Osbaldestone of Chadlington (died 1619). Ann later married Thomas Atkinson, and in 1661 her heirs sold the house to John Jordan, gent, who was tenant by 1652. The existing mansion was erected for a later John Jordan *c*.1725, recalling the influential design of Powis House in Bloomsbury (*c*. 1714).

Jordan apparently fell into debt, and around 1746 the house passed to John Hyde following foreclosure of a mortgage. Hyde's widow sold it in 1766 to William Chapman (died 1792), who was succeeded by his wife (died 1811) and son John (died 1845, aged 79). The next owner, the Burford cooper Edward Bayliss, died *c*.1848, when the house was sold to the Wesleyan Methodist circuit for conversion into a chapel. The domestic interior was removed, creating a large open space, and the sash windows were replaced. The Oxford architect Thomas Rayson further remodelled the interior in 1949. [*Hearth Tax Oxon*. 218; Gomme, A., *Smith of Warwick* (2000), 396; List; *BR* 403, 452, 454; RM; above, Figure 114]

In 1552 this may have been the half burgage-plot belonging to Thomas Chadwell of Little Barrington (Glos.). From the 1730s to 1840s it was owned with No. 75 (above), and the two plat-bands and Georgian window surrounds (one of which has been converted to a shop window) suggest that it was rebuilt around the same time as the Jordans' mansion house at No. 75. Jonathan Banbury, variously described as hairdresser, surveyor, relieving officer, and insurance-, house- and estate agent, bought it in 1848 and extended it the following year, using materials removed from No. 75 and its outbuildings at its conversion into a Methodist chapel. Re-used timbers can be seen in a rear room. Banbury still lived here in 1903, but by 1908 a grocer owned it, and from 1955 to *c*.1970 it housed an antiques business. It subsequently became a delicatessen and Indian restaurant. The shop window is early 20th-century. [*BR* 404, 449, 458, 634; RM]

Beams and a 16th-century doorhead with a four-centred arch, both in the side passage, suggest a medieval origin for this house, but no details are known before the 1730s when it was owned with Nos. 75-81 (above). Tenants included a poulterer (1740s-70s), an ironmonger and coal man (1820s-40s), and a grocer (1860s-90s), and in the late 20th and early 21st centuries it was a post office. The façade, which retains fragments of limewash, is early 19th-century, while the Welsh-slate roof, shopfront, and bordered sash windows date from the later part of the century. The rear outbuildings, now two cottages, are also 19th-century. [RM]

No. 83

No. 91

Behind the 18th-century ashlar façade, rebuilt in the 1970s after a collapse, is a five-bay late medieval house, whose roof has principal-rafter trusses, windbraces, and clasped purlins. Vestigial smoke-blackening indicates a medieval open hall: fireplaces and floors were inserted only in the early 17th century. Documentation from the 1650s to 1840s suggests that by then the site comprised two properties, each separately owned and occupied, though this is difficult to reconcile with the smart, unified 18th-century frontage. Owners of the northern part included members of the Bartholomew family (1650s-1723), the butcher John Whiter (1723-37), and the maltster William Upston (from 1741), and in 1723 there was an attached malthouse, barn, and garden. From the 1840s the whole site was occupied by successive members of the Hunt family, wine and spirit merchants related to the owners of Hunt Edmunds Brewery in Banbury, which owned the premises by the 1890s. By 1910 it was called the *Golden Ball*, and was still run by one of the Hunts in 1939. The name was changed to the *Golden Pheasant Inn c.*1980. [*BR* 449, 457, 499; RM]

No. 93

In origin this is probably a small 17th-century cottage (cf. Nos. 23 and 65), remodelled with a built-out ashlar façade and internal doors of *c.*1730. Beams of probably 17th-century date survive in a rear room. From the late 17th to mid-19th centuries it was a bakery (cf. No. 61): bakers were recorded as tenants in 1685, 1727, and (intermittently) from 1800 to 1861, and in 1793 it was described as a 'messuage, bakehouse and stable'. Other tradesmen included a miller (owner in 1738), corn dealer (owner 1815), cordwainer (occupant 1841), and ironmonger (owner in 1842). The bow-front shop window, like the 10-over-10 sash window above it, are early 19th-century additions, presumably for one of these businesses. From the 1880s to 1920 the house and shop were occupied by a shoemaker, and in the late 20th century it was briefly a china shop. From the 1980s it was the *Stone Gallery*, selling jewellery and fine art. [*BR* 449, 457; RM]

No. 95

A building here was probably occupied by a tailor in 1861, but was apparently demolished soon after: in 1901 the plot was vacant, with a wall in front. The existing coursed-rubble building (Barclays Bank) was erected in the 1970s. In an attempt to blend in the architect has adopted a simplified form of the Georgian window-surround on the first floor, and the roof has stone slates laid in traditional diminishing courses. [Jewell 14; RM]

No. 97

This 2½-storey house is of 17th-century origin, with early 18th-century window openings standing proud of the rendered façade. The sashes and shopfront are 19th-century additions, made probably by the jeweller and clock- and watchmaker John B. Walter, who lived here from the 1860s to 1890s. A descendant was still a watchmaker here in 1920, followed by *Woodward's* shoe shop (1930s-60s) and *Horseshoe Antiques*. [RM]

No. 99 Burford House

This extensive corner site was assembled from three separate narrow properties in 1839-41, by the linen draper William G. Westrope. Eighteenth-century occupants had included the apothecary Nicholas Willett (on the north), the hatter Moses Smith (middle), and the saddlers Solomon and James Jeffs (corner plot). The combined buildings remained a draper's until the early 20th century, run at first

No. 97

by Westrope (1840s to 1890s), and later by Alfred Parsons (1880s) and Alfred Thomas (1890s-*c.*1911).

Some surviving internal features (such as the massive beams supporting the first floor) suggest 16th-century origins for the building, and outbuildings along Witney Street are of 17th- and 18th-century date. The main building and High Street frontage were almost completely rebuilt in the 1920s by E.J. Horniman of The Priory, however. Despite the authentic Burford mix of stone and timber, traditional methods were not used: the wall-plate is not a continuous or jointed timber, the studs are not pegged into it, and several iron bolts are visible. By 1939 the rebuilt property was established as the *Corner House Hotel*, which remained open in 2007 as the *Burford House Hotel*. [RM]

The Burford House Hotel, one of several buildings restored by E.J. Horniman during the 1920s and 1930s. Though Horniman did not adhere to traditional building techniques, such restorations give Burford much of its present-day character.

East Side: Witney Street to Swan Lane

This prime stretch of High Street, close to the central crossroads, the medieval market place and the Tolsey, contains the most remarkable run of high-status late medieval buildings in Burford. Most are at least partly timber-framed, and date chiefly from the late 15th century. Three were major inns, and several are connected with prominent merchant families such as the Pinnocks or, in the 16th century, the Silvesters and Simon Wisdom. A few are concealed behind later façades, but most remain clearly visible. The most prominent later fronts are those of the *Bull* (18th-century brick) and No. 115 (Georgian), while the *Highway Hotel* (No. 117) is another example of early 20th-century remodelling. Several have 19th- or early 20th-century shopfronts, while Nos. 111-113 contains remains of the only medieval shopfront discovered in Burford.

The view south from Witney Street, including the *Bull Inn*, London House (No. 109), and Wysdom Hall (No. 115). Every building shown has a medieval core.

Nos. 101-103 (former *Angel Inn*)

This prime corner-site was an inn from the 15th to late 18th centuries, recorded first as the *Bear* (in 1489), and from 1539 as the *Angel*. Fifteenth- and early 16th-century owners were members of the prominent Pinnock family, followed by various owners or licensees. After 1773 it was absorbed into the neighbouring *Bull Inn*, with which it probably remained connected until the 1850s.

There is very little evidence of the medieval building, although a ground-level cellar window is early, suggesting that the inn may have had a cellar from the outset. There is also a small blocked window near the ground facing Witney Street. The rendered 18th-century front conceals twin gables.

From the 1860s the building was occupied by an upholsterer, a stationer, and (from the 1890s) by George Hambidge's grocery business, which continued here until *c*.1960. In 2007 the building housed two shops, Walker's Antiques (No. 101), and a clothing and gift shop (No. 103). The shopfront to 101 is 19th-century, as are the sash windows, datable by their 'horns'; the bow window at 103 is 20th-century. The cellar has a central passage between concrete platforms, typical of a modern beer cellar, and steps lead to where there was once a lift to street level. [*BR* 319, 321, 373, 429, 451, 459, 631; *Oxford Journal*, 27 Feb. 1768; *Inns* 10; RM]

No.105 (*Bull Inn*)

A house here is documented from 1473, when the prominent Burford merchant John Pinnock left it first to his son and granddaughter, and then to the parish church; the church received the rents from 1489 in return for an annual mass for Pinnock's soul. The town lost the property at the Reformation but later recovered it, and in 1599 leased it to the occupier, Andrew Ward, who had married the widow of a previous tenant. The building's medieval origins can be seen from the courtyard, in the deep jowled posts to the rear of the small gatehouse over the carriageway. The cellar under the front bar could also be medieval in origin. The first-floor gallery, originally open, would have given access to the upper room(s) (Panel 9). Though the overall layout would fit that of a medieval inn there is no documentary evidence for an inn here before the 17th century, and in 1539 the tenant was a butcher.

In 1610 John Silvester (who had acquired Ward's interest) opened the *Bull Inn* here, transferred from Nos. 111-113 nearby. A later John Silvester rebuilt it *c*.1620, perhaps the date of the small, low-ceilinged rooms behind the street frontage with their 17th-century fireplaces and panelling, some of it brought from elsewhere. The striking brick and stone façade was added in the 18th century, probably around 1715 by the innkeeper William Tash (Panel 9), and in 1768 £196 was spent on further building work. Some regular bricks in the upper part of the façade are modern replacements, following a major fire in 1982.

The *Bull* was sold by the charity trustees in or after 1820, and by 1910 was owned by Clinch & Co. of Witney. It remained open in 2007. [*South Midlands Archaeology* 13 (1983), 88-90; Laithwaite 61; *Inns* 20-32; *BR* 319, 321, 358-9, 366, 372-3, 428-30, 433-6, 519]

No. 107

The rendered façade of this tall narrow building hides a medieval timber-framed house, owned in 1489 by John Bishop. The rear wing is late 15th-century, but was cut off *c*.1600 when the present three-storey front range was built, originally with a jetty. Possible candidates for the rebuilding are Robert Silvester, Edward Reynolds, and Edmond Serrell, recorded as owners or occupiers between 1577 and 1630. A further refronting in the 18th century destroyed the jetty. By then the house was almost certainly let to tradesmen, and in the 19th and 20th centuries variously accommodated an apothecary, a grocer and linen draper, a cabinet maker, and (from the 1870s) booksellers, stationers and printers, including the long-lived stationery business of George Packer & Son (recorded *c*.1900-39). In 2007 it was a newsagent's. The shopfront is late Victorian, though the building was damaged by fire in 1982 and has been reconstructed. [*South Midland Archaeology* 13 (1983), 88-90; *BR* 319, 428-9, 433, 435, 450, 454; RM]

No. 109 (London House)

This impressive late medieval house may have been owned in 1552 by the clothier Edmund Silvester: his descendants certainly owned it in the early 17th century, when it was let to the Jordan family. On stylistic grounds the house was built *c*.1485 for someone of high status. The exposed timber frame originally had rows of windows to each upper floor: two cusped lancet pairs remain at first-floor level, while peg-holes and shaped

Nos. 109 and 111-113 now (above) and in 1885 (above right), when the timber framing at 109 was still concealed with render. No. 109 was Thomas Chandler's draper's shop and 111 was Lomas family butcher's.

studs show where the second-floor windows were. At a time when glass was expensive this was a high-status statement. Blocked mortices mark the location of brackets which once supported some form of canopy at eaves level. Of similar date are the large vaulted undercroft (Figure 38), probably let as a tavern, the carved stone fireplace in the first-floor front room (Figure 31), and stone arched doorways giving access to the stairs. The dog-leg stairs themselves are (late) 17th-century.

Later occupants included the mercer Timothy Bevington (1787) and, throughout the 19th and early 20th centuries, a succession of drapers. The current shopfront dates from soon after 1900, around the time that W.H. Akerman (a 'grocer and provision dealer') replaced the draper Thomas Chandler. Later occupiers included furniture dealers during the First World War, a cycle agent in the 1930s, and from c.1980 *Manfred Schotten Antiques*, still there in 2007. The name 'London House' was used from around 1876. [Wood, M., *English Medieval House* (1965), 268-9; *BR* 401, 451, 475, 637; Pevsner 515; RM]

No. 111-113

15th-century cusped lancet windows at 109 High Street. Below: Carved heads on two of the late 15th-century bargeboards at 111-113 High Street.

No. 115 (Wysdom Hall)

In origin this is another jettied, timber-framed building with fine carved bargeboards of the late 15th century, built for an unknown owner and incorporating a shop from the outset. Traces survive inside of the medieval timber shopfront (Panel 3), and there are more medieval buildings to the rear. As a shop, the ground floor would originally have been unheated, but fireplaces and chimneys were added in the southern part (No. 113) in the 16th century, along with some fine wallpaintings. By 1607 and possibly much earlier the building was an inn called the *Bull*, occupied by the John Silvester who, in 1610, transferred to No. 105 (the surviving *Bull*). Internal investigation in 2002 showed that the three gables to the street were altered about that time, and the oriel windows added to the first floor.

From 1703 the house was divided into two unequal parts. The northern two thirds (No. 111) were let to an ironmonger and from the 1790s to a succession of butchers, while the southern part (No. 113) became the *Wheatsheaf* inn, possibly by the 1730s. Despite this division and a later (unrelated) division of ownership, the uniformity of the front was preserved. The 18th-century render has quoins picked out in a fine-textured material on both parts (e.g. around the oriel windows), while the stone-slate lean-to roof is also 18th-century.

The boxed-out shopfronts were added in the 19th and 20th centuries. At No. 111 the long tradition of butchering was continued first by the Warmington, Wiggins and Lomas families (1830s-c.1900), and from before 1911 by the Castles, who remained there (as W.J. Castle Ltd) in 2007. Outside the shop are rails and hooks from which the carcasses hung, and at the rear is a former abattoir. At No. 113 the *Wheatsheaf* closed before 1871, when the building was occupied by a cooper: probably he used the well-lit structure which survives at the rear. By around 1938 No. 113 was a confectioner's, and in 2007 a shop called *Glass Heritage*. [Pevsner 515; *BR* 401-2, 445, 454, 474-5, 633; ORO QSD V/3-4; RM]

Behind the Georgian façade is one of the most important medieval houses in Burford. Around a narrow courtyard are jettied structures from the 15th and 16th centuries (Figure 32). One room has panelling of 1555, with the initials of the prominent merchant and townsman Simon Wisdom (died 1586 or 1587), who almost certainly lived here. Later owners included Hugh May, gent (late 16th century), and members of

Right: the 18th-century front of 115 High Street hides a medieval house occupied by Simon Wisdom. Below: 'Funerals Furnish'd', painted inside the doorway: one of many businesses run here from the 1880s.

the Bartholomew family, whose tenant in 1685 was a mercer, Francis Keble. The grand façade dates from around 1720, when Richard Whitehall, another mercer, bought the house. Its symmetry hides some of the earlier structure: a second floor cuts across the tops of the two windows to the left, though the elongated sash windows to the right light a full-height room. From the central doorway a passageway led, until the mid-20th century, to the courtyard. The junction with No. 117 next door (once also owned by Wisdom) is complex, a variant on Burford's many 'flying freeholds'. The roof extends over both properties, and part of No. 115 lies behind No. 117. The bowed shop fronts are probably not original to the front.

The building housed a mercer's business in 1805 and possibly for much of the 18th century. In the 1840s-50s it was a grocer's, and from 1861 to 1887 it was owned by John and Philip Hollowell, cabinet makers. A barn-like building at the rear, with 19th-century windows, was probably their workshop, and from 1887 to the early 20th century was used as a mattress factory and cobbler's shop by the Sharp family (successors to the Hollowells), who were boot, furniture, and china dealers. Faded painted signs to the street, in the house's central doorway, read 'Funerals Furnish'd', a common side-line for cabinet makers or upholsterers. In 1935 the house was sold to Marjorie Warner, whose son Roger ran an antiques business there until 1986. An antique shop continued in 2007, though the house was separately occupied. [Pevsner 515; BR 402, 445, 463; RM; Warner, R., 'Memoirs of a Twentieth-Century Antique Dealer', Regional Furniture 17 (2003), 1-175]

No. 117 (*Highway Hotel*)

Late 15th-century stone doorway at 117 High Street: part of the original building, unless re-used from elsewhere.

The façade is almost entirely of the 1920s (below), but the structure contains remains of another late 15th-century building, whose jetty survives above the 19th-century shopfronts. If the off-centre stone arched doorway with quatrefoil decoration in the spandrels is in its original position, then the original ground floor may have been of stone. A separate 16th-century doorway to the north is of timber, however. The earliest identifiable heat-source is a fireplace in the north ground-floor room. An earlier open hearth would have been impossible in a 'longwall' jettied building of this type, though the room may originally have been an unheated shop.

In the mid-16th century this was one of numerous buildings owned by Simon Wisdom (cf. Nos. 115, 123), who left it to his nephew Ralph. From the 17th century to 1824 it was owned by the Hunt family, some of whom lived here, though the property was sometimes divided: in 1727 the occupants were Thomas Hunt, ironmonger, and William Leach, hatter. From 1824 to the 1890s it was owned and occupied by the Bowl family, grocers and tallow chandlers. Later wings were added to the rear in the 16th and 17th centuries, and a rear room contains a kitchen range of the 1890s.

117 High Street shortly after E.J.
Horniman's alterations c.1922.

In 1922 the building became the *Highway Private Hotel*, and around that time E.J. Horniman of The Priory extended it upwards to create an apparent second storey. The original roof can still be seen (and felt) within the bedrooms at this level. The first-floor oriel windows, despite their 19th-century appearance, are also of the 1920s, though the frames of the Georgian sash windows between them may date from an 18th-century refronting of the upper floor. The sash windows themselves are late 19th- or early 20th-century replacements, datable by the 'horns' to the upper sash. The hotel remained open in 2007, but a needlework shop which occupied part of the first floor and basement closed after a change of ownership. [List; ORO MS Wills Oxon. 61/4/42; *BR* 449, 458; RM; *Inns* 66-7; Jewell 19]

No. 121

A timber-framed building of *c.*1500 lies behind this tall frontage. A thick moulded beam of the period can be seen in the side passage, and a 16th-century stone mullion window from the passage to the south (under No. 123). The façade is early 18th-century, with raised timber panels suggesting pilasters, and four large sash-window frames standing proud of the surface. The shop windows and stone walling at ground level are late 18th-century. No occupiers are known before the 19th and 20th centuries, when it was successively a grocer's (1850s-70s), tailor's (1880s-1920s), and butcher's (1930s). By 1939 it was a handicrafts shop, after the Second World War the *Gay Adventure*, and in 2007 a tea shop called the *Copper Kettle*. [Pevsner 514; local inf.]

No. 123

This remarkable run of late medieval buildings continues with No. 123, a double-jettied building whose late medieval timber frame is exposed at first-floor level. The close studding was meant to be seen. It had two timber mullion-windows, and the jowled posts suggest that it may also have had twin gables. In the 16th century this was yet another of Simon Wisdom's houses (see above), and he was responsible for its remodelling. A cruder timber structure was inserted to build out the first floor (the earlier building-line is visible inside the shop), but would have been plastered over. The stone archway, with Wisdom's initials and mark and the date 1582, completed the rebuilding; chamfered beams possibly from that phase can be seen in the passageway. No other details are known before the 19th century, when it was occupied by the bank agent William Ward (1830s?-60s),

a saddler and farmer (1860s-70s), a plasterer (1880s), and a slater and decorator (1890s-1920s). In 2007 it was a women's clothing shop called *House of Simon*. [Jewell, 80, 112]

Nos. 125-125A and 'Chevrons'

No. 125 includes another late-medieval building, encased in stone in the 18th century or earlier. The paintwork of the wall above and to the side of the shop shows that the doorway (marked 125) is the entrance to the flat above: another of Burford's many 'flying freeholds'. In the 19th century it was a tailor's, and a saddler, harness maker, and grocer's, and in the later 20th century it became a petrol station and garage (Figure 103). The unusual curve on the shopfront and the bracket and post to the right date from that period. It closed in 1997 when part of the shop window was reglazed, and in 2007 it was a shop called *The Hideaway*.

'Chevrons' next door belonged to No. 125 and contains features of many periods, including painted chevrons (which gave it its name) on some of the floor joists. The High Street wall was rebuilt after a collapse in the late 20th century. A low doorway and late 18th-century sash window on Swan Lane were possibly for a shop. Nineteenth-century occupants included plasterers, coopers, a linen draper, and (in 1891) a postman. [RM]

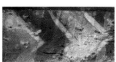

'Chevrons' is named from the chevrons painted on some of its floor-joists, at an unknown date.

West Side: Priory Lane to Sheep Street

The western side of central High Street, rising gently from Priory Lane, also contains several medieval buildings, although most are hidden behind later façades and shopfronts. The row included two of Burford's principal medieval inns, both near the crossroads: the *George* (No. 104) and the *New Inn* (No. 124), later renamed the *Crown*. A small nearby building (No. 96) bears the mark of the prominent 16th-century mercer Simon Wisdom. Four other buildings became inns or pubs in the 18th or 19th centuries, when most neighbouring buildings were shops. Two of Burford's cramped 19th-century cottage yards grew up behind Nos. 56 and 64 (The College) and No. 104 (George Yard).

No. 96 (Huffkins tea room) and the former *George Inn*, looking south. The *George's* timber-framed wing is 15th-century.

Nos. 46 (*Cotswold Arms*) and 48

These two buildings probably began as a single late-medieval range: No. 48 (left) extends over the doorway of the present *Cotswold Arms*, which has a deeply moulded Tudor-arched surround with carved spandrels. Both parts were substantially remodelled from the 17th century: the *Cotswold Arms* has stone mullion windows facing Priory Lane and a blocked one on the façade, while No. 48 was entirely refronted in ashlar. Its three first-floor mullion windows with drip-moulds are not symmetrical, suggesting an earlier layout behind. The two-storey canted bay window (extreme left) is of unusual design: the upper window has a drip-mould over, while the lower is set into a recess to allow light in, possibly for the tailors (the Deanes) who lived here from before 1851 to *c.*1911.

In 1800 No. 46 was the *Lower Mermaid Inn*, and was called the *Mermaid* until the 1870s; it was renamed the *Cotswold Arms* before 1881. Its ground-floor bay window and the upper-floor sashes are all 19th-century. In the 1960s No. 48 was a haberdashery shop, and in 2007 it sold travel goods and country clothing. The shop window and stone door-hood are early 20th-century. [List]

Nos. 50-56

Behind the 17th- and 18th-century fronts of these four separate houses and shops are remains of more medieval buildings. Nos. 50 and 52 (right), now linked as Jonathan Fyson Antiques, both started as late medieval single-cell units on the street, presumably used as shops. Both have later back wings, and at the side of No. 50 a doorway (which has been reduced in width) leads to the back of the plot. Both were refronted probably in the 17th century, though at No. 52 the large ashlar dressings around the first-floor windows show its separate development.

Nos. 54 and 56, with a higher roofline, were separately refronted in the 18th century, the former in large blocks of carefully squared and smoothed limestone, the latter in squared and dressed limestone rubble blocks, laid in courses of varying widths. No. 54's first-floor windows (datable by their wide glazing bars) were probably part of the same remodelling, though a 17th-century cupboard inside No. 56 suggests an earlier rebuilding, too. At No. 54 the refronting hides a medieval timber frame, whilst at No. 56 a two-centred 14th-century archway to the street (see below) points to medieval origins. Visible inside the archway are the timber joists of the room above, and blocked openings on its left may have contained small lock-ups for shops.

Nineteenth-century censuses show all four houses occupied by trades- and craftspeople, including shoemakers, slaters and plasterers, tailors, and grocers. The shopfronts (and some first-floor windows) are all 19th- or 20th-century: at No. 56 the ground floor was extended out onto the pavement with a new doorway and shopfront, probably for the watch- and clockmaker Richard Griffin (recorded there 1910). At No. 50, new outbuildings along the edge of the plot included one with a chimneystack, used probably by the blacksmiths (all members of the Barnes family) recorded there from the 1820s to 1850s. The Barneses were succeeded by the Banbury family, who ran a long-lived clothing business and (by 1891) a cycle depot. The building's Cotswold-slate roof contrasts with the 20th-century Welsh slate of No. 52, substituted before the enforcement of guidelines on use of traditional materials.

Cottages behind Nos. 56 and 64 (formerly 'The College')

(Right) the medieval entrance to The College and (above) the cottages today.

Through the medieval archway to the left of No. 56 is a group of cottages which by the 19th century formed one of Burford's several cramped cottage yards (cf. Nos. 135-137 and 153). In 1793 there were four dwellings here, but by 1841 the yard contained 11 separate households containing 44 people; 20 years later there were still 10 households and 40 people, including agricultural labourers, a stableman, and a gardener. By the 1870s and 1880s some of the cottages had been combined into a licensed boarding house accommodating around 20 lodgers, and the overcrowding diminished as Burford's population fell. Even so there were still four separate dwellings and 16 inhabitants in 1901, including the lodging house (with 12 inmates), and cottages to let. The name 'College', used ironically as in many such cases, was in place by the 1790s [RM].

The cottages themselves are probably 17th- and 18th-century in origin, built in random rubble limestone,

Occupants of 'The College' c.1900; the man of Afro-Caribbean descent (right) has not been identified.

and with some timber lintels. In the 1970s the yard was 'gentrified' and the passageway blocked. Apart from a three-light mullion window at the back of No. 56, all the existing doors and windows are 20th-century, and the roof, too, has been raised.

Though a shared Cotswold-slate roof now links this range with Nos. 54-56, the varied stone façades confirm their separate histories. No. 64 began as two separate cottages dating probably from the 16th or 17th centuries, and throughout the 19th century was occupied by boot- and shoemakers. From c.1915 to the mid-20th century it was Foster's motor garage (owned in 1939 by R.G. Paine), and its early building history is largely concealed behind the 20th-century frontage: the central porch, reminiscent of a miniature threshing barn, was inserted for the garage in the 1920s. Beneath the eaves are applied timber struts, another feature of the Edwardian 'vernacular' fashion seen in many of Burford's buildings. A roof dormer was removed some time after the 1930s. In 2007 the building was occupied by the *Oxford Shirt Co.* [RM]

No. 64

Nos. 66-68

This imposing, early 18th-century ashlar front in Taynton stone hides remains of a 15th- or 16th-century building behind. The only surviving feature is an arch-braced roof truss, but an external clue is the asymmetric frontage: the off-centre doorway indicates

Robert Foster's chemist's shop and post office at 66-68 High Street, c.1905.

the position of a former through-passage, while the deep cornice and parapet hide an earlier roof. Small windows in the north and south returns allowed the occupants to see up and down the street. The fashionable 18th-century doorway and sash windows, typical of Burford in this period, are illustrated above (Figure 88).

Probably this was the town house of a professional person, but no owners are known before the 1850s when it was a chemist's, occupied first by Richard Yerbury and later (1860s-90s) by Robert D. Foster. By 1887 Foster was also postmaster, and his family still ran a post office here in 1940 [RM]. Some of the original ground-floor windows have been replaced by a projecting late 19th-century shopfront with its own door; apparently the chemist made a shop in the left-hand part, while retaining the rest as his own house.

No. 70

Right: Bowerman's furniture and antiques shop at 70 High Street in the early 20th century; and (above) the premises today.

The squared and dressed stonework visible above the projecting 19th-century shopfront, laid in regular courses, is probably late 17th-century. The first-floor windows are 18th-century, but unlikely to be original, since they are somewhat clumsily set into the wall. The alleyway to the left led to the rear of the plot, a common feature of Burford houses, and under the shop window are openings to a cellar. In the 1840s-50s this was James Allen's grocery shop (combined, by 1851, with a boot and shoe warehouse), and from the 1860s it was a draper's, run from the 1880s by the Bowermans. The slogan 'Established 1870', on glass over the doorway, refers probably to the Bowerman family business, which must have started elsewhere. By 1920 Gilbert Bowerman was an antique dealer, and in the later 20th century this was a tea room. In 2007 it was part of the *Oxford Shirt Co*.

Nos. 74-76

A 17th-century front (now rendered) hides another building of medieval origin. Nothing is known before the 1840s, however, when the range was occupied by William Hemming, a smith and (later) 'engineer, ironmonger, and plumber'. From the 1880s the firm was taken over by Charles East and his relatives the Hollises, ironmongers, engineers, and waterworks contractors. A long range of outbuildings at the rear is entirely 19th-century, as are the first-floor sash windows at the front. The building was gutted for conversion into a supermarket *c.*1970, when two separate ground-floor shops were thrown into one; it continued as *Budgens* supermarket in 2007. [RM]

Nos. 78 (*The Mermaid*) and 80

Though substantially remodelled, both buildings are of medieval origin and were apparently of moderately high status. The *Mermaid* contains late-medieval cruck timbers, but in the 17th century it was largely rebuilt in stone; the remodelling probably included insertion of an upper floor (replacing an earlier open hall) and raising of the roof. The two-centred arched doorway is 14th-century, but may have been reset. The street-front's Tudor aspect, with its mullion and transom windows, results largely from a remodelling in the 1930s, while the untraditional Welsh-slate roof is also 20th-century.

The building was an inn or public house by the 1820s and possibly earlier, as indicated by a worn mounting-block outside. Until the 1940s it was the *Three Pigeons*, renamed the Mermaid after the Second World War.

No. 80 to its left (a fishing and clothing retailers in 2007) has a 14th-century arched stone doorway to the rear of the shop. The medieval building was only one room deep, possibly already used as a shop, and the arch was probably the back door of a through-passage to the yard behind. A heated rear wing was added in the 15th century, its Perpendicular fireplace altered in the 16th century when a new lintel was inserted. The ceiling beams in the shop are a 17th-century insertion to provide an upper room, and the rubblestone façade (which originally incorporated part of the house to the south) dates probably from the same period. In the 18th century the upper part of the façade was raised to form a parapet, and sash windows (replaced in the 19th century) were inserted. Nineteenth-century occupants included a printer and book-setter (1850-60s), a teacher with four pupils (1870s), and the cabinet-maker and house-builder William Smith (1880s-1910s), whose wife was a toy dealer. By 1915 it housed *The Wychwood Toy Co.*, for which the 20th-century shopfront may have been added. [Pevsner, 517; Laithwaite 72; List; *Inns* 58-9]

Nos. 82-84

This united rubblestone front conceals a jumble of rooms and phases and some re-used timber. As the ridges either side of the chimney stack do not quite match up, probably there were once two separate houses on the site. Both had medieval origins: the roof structure of No. 84 has been dendro-dated to 1432, while No. 82 is about 100 years later.

The right-hand part of the building may once have been part of No. 80, since the rubblestone façade extends across both buildings, and a blocked opening in the north gable can only have connected them. When Nos. 82 and 84 were united, probably in the 18th century, the present rubblestone façade with ashlar quoins was built out beyond the earlier building line to link them. The canted bay windows to each floor, and the parapet with a small pediment, could be later additions of *c*.1800. In the 1840s-60s the house was occupied by Richard Minchin (a hotel proprietor) and his sister Susannah, followed in the 1880s by a wheelwright. By 1910 William Smith owned it with No. 80. The shopfront is 20th-century, the pattern in the paving stones suggesting that its predecessor once had a central doorway. A safe remains inside from when the Burford Bank operated from here.

A building at the rear, converted into a new County Council library in 2005, was linked to No. 82 by a series of ad hoc spaces. Like many rear outbuildings it shows signs of light industrial use, including taking-in openings at first-floor level and wide doorways to the ground-floor passages. Two round-headed doorways faced west. Unusual features such as sink-like depressions and darkened timbers suggest it may have been the studio and darkroom of Henry Minchin, a mid-19th-century photographer who did not live here, but who may have been related to Richard Minchin. [*PO Dir* 1864, 1869]

Nos. 92 and 94

At No. 94, now called Christmas Court, the canopy with supporting columns, the boxed shopfront, and the bay windows are all 19th-century. Possibly they were added when part of the building was a hairdresser's (1850s-1910s or later). The central passageway may have also been cut through during the 19th century, and gave access to a blacksmith's forge at the rear: blacksmiths were recorded on part of the premises by the 1850s, and continued until the 1910s or 1920s. By the 1950s-60s the whole site belonged to Charles Pether's builders, the rear outbuildings becoming works and offices, and the front a store and retail shop. The premises were redeveloped in the 1980s by Aubrey Newman, and the shopfronts in the passage are now all late 20th-century [RM].

The main building itself is considerably earlier. The low roof-line suggests an early date, and in the right-hand shop, on the ground floor, is part of a doorway with ball-flower decoration, typical of the late 14th century. The roof has upper crucks, and may also be early. The blocked archway to the left of the stone front was an early 16th-century doorway, and in the 17th century the building was modernised with a new staircase and mullion windows, which can be seen from the central yard. The doorway to the right-hand shop is also 17th-century, and two small windows, now blocked, can be seen beside the bay windows to the first floor facing the street.

No. 92, on the right (or north), began as a narrow, 16th-century timber-framed building on the corner of the larger plot occupied by No. 94. Its stone cellar is medieval, and was perhaps for storage. The stonework of the adjacent building extends over the façade, suggesting that the properties were once united. A 17th-century fireplace survives on the ground floor, but the shopfront under a slated lean-to roof, the dormer, and the first-floor bay window were added in the 19th century, when the building was successively occupied by a confectioner, baker, and wine and tea merchant (1840s-70s), a carpenter and wheelwright (1880s), and a printer (1901). A rear outbuilding has a 17th-century fireplace, but may have been a bakehouse or kitchen.

No. 96

From the late 18th century to c.1918 this was the *Rose and Crown* inn. The lean-to and stone plinth with windows above look late 19th-century, added perhaps when extra space was needed to cater for the burgeoning tourist trade; the front door bears the date 1915, with a rose and crown formed in nails. In origin, however, this was one of several houses built by the wealthy Burford merchant Simon Wisdom, whose mark, with the date 1578, can be seen in the spandrels of the stone doorway. A timber doorway of similar date survives at the rear, and another interesting feature of the period is the decorated lintel above the five-light front window at first-floor level. In 2007 the building was a shop called *Peter Rabbit and Friends*. [Laithwaite 72, 75; *Inns* 60]

No. 98

The earliest feature is a stone Caernarvon archway in the right-hand front room, with the characteristic 'shoulders' of the late 13th century (Figure 27). Probably it has been re-set, as nothing else is visible from such an early date. Most of the structure has 16th-century origins (e.g. the fragment of moulded stone plinth near the doorway to the rear courtyard), but has been much altered. The rubblestone façade was raised in height in the 17th century, and at first-floor level three long timber lintels can be seen above blocked windows; before their replacement by 18th-century sash windows they may have lit a workroom. A large fireplace (now blocked) in the rear room may have served a bakery business recorded here from the 1870s. The central doorway and the shopfront with fluted pilasters were added in the early 20th century, but evidence of further doorways (now blocked) can be seen at either end. In 2007 it was a baker's, confectioner's, and restaurant called *Huffkins*. [List]

No. 104 (former *George Inn* and George Yard)

From the Middle Ages to its closure c.1800 this was one of Burford's most important inns, located close to the Tolsey and opposite Witney Street. When first recorded in 1485 it was owned by William Brampton, and since the family were leading inhabitants from the late 14th century the inn may go back that far. Later keepers included Agnes Charleye (died 1572), sister of the prominent Burford merchant Simon Wisdom; John Collier (died 1634), who in 1608 added Nos. 110-112; and Robert Aston (keeper 1674-97).

The large stone gatehouse was designed to be noticed by travellers arriving from the east. Under the arched carriageway, on the left, is a pair of blocked arches of c.1300, and similar arches survive inside the stone and timber range (now an antiques shop) to the right of the gatehouse. Possibly they lit small lock-up shops (Panel 3). The timber-framed and jettied 15th-century wing sits on a later stone ground floor, its moulded jetty beam (supporting the protruding upper floor) just visible above the present shop

The George's street front and former carriageway, with (right) the former courtyard, converted into cottages in the early 19th century. (See Map 17 and Figure 91)

window. Other early features include the tops of timber mullions, and vestiges of four sets of windows with traceried heads. A window at ground level lit the cellar, which may have been a tavern; fragments of a stone newel stairway leading down to it can be seen inside. In an upper room is a blocked opening with 15th-century quatrefoil spandrels. All these front rooms were used for eating and drinking, with accommodation round the courtyard to the rear (Panel 9).

In the early 17th century the gateway was altered by the addition of a stone gable with decorative finials, lit by a three-light casement window with drip-mould. Below is part of the original window to the room above the gateway, which had fluted jambs and probably one or two stone mullions. The asymmetric position of the window and archway suggests that an earlier layout dictated the position of the new work, which was probably contemporary with the incorporation of Nos. 110-112 next door (see below). The carriageway's right-hand wall seems to be part of the 17th-century alterations, and visible in its roof are the timber supports for a hearth-stone in the room above. Iron pintles (or pivots) for gate hinges survive in the left-hand jamb.

Looking back from the rear yard, the original line of the gatehouse roof can be seen running parallel to the street (see photograph). Behind the gatehouse, two steeply sloping roofs have a later linking section in front. This was probably built as a covered way around 1608, when Nos. 110-112 (right of the gateway in the rear-view picture) were added. The long range on the right was probably stabling, with sleeping accommodation above, and a kitchen mentioned in 1632 would have been in this part. The jettied row on the left was possibly a 15th-century dormitory range, though a stone-mullioned window in the centre suggests an early 17th-century rebuilding. On the street front, fashionable tall sash windows with thick glazing bars replaced the original windows of the jettied wing in the 18th century.

After the inn's closure the front part became a shop, occupied in the 1850s by a milliner and dressmaker and in the 1860s-80s by a clockmaker. The shopfront is mid-19th-century, and some of the timber-framing and the bargeboards were renewed in the 20th. The yard was turned into cramped cottage accommodation: from the 1840s to 1890s there were up to 12 households and 53 people here, including masons, labourers, seamstresses, and quarrymen. In the 1920s it was old people's accommodation, and in the 1960s the cottages were bought by public subscription and renovated as low-rent housing, many of them being combined. [List; *Inns* 12-20; Panel 9]

Nos. 110-112 (formerly part of George Inn)

A deed of 1608 records that this house had been recently rebuilt by John Collier (died 1634), keeper of the *George Inn*, who incorporated it into the *George* around that time. The stone-mullioned window to the cellar at pavement level seems earlier, but is part of a plinth which is later than the gateway jamb. In the 18th century the building was modernised with several sash windows. After the *George* closed it became a shop, successively occupied by a watchmaker, butcher, cabinet maker, and (in 1881) saddler (Figure 67).

The 17th-century building replaced a medieval predecessor with arched openings to the central passageway, owned in 1404 by William Brampton of Oxford. In the early 15th century it was apparently divided, and in 1495 (when acquired by Thomas Poole of London) it included a shop, cellars and solar (or upper chamber). [*BR* 333-6, 343, 352-3, 356-7; *Inns* 13; Jewell 13]

Nos. 118-122 (former Red Lion Inn)

The early-to-mid-19th-century ashlar façade of this tall three-storey building hides elements of a medieval house, including two 15th-century fireplaces (both in their original positions) in the private house above the shop. Owners included Henry Cutler in the early 15th century, in the late 15th John Pinnock the younger, of a prominent merchant family, and by 1580 a chandler, Robert Brewton. The modern-day doorways reflect the 15th-century arrangement. That on the right leads to a passageway through to the rear of the plot, so that the present shop-door would have been characteristically off-centre to the medieval house.

Between the 1770s and 1860s this was the *Red Lion Inn*, and the façade dates from that period. From the 1880s to 1910s it was Frederick Drinkwater's butchers, the faint outline of his painted sign still visible between the second-floor windows. From the 1930s to 1970s it was Barclays Bank, and in 2007 a bookshop. Rubblestone outbuildings at the back, related to the inn and butcher's, were bought in 1938 for conversion to cottages. The architect also remodelled the façade and recreated the passageway and door to the right, replacing the former butcher's shop window. [*BR* 333, 335, 338, 421, 425; *Inns* 62; local inf.]

No. 124 (Reavley's chemist, formerly *New Corner* or *Crown Inn*)

Externally there are few clues to the age and interest of this building. The shape of the roof is unusual, however, and hides a medieval structure with arch-braces and smoke-blackening (Panel 8). The building was recorded as the *New Corner Inn* in 1423, and as the roof has been tree-ring dated to 1401 it was probably purpose-built as an inn. Certainly this is a prime site, right by the Tolsey (or market house) at the central crossroads. Behind the render at first-floor level is a jettied timber frame, and rear wings and outbuildings along Sheep Street derive from its use as an inn. Charring of joists over the cellar marks the location of a ground-floor open hearth.

By 1501 the inn was renamed the *Crown*. It closed soon after 1734 when it was leased to an apothecary, Nicholas Willett, and has remained a druggist's or chemist's ever since – reputedly the oldest functioning chemist's in England. Just inside the shop is a massive elm 'samson post' with some carved decoration, possibly inserted to support the upper floors when the original front wall was replaced with the present panelled frontage and windows, on the building becoming a pharmacy. The first-floor sashes and timber shopfront are also 18th-century. The pharmacy shop fittings inside are an important survival. [*Inns* 6-9; *BR* 422, 425, 435, 679]

West Side: Sheep Street to No. 152 (former *New Inn*)

These further High Street plots, rising up the hill from Sheep Street and the Tolsey, were part of a medieval extension of the town, and originally had relatively wide frontages (Chapter 2). Several are documented from the Middle Ages, though all have been substantially rebuilt. Commercial and industrial buildings include a former inn at No. 152, a former rope factory at No. 142, and Nos. 130-132 with their impressive 19th-century shopfronts. The Tolsey itself, built in 1525 at the corner of Sheep Street, is discussed in Panel 6.

The view from the Tolsey (on the right), looking southwards up the hill.

Nos. 128-132

Occupying the whole of a wide medieval burgage plot, this long frontage dates from after 1863, when the building was Newman's drapers. Though the Tuscan columns at ground-floor level are well-crafted, tapering towards the top, the handling of other classical elements is idiosyncratic. The shopfront of Nos. 130-132 (iron columns within) and the doorway of No. 128 (with mosaic floor) are contemporary with the rest of the front, and vertical metal shutters survive in their housings above the door and windows. The arched shopfront of No. 128 is early 20th-century, replacing two domestic windows.

Robert Cutler owned an earlier house here in 1367, and in the 1580s the clothier John Floyde the elder lived here. Later owners or occupiers included John Hughes (1671), Robert Castle (1753), and (reputedly) the doctor Thomas Cheatle (c.1819), succeeded by drapers (the Tanners and Newmans) from the 1820s. Fragments of a 16th-century house remain inside and at the rear, while a rear wing to the north has 17th-century mullion windows with drip-moulds. In 1665 the house probably had five hearths. [*BR* 368, 669-70, 673; *Hearth Tax* 215; RM; Jewell 9, 97]

No. 134

This small building is probably Burford's best-documented property, because of its acquisition (with earlier deeds) by Brasenose College, Oxford, in the early 16th century. An earlier house occupied this half-burgage plot by 1250, when it belonged to Cold Norton Priory, and in the 1360s and 1420s the Cutlers held it with Nos. 128-132. Later lessees included Simon Wisdom (1552), the clothiers William Wisdom (1567) and John Templer (1600), and John Jordan, gent (1732), who probably all sublet it. The existing building is 16th-century; part of its timber frame is visible above the side passageway (inserted later), which in the 19th century led to outbuildings at the rear. The timber frame was rendered in the 18th century. In 1768 there was a periwig maker here, and in the 19th century the Holland family of gunsmiths and ironmongers, who had a forge at the rear. The projecting first-floor windows are late 19th-century and the shopfront early 20th. By 2006 the various outbuildings (wash-house and kitchen, coal-house and chaff house, and stable, warehouse and forge) were three separate premises. [Laithwaite 87-8; *BR* 669-70, 673; List]

No. 142 with rope factory and Holland's Yard.

142 High Street, with (below) the former rope factory built on its back plot in 1903.

Until unified as a single shop in the 20th century, these properties were quite distinct. The right-hand house, behind its smart late 18th-century ashlar façade and late 19th-century shopfront, is 17th-century, though a predecessor was occupied by the Cutlers (with premises to the north) in the 1360s and 1420s. From the late 17th to mid-18th centuries it was the *Three Goats' Heads* inn, run by the Daniel family with a hemp-dressing and sack-weaving business. Its neighbour is of similar date, refronted in a more vernacular 18th-century style, and with 19th-century sash windows and 20th-century shopfront. At the back in the 19th century was another of Burford's cramped cottage yards, called Holland's Yard after ironmongers living in the left-hand house in the 1820s-70s. Three households lived there in the 1860s-70s, including a pauper, labourers, groom, and laundress.

James Wall of Eynsham acquired the right-hand house in 1811 and set up a rope-making business. In 1903 a successor built a new brick rope-factory at the rear, possibly replacing the cottage row. The wide side doorway led to the rope-walk, where strands of hemp were laid out for twisting into rope. The factory, visible from Sheep Street, closed after the Second World War and was used as a printing works, becoming a private house in the late 20th century. The left-hand house was a cycle-makers in the 1890s-1910s, before the two parts were combined as a Co-op stores after the Second World War. [List; *BR* 455, 669-70; *Inns* 69; RM]

Nos. 144 and 150

150 High Street (Brian Sinfield Gallery), with (right) No. 144.

William Cox, an upholsterer and cabinet maker, rebuilt and enlarged No. 144 in the early 19th century, creating a plain ashlar front with tall sash windows to the first-floor *piano nobile*. The iron tie-ends and shallow-pitched roof suggest, however, that the façade hides an earlier building, which from the 1740s to c.1801 was occupied by a saddler, Solomon Jeffs. Occupiers from the 1850s to 1910s included shoemakers, bakers, and a harness-maker, though the shopfront (*Burford Woodcraft* in 2007) is early 20th-century.

No. 150 next door, similarly three-storeyed, was also refronted in the early 19th century, this time in rubble stone, and the roof pitch was altered to create larger attic rooms. The carriageway and former stable to the rear are of similar date, the ground-floor canted bay window added some decades later. The core is probably 17th-century, the date of a large beam and alcove (formerly a fireplace) in the carriageway. From the 1840s this, too, was occupied by shopkeepers (bakers, confectioners, tailors), and in 1901 by a blacksmith. *The Brian Sinfield Gallery* opened here in 1972.

In the 19th century some dwellings seem to have lain behind No. 144, associated possibly with neighbouring Holland's yard (see No. 142). Inhabitants in the 1840s-90s included craftsmen, tradesmen, and a farm bailiff. [RM]

No. 152 (former *New Inn*)

In the late 17th and 18th centuries this may have been the *Quart Pot* inn, and by 1830 it was the *New Inn*. Medieval roof timbers (possibly re-used) survive in a rear wing, but the front range seems to have been built in the 17th century, and the façade with central doorway is early 19th-century. The 'horns' on the window sashes show they have been renewed, probably in the 20th century. After the Second World War the inn was renamed the *Rampant Cat*, after the town's (and Robert FitzHamon's) heraldic symbols. In the later 20th century it became the *Dragon Inn* Chinese restaurant. [List; *Inns* 69-70]

UPPER HIGH STREET AND THE HILL

East Side: Uphill from Swan Lane

This far up the hill settlement may have thinned in the later Middle Ages, following falls in population (Chapter 2). At least two houses are part-medieval, however: No. 127 and, most strikingly, No. 139 (Hill House). Most others are of 16th-, 17th-, and 18th-century origin, and include former inns or public houses (Nos. 127, 141, 155), smart private dwellings (Nos. 127, 131, 153), and cottages (Nos. 143-5). In the 19th century many were subdivided to accommodate labourers or lesser tradespeople, and behind Nos. 135-7 and 153 were two of the town's cramped cottage yards. No. 157, at the top of the hill, is another example of early 20th-century remodelling in vernacular style.

Looking up the hill from 135-7 (left) and 139, in origin a large medieval house with an open hall. Behind 135-7 was one of Burford's 19th-century cottage yards.

**Nos. 127 (former *Swan Inn*)
and 129**

No. 127 contains probably 15th-century remains, notably an internal two-centred archway at the back of the shop and a nearby rear-facing window. Some of the front may be 16th-century but has been much altered, and an early 17th-century oak window-frame is visible in the gable. In 1652 this was probably the 'mansion house' of John Hanns or Hannes (died 1660), and by 1685 it was the *Greyhound* inn, which continued as the *Swan* from the 18th to the mid-20th century. In the late 19th century it was also a butcher's: the industrial paviors outside are of that date, providing a non-slip surface when the pavements were washed down. Ranges of various dates extending down Swan Lane were presumably stables and outbuildings for the inn. The first-floor sash windows are early 19th-century, and above them changes in the stonework show that the roof was raised when dormers were inserted, to increase headroom in the attics. The sashes in the ground-floor bays are 20th-century replacements, and fragments of moulded stone in the wall to Swan Lane were probably also inserted in the 20th century. In 2007 the ground floor housed *Swan Gallery Antiques*.

No. 129 next door, tall and narrow, seems to have once formed part of No. 127, as they share a plot and the second floor extends over the party-wall. A fireplace hints at a 16th-century date, though the façade and sash windows are early 19th-century. By then it was a separate house, occupied in the 1840s by a schoolmistress, and in the 1850s-60s by a land surveyor. [List; *BR* 451, 460; *Inns* 67]

Nos. 131 and 133

The elegant three-storey house now called No. 131 seems to have been entirely built in the late 18th century by an unknown owner, its central windows featuring raised architraves to accentuate the symmetry. Nineteenth-century occupiers included a tailor and woollen draper (1870s-80s), and later a schoolmaster. No. 133 next door may have 17th-century origins (hinted at in small blocked openings under the eaves), but the sash windows are early 19th-century. The shopfront and pentice (lean-to) roof over it date from the 1870s, around the time it became a baker's.

**Nos. 135-137 (including
Wiggins' Yard)**

Behind this house in the 19th century lay one of Burford's cramped 'cottage yards', home to labourers, hawkers, and other impoverished inhabitants and their families. Eight small households lived here in 1841, that of Richard Wiggins, shoemaker, probably in the main house, with the rest in the yard behind. The Wiginses were still here in the 1870s but had gone 10 years later, when there were apparently five households and one unoccupied house. Multiple occupation ended before 1910, and Wiggins' Yard now forms one property. The main street façade dates from *c*.1800, though the plank door with late 17th-century hinges suggests an earlier building behind, and the ends of timbers visible in the stonework may indicate the position of an earlier floor. The large boxed-out bay window is 20th-century, and may have been a shopfront. [List]

No. 139 (Hill House)

This late medieval stone and (probably) timber-framed house has been much altered, but its medieval plan can still be discerned. In its right-hand part, a late 15th-century arch-braced roof with two rows of purlins survives above an (inserted) ceiling over the former open hall. The private parlour would have been the room to the left, which has deeply moulded beams and a six-light window. (Restored tracery survives in two of its lights; the rest was lost when a bay window was inserted in the 18th century.) The medieval private chambers above were probably in a jettied and gabled timber-framed cross wing, the cut-off joists for which can be seen in the external stonework. The medieval service rooms and entrance would have been on the right, where the carriageway belonging to No. 141 is now. The present doorway has been reset, and a traceried window of *c*.1320 at the rear and a 14th-century carved head corbel at the front may also have been reset from an earlier building. The original owner is unknown, but was presumably a merchant or someone of similar status.

As so often there was considerable modernisation in the 16th century, when the parlour gained a fireplace and a first floor was inserted into the hall. In the 18th century the jetty was removed and the wall rebuilt in stone, with sash windows. None of the people responsible is known, and by the 19th century, like many of Burford's larger buildings, the house was divided between relatively humble tenants, including a tailor and shoemaker (1840s), and a tailor and builder or broker (1860s). In 1850 Elizabeth

Hill House. The medieval hall was in the right-hand part, with a (now lost) entry and service rooms beyond. Private chambers were in the left-hand part, where the row of sawn-off joists above the ground-floor window probably supported a projecting, timber-framed upper storey. The existing doorway was inserted later.

Clare applied for a licence to use part as a Nonconformist meeting house. The house was heavily restored in the 20th century by Lady (Susan) Tweedsmuir, widow of the writer John Buchan (Lord Tweedsmuir), who lived here from c.1940 until her death in 1977. The stone mullion-windows to the ground and first floors, despite their authentic Cotswold 'feel', are of that period. [Sturdy, D., 'Houses of the Oxford Region', *Oxoniensia* 36-7 (1961-2), 319-20; Wood, M., *English Medieval House* (1965), 354; *ODNB*]

No. 141 (former *White Horse*)

The house has 17th-century origins, and in 1703 was owned by a carpenter and apparently let as four properties. By the 1760s it was the *White Horse* inn, and the carriageway and façade probably date from then. A chain and pintles (or pivots) for the door to the carriageway survive, and a stone niche may have been for a lamp. The *White Horse* continued until the late 20th century, though in the 19th century various tradesmen and their families seem to have shared the premises, including carpenters, drillmakers, and a corn merchant. In 1781 it was partly sublet to the overseers of the poor for Upton and Signet, who perhaps used some of the outbuildings as a poor house. Multiple occupancy may explain a blocked doorway apparently replaced by the ground-floor left-hand window (see straight masonry-joints below). In 2007 it was a single private house, and the timber transom windows are 20th-century. [List; RM; Oxf. Journal Synopsis 12 Oct. 1765; ORO QSD V/2-4]

Nos. 143 and 145

Both these buildings probably began as 17th-century stone cottages. No. 143 was substantially rebuilt in the first half of the 19th century: timber lintels for earlier doors and windows can be seen in the stonework, and the stylish doorway is slightly off-centre, suggesting an earlier plan. No details are known before the 1840s when it was occupied by a sawyer and his family, followed (amongst others) by a gardener, plumber, and shoemakers. The much smaller No. 145 comprised a single ground- and first-floor room, the doorway leading to a passage to the rear. It does, however, have a cellar, and in the 18th century a rear wing was added, followed by a separate cottage in the 19th century on a diminutive back plot. Throughout the 19th century this tiny property seems to have been in multiple occupancy: six people and three small households were listed in 1841, and in 1891 two agricultural labourers with their families, and a widow with her son. The sash windows are early 19th-century.

Nos. 147-149

At the heart of this building is a 16th-century two-roomed house with a cross-passage behind the left-hand doorway. A kitchen wing was added in the 17th century, and in the 18th a cottage was built at the rear. By 1803 there had been extensive sub-division: the cottage was divided into two, and the kitchen was a separate dwelling. To give access a new doorway was made from the street, its position marked by straight masonry-joints under the left-hand window. The surviving right-hand doorway was inserted later in the 19th century, when the main range was divided between two families. Nineteenth-century censuses list up to four or five families here, headed (among others) by sweeps, agricultural labourers, paupers, machinists, carpenters, a quarry worker, and a glovemaker. In 1968 the house was almost ruinous, but was rescued and returned to a single dwelling. [Laithwaite 88]

No. 151

This is a mid- to late 17th-century house with contemporary attic windows in the twin gables. The other stone mullion windows are 20th-century interpretations, and postdate the slumping of the façade which has caused the left-hand attic window to tilt dramatically. Its history is unknown before the 1840s when it seems to have been temporarily sub-divided; later 19th-century occupants included a gloveress, shoemakers, an agricultural labourer, and a milkman. [List]

No. 153 (including Perrin's Yard)

As at Nos. 135-137 (above), in the 19th century the carriageway gave access to a cramped cottage yard containing at least five dwellings. Occupants recorded in 19th-century censuses included a ragman, agricultural labourers, shoemakers, and carpenters, all with their families. By 1861 the main house was occupied by Thomas Perrin, a builder after whom the yard was named; possibly he developed it further, since more households seem to have been listed than earlier. In 1901 the yard still accommodated two households, but two other cottages there were empty. Stylistically the main house seems to be of the 1750s, but maps show a different layout in the 1920s, and the incorrect (by 18th-century standards) proportions of the ground-floor windows reinforce suspicions that this is partly a 20th-century pastiche. A doorway in the façade was blocked in the late 20th century.

No. 155 (former *Chequers Inn*)

By 1753 this building was the *Chequers Inn*, still open in 1782. The façade dates from that period, though a Tudor-arched fireplace inside points to earlier origins. By the 1820s, when sold to a Bampton maltster, it had been divided into cottages, and throughout the 19th century seems to have accommodated three separate households including agricultural labourers, dressmakers, cordwainers, carpenters, and (in the 1890s) a chimney sweep. In 2007 it was a single house called Chippings. [List; ORO QSD V/2]

No. 157

This three-gabled house looks quintessentially 17th-century and retains some genuine features, such as the drip-moulds over the windows. However, what we see today is largely the result of a comprehensive 20th-century remodelling, comparable with that undertaken in several other Burford buildings. Nothing is known of the building's earlier history, save that in the 19th century, like several nearby houses, it was apparently divided into small cottages: four or five households were recorded on or near the site, headed by labourers, glovers, joiners, laundresses, and chimney sweeps. [*Mallam's & Co. Sale Particulars April 2003*]

West Side: Uphill from No. 154

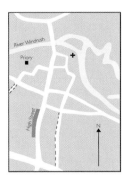

As elsewhere in the town, several buildings along this stretch hide medieval cores behind more recent façades, confirming that medieval settlement extended to the top of the hill. No. 174 (with its imposing 18th-century front) contains 14th-century features, while Nos. 160-162 have dated 15th-century roofs, and the ground plans of Nos. 154-8 and 184-192 suggest that they incorporate medieval hall-houses.

Most other houses are 17th-century or later, some of them built as cottages: No. 178 was a 17th-century encroachment on vacant land, while No. 194 seems to have replaced a barn some time after 1607. A few other houses were minor inns or pubs. Behind Nos. 160 and 174 were two more of Burford's 19th-century cottage yards, although No. 194's smart 18th- and 19th-century front, at the very top of the hill, shows the area's continuing appeal for well-off professionals. The stretch also includes one of the town's 19th-century public buildings (the Court House, No. 164), while Nos. 162 and 170 are among the numerous Burford buildings remodelled in vernacular style in the early 20th century.

Looking north from the top of the hill, Nos. 196 and 194 in the foreground. The neighbouring cottages (obscured behind trees) may include remains of a medieval hall-house.

Nos. 154-158

These three separate houses may have begun as a single large medieval hall-house, the hall (with cellar) on the site of No. 156 (middle), and the cross-wing at No. 154 (right). No. 156 is now 17th-century, with a 19th-century rubblestone front and shop window, though a medieval-style through-passage survives. At No. 154 a potentially early hipped roof is visible behind the parapet. Its ashlar front is 18th-century, however, and the ground-floor bay with sliding (Yorkshire) sashes was perhaps added in the 1870s, as a shopfront for a confectioner and seed dealer. No. 158 has an 18th-century rubblestone façade and 20th-century shopfront, an airbrick showing the location of a cellar which formerly had access from the street. Nineteenth-century occupants included a plumber/glazier and tanner at No. 154, a plumber, coal merchant, and wheelwright (No. 156), and carpenters and bakers (No. 158); earlier occupiers are unknown. [List; Laithwaite 80]

Nos. 160-162 (with Godfrey's Yard)

Both houses contain medieval cores behind later façades, which were further remodelled in the 20th century. The roof structure of No. 160 (right) is 15th-century, and a 16th-century window survives on the ground floor. Much of the front is 20th-century, however, including the first-floor windows and bay window. The location of the original doorway is unclear, the existing 20th-century doorway having been inserted into the 16th-century window opening.

At No. 162 (left) the cruck-framed roof has been tree-ring dated to 1459, and the front door is 16th-century with original ironwork. The distinctive twin gables are from a 17th-century refronting, probably when fireplaces and chimneys were introduced. From the mid-17th to mid-18th centuries the house was associated with the King family, and from 1774 to 1834 with the Beals (none necessarily resident). By 1778 it was evidently two dwellings, and by 1835 it was three, occupied by a shoemaker, stonemason, and widow. It remained subdivided until the 1870s. In 1928 E.J. Horniman of The Priory bought and extensively restored it, as he did several other Burford houses. Most of the window stonework is of that period.

A small cottage yard nearby was recorded intermittently during the 19th century, variously called Beal's, Bowl's, or Godfrey's Yard (the last two names apparently from occupants of No. 160). Up to two households were recorded, including a blacksmith, labourer, and washerwoman. [List; *BR* 450, 459; RM]

No. 164 (former police station and court house)

The police station and court house were built in 1869, on a site bought by the Oxfordshire Clerk of the Peace the previous year. The design is by William Wilkinson, a prolific architect responsible for Oxford's *Randolph Hotel* and numerous North Oxford villas. The rubblestone façade of the court house, with ashlar dressings to mullioned windows and a four-centred arched central doorway, is a deliberate attempt to fit in with the local vernacular, though the iron railings are more Oxford than Burford.

From the 1870s to 1970s the police house at the rear was usually occupied by two officers and their families, most commonly an inspector and constable. (Local wags in the 1960s nicknamed them 'Ploddy' and 'Noddy'.) The cells survived until the police house was converted to domestic use in 1978-9.

An earlier house here belonged apparently to the merchant Edmund Silvester (died 1558) and later to the Jordans, who let it; in 1665 it was taxed on five hearths, suggesting a moderately substantial building. Earlier 19th-century occupants were bakers. [Saint, A, 'Three Oxford Architects', *Oxoniensia* 35 (1970), 53-102; Laithwaite 110; *BR* 446, 455; *Hearth Tax* 216; RM]

Nos. 166-168 and 170-172

166-168 High Street with (below) Nos. 170-172.

Though substantially rebuilt, these two small cottages and two adjoining houses originated probably as two neighbouring medieval houses. Nos. 166-168 suggest the remains of a medieval hall-house, with the hall on the site of No. 168, and the cross wing at No. 166, which retains a through-passage. Most of the existing buildings are late 17th-century with 19th-century windows, however, and the street gable at No. 166 is a 19th-century addition. Nineteenth-century occupants were mostly agricultural labourers, but the earlier occupation history is unknown.

At Nos. 170-172, a single medieval predecessor probably occupied the entire burgage plot. The site of the doorway at No. 170, which led to a through-passage, may be a survival, while at No. 172 there is a cellar under the right-hand part, perhaps originally accessible from both house and street. Both houses were apparently rebuilt in the 17th century, and were substantially remodelled later. No. 170, which has internal evidence of timber framing, was the *Sun Inn* from the 1680s to 1807, and in the 19th century was variously occupied by a grocer, joiner, butcher, and chimney sweeps. In the 1920s it was heavily remodelled probably by the builder Charles Pether (owner-occupier in 1910), using elements of Cotswold vernacular such as stone-mullioned windows and a Tudor-arched doorway. Former stabling at the rear was converted to domestic use around the same time. The author David Ayerst lived here from the 1960s to 1992, and the house was further restored in the 1990s.

No. 172, owned from the mid-17th to early 18th centuries by members of the Jordan family, was temporarily divided, with a small stone one-bay cottage over the cellar and a separate, probably timber-framed part to the left (though visible timbers are re-used). In the 18th century it received its symmetrical ashlar front and a rear wing, and in the 1840s was probably occupied by an excise officer, land agent and servant. [List; Pevsner 513; *BR* 447, 461; ORO QSD V/1-4; *Inns* 70; RM]

No. 174 High Street (Glenthorne) and Wells' Yard

In the 17th and early 18th centuries this was the *Star Inn*, owned and sometimes occupied by members of the Taylor family. The fine ashlar façade was added in the later 18th century, its closely paired windows probably designed to count as one for window tax. Behind, however, is a much earlier house: medieval elements include a 14th-century arched doorway and fireplace, and a decorated beam. Possibly it began as a timber-framed jettied townhouse with twin gables and a stone rear wall. It was remodelled in the 17th century when a stair turret (visible at the side) was added at the rear; the stone walls and stone mullioned side window were probably also built then, and a carriageway

174 High Street, with (far right) an internal 14th-century doorway and fireplace, both apparently in their original place.

(of which no external trace survives) was created to the north when it became an inn. In the early 18th century it belonged to the mercer Richard Whitehall (died 1736), passing to his daughter Maria (died 1768) and her husband Edward Patterson. In the 1890s-1910s the occupant was a painter-glazier.

A small cottage yard nearby was mentioned in 19th-century censuses, housing the family of an agricultural labourer and (later) of a poulterer. In 1901 it was called Wells' Yard, after the occupant of No. 174; presumably it occupied part of the side or back plot. [Pevsner 513; List; *Inns* 70-1]

Nos. 178, 180, 182

These three separate houses are probably all of 17th-century origin. No. 178 (right) is probably the 'little new-built house' mentioned in a will of 1684, its site carved from a wide open space called Cowpen Close, which led to the open fields and cattle pen. The stone-mullioned windows with drip-moulds are part of the original building, though they would then have had smaller pieces of glass in lead *cames* (strips). Twentieth-century alterations include the door, a rear extension, and a new brick chimney stack. No. 180 is of similar date, with sash windows inserted probably in the 18th century and replaced in the late 19th or 20th (since they have 'horns'). Stone infill around the ground-floor windows shows that they were originally wider (probably casements), while the swept dormers suggest an earlier thatched roof. Nineteenth-century occupants included agricultural labourers, shoemakers, and possibly (at No. 180) a shopkeeper.

No. 182, also mid-17th-century, has a central-passage plan, its roof possibly raised later to allow for taller first-floor windows. In the 19th century it was subdivided among three households which included agricultural labourers, laundresses, and slaters or plasterers. The windows reflect the division: to the left are 17th-century stone-mullioned casements and a canted bay window, and to the right a 19th-century Yorkshire or sliding sash. In the mid-20th century it was briefly a lodging house for female trainees working at the *Bay Tree Hotel* in Sheep Street. [ORO MS Wills Oxon. *67/2/4* (Nos. 178 and 182); *BR* 330-2, 346, 447, 563 (No. 182); List; Pevsner 513; RM]

Nos. 184-186

Until the 19th century this was a single house (as it still looks externally). The through-passage plan may have medieval origins, while the doorhead and a chimney-piece in No. 186 could be 16th-century. The rest seems 17th-century, though the first-floor mullion windows have been blocked. At some point the façade was 'pecked' to hold render. By 1607 this was part of the endowment of Burford Grammar School, and was leased in the 17th and 18th centuries to the Greenhills and Townsends (of whom one, in 1699, was a maltster). The dormers were perhaps added in the 19th century when it was two cottages, occupied (from the 1850s) by tradesmen and labourers. [List; Laithwaite 77-8; *BR* 328, 330-2, 346, 518, 562-3]

Nos. 188-192

The basic plan suggests that these three cottages began as a medieval hall-house, remodelled with fireplaces and first floor in the mid-17th century. The doorway to The Cottage (No. 188, right) leads to a through-passage, to the right of which was probably the service end. Hound Cottage (No. 190) replaced the hall, while Clematis Cottage (No. 192) was built on the site of the solar or high-status room. The casement windows are all replacements, and the ground-floor window to The Cottage was once taller. The door is 20th-century.

From the late 16th century to *c*.1862 the property belonged to the trustees of Burford Grammar School. Lessees, recorded from 1587, included Matthew and Richard Winfield, sieve-makers (1650s and 1680s-90s), and the masons Jonathan and Robert

Osman (1704 and 1727). In 1651 it was described as a 'house'. Its division into three cottages probably took place in the early 19th century, and occupiers from the 1840s were masons, sawyers, agricultural labourers, and carpenters. In 1859 No. 192 was 'very dilapidated'. [Laithwaite 80; *BR* 323, 328, 330-2, 346, 458, 519-20, 562]

No. 194

From 1587 to 1628 the site belonged to William Hewes alias Calcott, and in 1607 seems to have had only a barn. Possibly a house was built in the 17th century, but sporadic references to owners from the mid-17th century to early 18th give no details. The present house's symmetrical façade has 18th-century features such as the open-pedimented door hood and the first-floor windows with keystones. From probably the 1820s it was occupied by the solicitor John J. Ansell and other family members, and from the 1880s by the brewer Arthur Garne – probably it was Garne who remodelled it in the late 1880s, adding the canted bay windows. The iron railings are mid-19th-century. [List; *BR* 323, 328, 330-2, 346, 450, 562-3]

No. 196

The apparently symmetrical front conceals a 17th-century house, with a stair turret leading to the upper rooms. Mid-18th-century changes included the doorframe and front window openings, and the shadow of an earlier building line in the south gable suggests that the roof was raised around the same time. The casements are 19th-century. In 1910 it was owned by Thomas W. Porter (who lived next door at No. 194), and leased. No earlier history is known. [List]

SHEEP STREET

Sheep Street was laid out early in Burford's medieval development, and in No. 25 (Calendars) includes a notable late medieval house. Another survives behind the façade of Nos. 33-35. Most of the street's buildings are later, however, and at the far end Nos. 39-53 represent 16th- and 17th-century development of what was then vacant pasture. The northern side is notable for some extensive commercial developments incorporating what were once separate houses: in particular the long frontages of the *Lamb Inn* (assembled in the 18th century), Garne's Brewery (created in the 19th), and the *Bay Tree Hotel* (created in the 20th). Hanover House (No. 11), on the south side, was also associated with the Garnes. Less typical is No. 9 at the High Street end, a modern house which employs a range of period features derived from other Burford buildings (Figure 102).

Sheep Street's south side, the 15th-century timber-framed front of No. 25 (Calendars) visible between the later stone buildings on either side.

North Side

Lloyds Bank

Constructed for the County of Gloucester Bank Ltd in 1878, possibly to designs by James Medland of Gloucester, this commercial building displays a domestic Gothic style which is unique in Burford. The interior was replaced in the late 20th century. The site itself is documented from 1598, when a house here (owned by charity trustees) was occupied by Robert Serrell, and before him by a slater. Later lessees included the clothier Simon Partridge (1684), who may have sublet it. Occupants in the 1840s-70s included a wheelwright, a cow keeper and horse-breaker, a hawker, and the bell-founder Henry Bond. From the 1880s the new building was occupied by successive managers of the Gloucester and (from the 1890s) Lloyds Bank. [BR 329, 340, 430, 434]

Titcombs

As so often in Burford, the house's 18th-century façade conceals an earlier building. To the rear is a cruck-framed barn dendro-dated to 1571, while an archway of *c.*1500 in the garden wall may be a remnant from a lost medieval house on the site. The thick glazing bars in the first-floor sash windows survive from the 18th-century remodelling, and the ground-floor sashes are of sliding or Yorkshire type, seen elsewhere in Burford. The house is documented from the 1590s, when it belonged to Richard Chadwell, gent. In the 19th and early 20th centuries it was occupied by bakers, among them George Titcomb, who is recorded here from the 1890s to 1920s. The cruck-framed barn was converted to domestic use by the architect Russell Cox in the later 20th century. [List; *BR* 340, 430, 434, 447, 455]

Bay Tree Hotel

Established in 1935, the *Bay Tree Hotel* encompasses two earlier houses. Its detached right-hand part (east of Lavington Lane) began probably as a late 17th-century cottage, which has a later north range and an east wing of *c.*1936. The doorway in Lavington Lane is 20th-century. The hotel's main part incorporates on the right a house built soon after 1649, when it was leased to the yeoman farmer Thomas Baggs. Constructed on a two-room cross-passage plan, it has three attic gables to the street with mullioned windows and drip-moulds, and two 17th-century fireplaces survive inside. As noted in a modern wall plaque, an earlier house here belonged to the Tanfields: in 1629 Lady Elizabeth Tanfield bequeathed it for maintenance of the Tanfield family tomb in Burford church. None of the fabric is that early, however, and despite local tradition there is nothing to suggest that any of the Tanfields (who lived at The Priory) were particularly associated with the house. The lower part of the present hotel range, on the left, is a 20th-century extension.

In the 1660s Baggs still occupied the gabled house with an adjacent barn, and in the 1680s the lessee was Henry Godfrey, gent. From the 1830s the occupiers were solicitors: first James Scarlett Price (died 1876), who bought the freehold in 1860, and later Thomas Brown (1870s-1920s). Occupants of the separate cottage beyond Lavington Lane included a solicitor's clerk in 1851 (son of the head of household), who presumably worked for Price. In 1935 the main premises were bought by Miss Sylvia Gray, founder of the *Bay Tree Private Hotel*, and the buildings were further extended to the rear. Also at the rear are several renovated 19th-century outbuildings, including stables and a cart shed.

A large classical entrance-way down Lavington Lane, behind the 17th-century cottage, was part of the 19th-century court house (Figure 97). [List; Laithwaite 77, 79; *BR* 391, 453, 461, 479; *ODNB* (Lawrence Tanfield); *Inns* 74-7; Fisher , *Hist. Burford* (1861), 35]

Baracca (formerly Brewery House)

Despite the early 18th-century style of the window surrounds and a broken pediment above the doorway, this is a mid-19th-century rebuild of an earlier cottage, documented from the 17th century when it was owned by a Little Faringdon yeoman (William Ford). In the 18th century it was used as a farmhouse, and in 1813 it belonged to the maltster John Bateman, who went bankrupt five years later. In the 1840s-50s it was occupied by a tailor and later by an Inland Revenue Officer, the latter with his wife and nine children.

In 1858 the cottage was bought with four barns and an orchard by the brewer and maltster Thomas Henry Reynolds, who had recently acquired the brewery next door. He demolished the barns and replaced the cottage with the present building, renamed Brewery House. The off-centre doorway suggests that an earlier plan was retained in the remodelling. From 1880 Reynolds was succeeded here by George Garne, new owner

Left: Garne's Brewery and Baracca (Brewery House) in 1931, with Oswald Burton and Frank Wilkinson (later managing director) outside. Right: George Garne (1823-1902), who took over the brewery from Thomas Reynolds in 1880.

of the adjoining brewery, whose family occupied the house until 1958; the modern house-name Baracca dates from *c*.1918. The cross-mullion windows are 20th-century replacements. [List; *BR* 450, 458, 479; *Inns* 93-4, 96]

Former Garne's Brewery and Malthouse

The Malthouse, converted into a house for William Garne in 1946.

Two cottages here in the 1650s were replaced in the early 18th century by a single farmstead, where malting was carried out long before the establishment of a brewery in the mid-19th century. An early 18th-century kiln and malthouse survive at the rear near Priory Lane, and in 1774 the site contained 'houses, malthouses, granaries, and gardens'. In 1802 the hop merchant Richard Tuckwell bought the premises, and was succeeded by his brother John, a maltster, and before 1840 by Humphrey Tuckwell of Signet, farmer. By then the site was let to Thomas Streat, a maltster and brewer who probably set up the brewing business.

The central archway (now with a plank door of *c*.1946) was inserted in the 1840s, though the façade itself may be an 18th-century refronting of an earlier house. This is suggested by the asymmetry of the upper windows, while the left-hand casement has a sill re-used from a 16th-century mullion window. The upper right-hand window is identical to those of Baracca next door, rebuilt as a house for the brewery *c*.1858; possibly the house originally extended over part of the brewery, forming yet another of Burford's 'flying freeholds'.

Streat was succeeded in 1858 by Thomas H. Reynolds and from 1880 by the Garnes, who ran the brewery until Nelson Garne's death in 1958. A malt store, granary, and wine-and-spirit store were added in 1895. On-site malting ended in 1936, and 10 years later part of the adjoining malthouse (along the street on the left) was converted into a flat for William Garne, then well in his 80s. A datestone over the first-floor oriel window (with the initials NG for Nelson Garne) commemorates the rebuilding. The Wadworth sign dates from 1969, when Wadworth's (of Devizes, Wiltshire) acquired the firm of Garne and Sons. In the mid-1990s the site was redeveloped as small business units, and the front became a tourist information office and house. [List; Laithwaite 62, 64; *BR* 449, 459, 479; *Inns* 91-8; above, Figure 78; local inf.]

The *Lamb Inn*

Like the *Bay Tree Hotel* two centuries later, the 18th-century *Lamb Inn* comprises an accumulation of several properties. Three of them, running northwards and eastwards from the corner of Sheep Street and Priory Lane, were bought up by Thomas and Susannah Hucks between 1720 and 1734, perhaps in connection with the inn's creation. The oldest is a range facing onto Priory Lane, which includes a medieval window with four cinquefoil traceried lights under a label. The twin-gabled range in which it sits was probably a dwelling called Ivy House in the 1540s, and seems to have originated as a lodging for the medieval hospital nearby. Owners included John Barker (lessee of the former hospital in the 1540s), the clothier John Templer (died 1626), and the Davis and Glyn families, from whom the Huckses bought it in 1723. The main Sheep Street range, bought in 1720 and 1734, is of 17th-century origin, with ovolo-moulded

Above: Medieval (probably late 15th-century) window facing Priory Lane, possibly part of a lodging house for the medieval hospital which became part of the *Lamb Inn*. Below: Blocked doorway at the former *Three Towers*, now also part of the *Lamb*.

windows to the rear, and formerly comprised two houses. That on the corner was owned by a broadweaver in 1715, and that to the east by a chandler in 1734. The inn itself was established by the late 1750s when the innkeeper was Thomas Merrick, and in 1760 the *Oxford Journal* reported the robbery of a traveller putting up there.

During the 18th century the building was remodelled for the coaching trade. In the front range is a small snug with a fireplace, perhaps a 'warming room' for coach passengers passing through Burford. A separate house to the east (or right), with a lower roof line, was incorporated in the early 19th century, having been a separate inn called the *Three Towers* from at least the 1770s. In origin it was a 17th-century house similar to its neighbours, occupied in 1734 by a cooper, and with an ovolo-moulded mullion window to the rear and Tudor-arched fireplaces inside. Twentieth-century alterations to the inn included rear extensions and a corridor, and stables in the rear courtyard were converted into accommodation. A mounting block survives outside. [List; *BR* 450, 458; *Inns* 77-85, 88; ORO QSD V/1-4; Moody, R., *A Burford Celebration in Camera* (1990); RM]

South Side

No. 11

Though apparently rebuilt in the early 19th century, with a smooth ashlar façade and contemporary features, this tall three-storeyed house shows signs of an earlier building inside, and has an attached barn at the back. The original house was evidently built across Sweep's Lane, a medieval 'back lane' running parallel to High Street: the pattern in the pitched stone pavement outside does not quite align with the doorway but continues at the rear, apparently preserving the lane's former course.

In the 1850s the brewer Thomas Reynolds briefly occupied the house with his family and two servants. He was followed probably in 1858 by a widowed proprietor of houses, and from the 1890s to 1940s by the brewer and spirit merchant William (or Willy) Garne, co-owner of Garne's Brewery across the street. Garne renamed the building Hanover House, reportedly after an early steamship, following his marriage to the ship's captain's daughter in 1883. The small attic dormer may have been a taking-in door for goods associated with the brewery. [List; RM]

Nos. 17 and 23

The ashlar façade of No. 23, with its large central gateway, dates from *c.*1845, when the building was occupied by the auctioneer, surveyor, insurance-agent and former brewer Thomas Streat (recorded here 1850s-70s). Streat's businesses must have required a variety of spaces, and the central archway leads to a passage through which the items he dealt in could be brought. The building itself is probably earlier, the slightly undulating ridge suggesting an 18th-century date. In the 1840s it seems to have been in multiple occupation like many other Burford houses, inhabited possibly by a basket maker, carpenter, blacksmith, and agricultural labourer.

In the early 1890s the occupant was Thomas Paintin, a cab and omnibus driver, who before 1899 opened it as the *Lenthall Temperance Hotel*. In 1908-9 it was also listed as a Cyclists' Touring Company house, reflecting the arrival in Burford of recreational

The *Lenthall Temperance Hotel* (23 Sheep Street) before 1910, with the unrestored Calendars (no. 25) beyond.

tourism. From the 1910s it became a private house called Greyhounds, the right-hand part housing the editorial offices of *Countryman* magazine from 1949 to 2003 (save for a short break). In 2006 it was still used for both domestic and business purposes.

No. 17, to its left, has a façade of similar date (early to mid-19th-century), including contemporary sash windows without the 'horns' which characterise later sashes. Nineteenth-century occupants included a sawyer and his family, a retired excise officer, the solicitor Walter Ansell (1860s), and the master of the boys' Board school (1880s). The name Lenthall House dates from the 1950s. The passage on the left, typical of many Burford houses, led to Nos. 13 and 15 Sheep Street, which have since been demolished. [List; *Oxon. and District Trades Directory*; Jewell 28-9; local inf.]

No. 25 (Calendars)

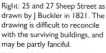

This notable late-medieval house is comparable with some broadly contemporary examples on High Street. The narrow entrance part (on the left) was formerly a separate 1½-storey cottage, heightened and almost entirely rebuilt *c.*1925 when it was taken into the main house. The house's principal part, however, was built soon after 1473, the felling date of the timbers in its front and rear ranges. The builder was presumably a prominent Burford merchant, and the rear south wing could have been a wool store (Figure 20).

Right: 25 and 27 Sheep Street as drawn by J Buckler in 1821. The drawing is difficult to reconcile with the surviving buildings, and may be partly fanciful.

Below: 25 Sheep Street today.

As in many 15th-century Burford houses, timber and stone are used together. The double-length front jetty rests on a stone wall, and the long, jettied back wing rests on stone corbels in the wall of the front range. The construction is so unusual that the artist and architect J.C. Buckler, in a drawing of 1821, showed a gable protruding over the longer jettied section at the front. There is, however, no internal evidence for this, suggesting that (as with Falkland Hall on High Street) the drawing is in part a fanciful reconstruction. The house's original plan was typical of the late medieval period, with a through-passage giving access to a hall (on the right) and to services (on the left). Another structure at the rear may have been a kitchen, which had a floor inserted later.

Sash windows were inserted in the 18th and 19th centuries, when the house had lost its original status and was possibly sub-divided. Nineteenth-century occupants included a blacksmith and a basket-maker (1840s), a glover and a furniture broker (1850s), and in the 1890s an engine driver and a basket maker, with their respective families and two boarders. Richard and Mary Gretton extensively remodelled it between 1912 and 1925, rebuilding the adjoining cottage as an entrance hall and stairway, and making an extension at the rear to link the cottage with the main house and south wing. The name 'Calendars' dates from this time, a reference to their 'calendaring' and publishing of Burford's voluminous historic records. Later occupants included the Revd Dr V.H.H. Green of Lincoln College, Oxford (1960s-2003), after whose death extensive internal renovations were carried out in 2005-6. [Jewell 28; Gretton, M S, *Burford Past and Present* (1945), 145; Laithwaite plate IV; RM]

No. 27

A house here may have been occupied in 1652 by Leonard Mills, carrier (taxed in 1662 on five hearths), and owned in 1685 by Robert Aston (of the *Bull*). The style of the windows and gables suggests a date *c*.1620, but the building was radically rebuilt *c*.1907 for Canon W.C. Emeris, vicar of Burford, by Groves the builders. The leaded lights are certainly 20th-century, and replaced stonework under the right-hand window suggests there was once a doorway here, made redundant when the present entrance was created in the east gable wall. J.C. Buckler's drawing of 1821 shows the range (without its front gables) extending eastwards to abut No. 25, with a doorway or passageway on the site of the present gateway. Map evidence confirms that the buildings were separate by 1881, however, and the drawing may be fanciful (see above). Certainly No. 27's east gable-wall shows no obvious scarring.

Nineteenth-century occupants included a baker and an agricultural labourer. A barn at the rear was used for folk dancing in the early 20th century, and in 1929 was bought by Mrs Conger Vanamee of New York for conversion into a house; in the 1940s-70s the folklorist Katherine Briggs lived there. The name Waynes Close was coined by 1920. [*BR* 449, 458; *Hearth Tax* 216; Pevsner 521; Gretton, M. S., *Burford Past and Present* (1945), 110, 145; RM]

No. 29

The ashlar façade is of 1696 (datestone), but masks an earlier building: note the position of the doorway and side passage, squeezed into a corner. The initials RAS refer probably to Robert and Sarah Aston, proprietors of the *Bull Inn*, who reputedly commissioned the refronting from the local master-mason and quarry owner Christopher Kempster, an associate of Sir Christopher Wren. At the rear is a timber-framed and gabled wing which has been claimed as 16th-century, though it may be later. The house was further modernised in the 18th century, but no occupiers are known before the 1840s when an attorney, Thomas Mann, lived here, followed by the stonemason Thomas Clark (1850s-70s), and by the retired drapers John Secker (1870s) and Alfred Parsons (1890s-1910s). The decorative finials on the dormers look late Victorian. [Pevsner 521; local inf.]

Nos. 33 and 35

Behind a remodelled 17th-century façade are remains of another medieval house, documented from 1492 when the guild of the chapel of St Mary in Burford church owned it. A passageway at No. 35 leads to a courtyard, to the left of which is a medieval Caernarvon arch forming a doorway through a thick rubble wall to the Masonic Hall behind. The upper room to the left has three cruck trusses with extended knees, probably of the mid-15th century. The guild presumably lost the building at the Reformation, and in 1550 the merchant Edmund Silvester (who owned several Burford houses) acquired it, leaving it in 1569 to his fourth son Thomas. By the early 17th century Thomas Bignell was probably owner, and in the 1680s-1710s Daniel Payton, Simon Partridge, and John Andrews.

The Sheep Street range may date from the late 17th century, and originally had a through carriageway to the rear courtyard. Possibly it functioned for a time as an inn. The carriageway was blocked to form two doorways in the mid-19th century, when a former doorway to the right was blocked to form two small windows. The drip moulds to the gable dormers extend awkwardly over the bargeboards, suggesting that they, too, are later additions. By then the house was apparently subdivided, occupied in the 1840s by a farmer, confectioner, and two cabinet makers, and in the 1860s by a servant (with his family), a female teacher with two resident pupils, and the attorney Thomas Mann. It remained two houses in 2007. The Masonic Hall was established in an outbuilding at the back before 1915. [List; *BR* 321-2, 334, 344-5, 352, 356-7, 359; PRO PROB 11/51, f. 40]

No. 39-43 (formerly Culverclose)

In contrast to the houses described above, buildings from here to the end of Sheep Street resulted from 16th- and 17th-century development of what was then largely open land. In the 15th and 16th centuries the site of Nos. 39-43 was part of a large pasture field next to the road, enclosed by a wall and hedge, and called Culverclose (i.e. Dove Close) after a nearby dovecote. Thomas Poole left it to his wife and then to charity trustees in 1500, and in 1580 it was leased to Ralph Wisdom, who built four houses along the frontage by 1598. In 1630 the close and four houses were leased to Edmond Redman of London, gent, and by 1659 (when the charity trustees leased the houses and close separately) there were evidently five houses.

Probably these were the houses known later as Nos. 39, 41, and 43, along with a since-demolished house further west. The gabled façade of No. 39 links two much-altered late 16th-century houses, probably united in the mid-18th century when this was the *Golden Fleece* inn. The inn closed *c.*1862, and in the 1880s-1910s the house was occupied first by a laundress and later by a journeyman cooper. No. 41 next door was built *c.*1600 and refronted in the 18th century, having been let to yeoman farmers; successive 19th-century occupiers included an agricultural labourer, a baker, and a former schoolmistress. No. 43, also of *c.*1600, was let between 1659 and 1707 to a chapman, yeoman, and hatter, and was remodelled as two labourers' cottages in the 19th century, reverting to single occupancy in the 20th. The fifth house, documented from 1659, housed labourers, a shoemaker, and a Greenwich pensioner in the 19th century, and in the early 20th probably included Henry Bond's bell foundry, which later moved to Witney Street. The building was later demolished. [*BR* 334, 336, 339-40, 342, 351-2, 355-9, 519; Laithwaite 64; List]

Nos. 45-53 (formerly the Leynes)

47-49 Sheep Street, with (below) 51 Sheep Street.

Like Nos. 39-43, these 17th-century houses were built on vacant land: in this case the Leynes, a large pasture close which in 1492 belonged to Keynsham abbey as part of the Burford rectory estate or glebe.

Both Nos. 45 and 47 were built between 1628 and 1652. Surviving 17th-century work in the former includes newel staircases and a barrel-vaulted cellar, the mullioned window to which can be seen near the pavement. Signs of two doorways towards Sheep Street show that it was a cottage-pair in the 19th century, when occupants included masons and agricultural labourers (eastern part), and a dressmaker, papermaker, and gardener (western part). No. 47 was refronted in the 18th century and its roof was probably raised, the off-centre doorway and different-sized windows surviving from the earlier building. The 'gothick' sash windows and door hood are late 19th- or early 20th-century, added perhaps when the mason Edwin Timms lived there in the 1890s. The adjoining No. 49 may have been the last of the 17th-century properties to be built on this plot, and was clearly a separate house, even though the stonework plat-band has been carried across its façade from No. 47, and No. 47's quoins have been moulded to form a door frame. The window keystones suggest an 18th-century remodelling, and in the 19th century it was occupied by (amongst others) a retired draper and grocer, a cabinet maker, and a cooper.

The 17th-century origins of Nos. 51-53 are well hidden behind its eastern part, whose front range was fashionably remodelled in the 18th century with a central doorway, an entrance hall, and stairs lit by a round bull's-eye window. Occupants in the 19th century included the maltster and brewer Thomas Streat (1840s), the banker William Ward (1860s-70s), and a female annuitant (1880s-90s), followed before 1901 by a retired governess. The attic storey with dormers is said to have been added in 1926, when the house was extended to the rear and to the west (right) with a new doorway. [*BR* 334, 339, 342, 344, 352, 356-7, 359; Laithwaite 64; local inf.]

WITNEY STREET

Formerly the main route into Burford from the east, Witney Street is now a quiet side-road lined for the most part with small 17th-century cottages, many of which have been much altered. Its south side, however, is dominated by one of the town's largest domestic buildings: The Great House, built on the site of a former inn for the physician John Castle in the late 17th or early 18th century. No. 34 beyond was adapted from its former stables. Other notable buildings include No. 12 (Bull Cottage), externally heavily altered, but in origin one of Burford's oldest surviving houses. Industrial premises included Bond's bell foundry, based at No. 45 in the 1920s and 1930s, while beyond the area included here was a tannery and the site of Burford Mill. The street also includes two nonconformist chapels: the Baptist chapel (still in use), and the 19th-century Plymouth Brethren meeting house at No. 17 (now a house).

Looking east along Witney Street, the large bulk of The Great House on the right, small cottages and houses on the left.

North Side

Nos. 3, 9, and 15 (with Hunt's Yard)

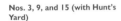

Several houses at Witney Street's north-west end (before the modern cul-de-sac of Sylvester Close) began as outbuildings for premises on High Street. No. 3 (The Coach House), now lit by 20th-century windows to the street, was a warehouse in the mid-19th century, associated probably with the *Bull Inn* and later with 99 High Street. Almost certainly the building has earlier origins, however. A cottage here was acquired in 1494 by Thomas Poole of London, who 10 years later conveyed it to trustees for charitable uses. During the 16th century it was usually called a woolhouse, and in the 17th century a barn. In 1580 the lessee was Burford's leading mercer, Simon Wisdom. [BR 335-39, 342-3, 351, 353, 518-19]

The 19th-century façade of No. 9 (York House), with its squared coursed rubble, stone lintels with keystones, and stone door-hood, probably also hides an earlier core. The arrangement is asymmetrical, and the blocked opening to a cellar is visible just left of the doorway. Further along, the long low range divided into Nos. 15 and 15A perhaps also began as outbuildings, its sagging roofline suggesting a pre-18th-century date. No. 15A's doorway replaced a larger carriage entry, whose outline is visible in the stonework.

Nineteenth-century censuses listed several households in the area, many of them probably in Hunt's cottage yard to the north: the yard lay behind 91 High Street (which was owned by the Hunts), but opened to Witney Street also. Eight households were mentioned in 1851, headed by a gardener, tailor, milliner, labourer, ostler, fishmonger, pauper, and retired servant. A ninth house was empty.

Nos. 17 (Old Meeting House) and 19

The large gable facing the street at No. 17 is unusual in Burford, and reflects the building's origins as the Plymouth Brethren Meeting House (opened by 1877). Further evidence is the regular coursed stonework and the pair of sash windows at first-floor level. The ground-floor window and door date from its conversion to domestic use in 1965, and the building was considerably remodelled in 2006, with the addition of dormer windows and a chimney stack.

No. 19 next door dates possibly from the 18th century, and there is evidence of early timber lintels. By the 1840s it had been divided into two cottages, the reason for the blocked doorway visible in the stonework. The western part seems to have been variously occupied by butchers, bakers, and a dressmaker in the 19th century, and the eastern by the postmaster and a tailor. The quoins on the right show where the front has been heightened to create more attic space, probably in the late 19th century. The first-floor boxed oriel window and Welsh-slate roof are 20th-century. [Moody, R., *A Brief Account of the Plymouth Brethren Meeting in Burford* (2004); List; above, Chapter 9]

No. 21

Most of the present house is late 17th-century, built probably by the chandler Thomas Parsons who owned and lived in it in 1708. The mouldings of the doorway and fragments of ovolo-moulded mullions visible at the ground-floor window are from that phase. Some thick internal walls may, however, be the remnants of a medieval house, and the line of an earlier steeply pitched roof can be seen in the west gable. Later owners included the slater John Green, whose family probably lived here from 1769 to 1831, and the glover and gaiter-maker Augustus Evans (here 1851-79), followed by an excise officer (1881) and a retired police inspector (1901). The present large ground-floor window is probably 19th-century; the sills of its 'Yorkshire' or sliding sashes are moulded, and may have been reset. A cottage at the rear almost certainly existed by 1708, when the site accommodated three households. [Private correspondence summarising deeds from 1708]

Nos. 23 and 25

In the 19th century this long range comprised two pairs of cottages. Probably it was the two tenements 'under one Raunge' given to the endowment of Burford Grammar School in 1571, which in turn were among three adjoining tenements left by John Pinnock the elder to his three daughters in 1486. If so, leases show that No. 23 was subdivided in the late 17th century, and No. 25 at a later date. The existing façades exhibit a confusion of former windows and doorways, with different types of stone. The gabled dormers with sliding sashes are identical in both properties, however, reflecting their common ownership into the 19th century.

Seventeenth- and 18th-century lessees included a currier, apothecary, and fuller (No. 23), and a rough mason, day labourer, and widow (No. 25). From the 1840s the four cottages were occupied by agricultural labourers, a groom, tailors, blacksmiths, and a butcher. No. 25 was in single ownership by 1910, and No. 23 by the 1920s, the probable date of its ground-floor windows. The triangular-headed doorways at No. 23 (one now a window) seem out of place: that to the left is possibly reset, and the other probably dates from when the cottage was re-united. The front was once lime-washed, and small patches remained visible in 2007. [*Wills* 39; *BR* 323-4, 327-30, 332, 346, 553, 563-4]

Nos. 27-33 (including former *White Hart Inn*)

Like many buildings on this side of Witney Street, these three houses on the far side of Guildenford began as 17th-century cottages. At No. 27 the main windows are 18th-century, but the labels over the basement openings are evidence of a 17th-century house, and the position of the doorway relative to the windows suggests that the façade was constrained by an earlier building. The gable end has chamfered 17th-century window surrounds. Nineteenth-century occupants probably included an agricultural labourer, butcher, machine worker, and baker.

Nos. 35, 37, 41, 43

No. 29 (the middle property) was heightened to three storeys in the early or mid-19th century when it became the *White Hart Inn* (recorded 1840s to 1871). The tripartite window and carriageway surround with matching pilaster strips are from the same period. Probably the carriageway gave access to a forge when a blacksmith lived here in the 1890s-1910s. No. 33 next door has 18th- and 19th-century sash windows and a Welsh-slate roof. Its large ground-floor window dates from its use as a baker's and grocer's shop in the 1850s-80s, followed by a shoe shop (1901) and saddlery (1920s-30s). Many of the stones in this group have been keyed for a covering of render. [List; *Inns* 104; Jewell 79]

The street continues with a further line of 17th-century rubble cottages, whose 19th-century occupants included labourers, a groom and gardener, and a dyer, stone mason, fellmonger, shoemaker, and plumber/glazier. All the buildings have been variously altered, as shown by a photograph of the 1920s [Jewell 79]. At that date No. 35, possibly once a cottage pair, had a large 18th-century carriageway to the left (its outline clearly visible around the present door and window), and a central doorway now replaced by a window. No. 37, with its 'Cotswold' mullioned windows, was also a cottage pair, but the present building is the result of an almost complete rebuild in the 1940s. At No. 41 differences in the upper courses of stonework show that the roof has been heightened, probably in the 18th century when the large casement windows were inserted. Probably the owners were of limited means, since one might have expected such improvements to include sash windows and a roof-line as high as neighbouring houses. The lower-quality work and the use of a cheaper sliding or 'Yorkshire' sash window point to the same conclusion. At No. 43 the sash windows are 18th-century in style (moulded architraves standing proud of the wall), but may be part of a 19th-century remodelling. [Jewell 79; List; local inf.]

No. 45 (including medieval archway)

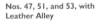

Right: An undated photograph of Bond's bell foundry, located here from c.1922. The main structure collapsed in 1955, leaving only the medieval doorway and window to the street (above).

This site formerly included two cottages, shown in 1920s photographs. That on the right collapsed in 1955 and was demolished, leaving only a stone-mullioned window and a 14th-century doorway. Both those features were part of the cottage shown here in 1926, though the medieval doorway may have been reset from elsewhere in the town. The surviving cottage is an almost complete rebuilding of the house shown here in the 1920s, which had a central front doorway. In the 19th century the two cottages were occupied by labourers, tailors, and by a grocer, innholder, millwright and furniture dealer, sometimes with multiple boarders including a fellmonger. From c.1922 to c.1941 the whole site was Bond's bell foundry: a carriage entrance occupied the site of the present gateway, with a taking-in door above. [Jewell 76, 79; Pevsner 521; drawing (1955) by B.C. Boulter in Tolsey Museum]

Nos. 47, 51, and 53, with Leather Alley

This further row of probably 17th-century cottages has also been repeatedly altered, re-divided, and recombined. No. 47 combines separate houses marked by different rooflines, the higher (right-hand) part once forming part of the adjoining building. The lower part was formerly two cottages, occupied in the 19th century by agricultural labourers, a leather dresser, and a milkman; the late 20th-century garage door on the left replaces a former door and window. The doorway and window opening of the higher part were there by 1926, but have remains of a large carriage entrance in surrounding stonework. One of the openings was a passage to another of Burford's 19th-century cottage yards, called Leather Alley, which in the 1850s-60s accommodated five households of labourers with another three to four cottages unoccupied.

Nos. 51 and 53 next door share a central entrance passage giving access to both properties. Both were refronted in the 18th century, with the pointing spread over the rubblestone and lined to suggest squared ashlar. Elegant new windows were also added, but the lack of fashionable stonework around the doorway and the window above signals its status as a common alley. Nineteenth-century occupants probably included a bone-gatherer, leather dresser, sawyer, and sack-mender (No. 49), and a cordwainer, labourer, and freestone quarryman (No. 51). [Jewell 76, 79; List]

Nos. 55, 57, 59

No. 55 probably has 16th-century origins, and shows evidence of timber framing. The gables are 17th-century, though the oriel windows (in place by 1908) are modern. Nineteenth-century occupants included a nurse (later a pauper) and her six children, one of whom worked as a gloveress, followed mostly by agricultural labourers.

Nos. 57-59 stand on part of the plot of No. 55, and before restoration in 2005-6 comprised two poorly built cottages at the town edge, dating probably from the 17th century. No. 57 may have begun as a low extension to 55; in the 18th century its roof was raised, and a wall was built within it to create a passageway to No. 55's rear garden (entered through the doorway in the front wall). No. 59 may have originated as a back wing, but by the 1840s the two parts were separate cottages, occupied probably by an agricultural labourer and a woman with three children and a lodger. Later occupants included other labourers, a leather dresser, and a sawyer. [Jewell 76; Ditchfield, P.H., *Vanishing England* (1910), 109]

South Side

No. 12 (Bull Cottage)

This small early 14th-century house, though heavily remodelled, may be Burford's earliest surviving domestic building, and is documented from the 1390s. A watercolour of 1840 shows that it had a two-centred arched doorway to the street and an adjacent window with ballflower decoration, whose top half was cut off in the 16th or 17th century when a floor was inserted. Part of a medieval column and capital survives just below the eastern (left-hand) apex of the roof, perhaps relating to an earlier roof structure. Fourteenth-century features inside (Figure 29) include archways, a chimneypiece, and more ballflower decoration, while the rear wing has a raised cruck truss with arched braces to a collar. A Decorated (14th-century) chimneystack shown on the eastern gable in 1840 belonged to the neighbouring house (No. 14), which has been largely rebuilt. Presumably the stack escaped demolition because the gable was shared with No. 12.

Bull Cottage now and (right) c.1840, when it retained its original 14th-century doorway and a contemporary chimney stack. The interior includes high-quality 14th-century stonework (Figure 29).

In 1396 John Cakebread left the house to his wife Matilda and others. Later owners included Thomas Spicer (1402), John Hill or Prior (to 1492), and Thomas Poole of London (1492-c.1504). By 1628 the house was a tavern or inn called the *Talbot*, run apparently by the cooper George Fowler who was tenant by the late 1590s. A 17th-century remodelling of the front may have taken place around that time. The name *Talbot* continued in use until the early 18th century, although named tenants included London gentry and a Burford clothier rather than innkeepers. If it was indeed still an inn, presumably they sublet it to local publicans. From 1707 it was held with the neighbouring *Bull Inn* and became associated with its stabling, which probably saved it from more radical rebuilding; in the 1850s it was inhabited by agricultural labourers, and from the 1870s by ostlers. It was brought back into full domestic use in the 20th century, when the present 17th-century-style windows were inserted. [Laithwaite plate I, 74-7; List; *BR* 333-6, 339-40, 342-3, 345, 351, 353, 355, 358-9, 366, 420-1; *Inns* 23-4]

Nos. 14 (former *Mason's Arms*) and 16

Like its neighbour, No. 14 is documented from the 1390s. In the late 15th century it was one of several properties owned by the prominent Pinnock family, who left it to the vicar and churchwardens in return for an annual mass for the souls of John Pinnock the elder (died 1473) and his wife. A 14th-century Decorated chimneystack survived on its west gable until the 19th century (see No. 12), and the through-passage plan and off-centre doorway also hint at an early building. Any early remains are well hidden behind an 18th-century remodelling, however: the ashlar façade and parapet date from *c*.1730, while the window pattern and cornice are of a similar period. The person responsible for the remodelling is not known, though members of the Jordan family owned it for part of the 17th century, and the occupier in the 1660s was probably a sieve-maker. Before 1707 it was divided among three separate tenants. In the 1840s it became the *Mason's Arms* pub, run by a succession of licensees and acquired, before 1910, by Clinch's Brewery of Witney. For a time it was not as clean as it might have been and was known locally as 'Sooty's', the landlord's wife being referred to as 'Sweep'. In 2007 it was an inn and restaurant renamed the *Angel Brasserie*.

No. 16 next door is modern, built *c*.1990 on the site of the former Agg's builder's yard. It blends in by incorporating local materials and vernacular features such as sash windows and dormers, though the flat stone window heads are incongruous: for authenticity, they should have been timber lintels. A house here was occupied in 1473 by Robert Coburley, hosier, and fireplaces from a more recent building survived in the external wall of the *Angel* when the site was a yard. [Pevsner 520; Laithwaite 77; List; *BR* 319, 333, 338-9, 342-3, 353, 355, 358-9, 366, 421, 455, 447, 671; *Inns* 99-100; RM]

Nos. 18 and 20

The blocked doorway left of centre shows that No. 18 was once a pair of cottages, erected probably in the mid-17th century. The original cottages were mirror images, each with a single room on the ground floor and heated by a deep fireplace in the gable wall. Also in the thickness of the wall was a winder staircase to the first floor, with a further one to the attic room. The front doorway is of *c*.1700, with 18th-century sash windows to first floor; the bay window to the right is probably early 19th-century. Later 19th-century occupants included a confectioner, plasterer, baker, and blacksmith.

The present right gable-wall looks like a buttress and has no chimney stack. This is because the adjoining house (No. 16) was demolished at some stage and its land used as a builder's yard: the end wall of No. 18 was presumably rebuilt to make it self-supporting, without the fireplaces and staircase which would have weakened it. As this would have removed all heating from the right-hand cottage, the pair presumably became a single house at the same time (*c*.1900).

The adjoining No. 20 has a rubblestone front of *c*.1800, though the doorframe is late 20th-century. Nineteenth-century occupants included the builder and insurance agent James Wickens (1851-81) and solicitor's clerk W.G. Burton (by 1891).

Nos. 24 and 26 (*Royal Oak*); former *White Hart Inn*

These now separate buildings were formerly the *White Hart Inn*, said to have been built and opened around 1615 by Richard Merywether. No. 24 retains medieval roof timbers, however, possibly from a building on this site. The inn was still in business in 1642 when it featured in a Civil War skirmish, but had closed 10 years later when Walwin Hopton occupied it. In 1685 the tenant was John Loder, gent, and the combined building continued as a gentleman's residence into the 18th century. Before the 1780s it was reopened as the *Royal Oak*, which remained in business in the range's eastern part (now No. 26) in 2007. Some 19th-century licensees combined it with other trades, George

Nos. 26 (in foreground) and 24 Witney St, with (far right) a ground-floor window at No. 24. Like many Burford buildings this one shows 'pecking' in the stonework, chiselled to help hold a coat of render. Note also the traces of an earlier, wider window opening.

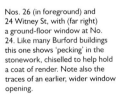

Pratley (1850s-60s), for instance, working as a carpenter, while his wife ran the pub. The building was remodelled in the early 19th century, the date of the present windows.

No. 24 (now Consitt House) may have been part of the inn until the 1850s, and graffiti near its rear doorway confirms its connection with James Strafford, landlord in the 1770s-80s. By 1861 it was apparently a separate house, occupied successively by a tea dealer and, in the 1870s-80s, by a tailor and a brewer's labourer. In the 1910s it was owned by the Burford brewers Garne and Sons. Its front was formerly rendered, as shown by 'pecking' around the right-hand ground-floor window; removal of the render has left the windows standing forward from the wall. The window-frames themselves could be mid-18th-century, that at bottom right replacing an earlier wider one, while the doorcase (with its slightly later door) was added c.1800. The house's four heated rooms probably all formed part of the inn's accommodation. [List; *Inns* 100-2; *BR* 447, 456; ORO QSD V/2-3]

Nos. 30-32 (The Great House)

A rear view of The Great House (above), showing the south-east wing added in 1994 (with the curved gable), and the two projecting wings added soon after its original construction. Both appear on an early but undated panel painting in the house (below).

The Great House is one of Burford's three most important gentry houses, and one of the few buildings in the town to have architectural pretensions. The site was occupied in the mid- to late 17th century by the *Black Boy* inn, owned in 1685 by the innholder, chandler, and burgess Thomas Castle (died 1690). Thomas's son John (1655-1727), a physician prominent in town affairs, built the existing house probably between 1695 and 1710: the front range fits those dates stylistically, and Castle lived here by the 1720s.

As one of the town's largest houses it continued to be occupied by professionals or gentry. Castle family members lived here until the 1750s, to be succeeded before 1790 (as tenant) by Mrs Sophia Gast. Nineteenth-century occupants included the Burford surgeons Robert Pytt and William Cooke (1820s-60s), Edward Marriott, JP (died 1887), and W.H. Hutton (here 1895-1915), historian and dean of Winchester. In the mid-20th century it was home of the financier Lord Piercy of Burford.

The house's main range presents a grand classical façade to the street, its central door reached up a flight of five steps, and the central three bays crowned by a pediment. The principal floors have elaborate window openings with projecting cornices and convex mouldings; the ground-floor basement is lit by oval *oeil-de-boeuf* windows, and the top floor (which forms a single long gallery) by round ones. Battlemented chimneys and a battlemented parapet are a reference to the family name, a visual pun continued in some of the internal decoration.

One of many allegorical panel paintings in The Great House, this one shows Hope overlooking a harbour scene. The battlemented tower in the background refers to John Castle, for whom the house was built.

Two rear (south-west and south-east) wings were added not long afterwards, the former c.1700-30 (in two stages), and the latter probably c.1720-40. The work was for John Castle or his cousin Edward (died 1758), to whom the house was left in 1727. The additions obscured some of the earlier arrangements, in particular the location of the original stair, since the existing stairway runs from the central entrance hall to landings in the new back wings. The service rooms were in the basement: a former kitchen with a blocked fireplace survives on the east, and a bakehouse with three separate hearths and two ovens on the west. Possibly they were left over from the inn, though as the basement arrangements correspond exactly to the room divisions above, it seems more likely that they were created as part of Castle's house. The only significant later additions were a small rear block and garden door (*c*.1950), and a studio wing added to the south-east wing in 1994, to house a collection of prints and drawings.

Late 17th- or early 18th-century decoration includes an exceptional series of paintings on wooden panelling or wainscoting, encompassing allegorical, devotional and scriptural images. Another panel painting shows the south (garden) side of the house with the back wings already in place, confirming that they were added before *c*.1730. Recent paint scrapes suggest that the original wainscot may have been the 'dull red colour' reported in the early 20th century, although a 'green room' facing Witney Street in 1726 was named presumably from its wall colour or furnishings. [Report by Nicholas Cooper for VCH (2006); *BR* 100, 356-7, 479-81; *Country Life* 98 (1945), 508-11; PRO PROB 11/615, f. 334]

No. 34

Until 1968-9 this was stabling for The Great House. In origin it was probably contemporary with the main building, but may have been largely rebuilt in the mid-19th century. The 20th-century conversion, by the architect Russell Cox, included insertion of new windows and chimneys and building of a new lower block on the west; a bullseye window in the east gable is modelled on those in the Great House. A former barn on the east side of the rear yard was restored by the owners *c*.1987, when dormers were inserted; an adjoining barn belonged to the neighbouring Baptist chapel, and was for a time used as a chapel school. Its Stonesfield slate roof was replaced with imitation slates in the 1990s. The Baptist chapel itself (built in 1803-4 on the site of an earlier meeting house) is discussed above (Chapter 9). [List; Pevsner 509; inf. from owners (2003)]

GUILDENFORD

Created as a medieval back lane which probably followed an early droveway (Chapter 2), Guildenford is very much a street of two sides. On the west, which was probably built up during the Middle Ages, is a run of vernacular cottages of various dates from the 18th century onwards, with entries directly from the pavement. On the east is the last remaining garage in Burford and, behind long front gardens, the much altered Castle's Almshouses, founded in 1726. Building materials are typical of Burford: the limestone rubble is often uncoursed, and supported by long timber lintels above small casement windows.

In 1841 the lane contained around 20 separate dwellings (some of them unoccupied), and from the 1850s to 1870s there were around forty, presumably because several cottages had been subdivided. Agricultural labourers headed many households, and craftsmen the rest: in 1851 they included slaters, carpenters, a glover, and a basket maker. From the 1880s the proportion of agricultural labourers fell, and by 1901 there were only eight.

West Side

This near-continuous run of cottages begins with Nos. 1-2, where stonework shows that a first-floor central casement has been removed. The central dormer was probably shared between the two attics, with a central partition forming the window's central mullion. Beyond, Homeleigh and No. 4 display a rusticated treatment typical of the mid-20th century; No. 4 has a memorial stone to Nan Meadows (1912-88), a former District Nurse and (latterly) peace campaigner. Fortey's Close, perhaps the most stylish house in the street, is followed by Nos. 5-8, built in the 18th century as two mirror-image cottage pairs but long since converted into two houses. The street's western side ends with Russell Cox's vicarage of 1937 (Figure 100), an excellent example of sympathetic 20th-century building in Burford.

East Side

Opposite Nos. 1-2, former commercial use can be seen in Weavers and Tiverton Cottages. Much of the street's east side, however, is taken up by the former almshouses (Figure 64) and by *Vick's Byways Garage*. Opposite the Old Vicarage are Ford Close and Emmanuel Cottage, another late 18th- or 19th-century cottage pair; each have long gardens, the former now displaying a Chinese influence.

Vick's Byways Garage: in 2007 the last of the half dozen motor garages once serving Burford.

BURFORD PRIORY

Built by Sir Lawrence Tanfield in the 1580s on the site of the dissolved medieval hospital, this is by far the grandest of Burford's houses, and was clearly a statement of Tanfield's wealth and prestige (Chapter 6). The building today is only a fragment, having been halved in size in 1808. Even so its only rivals are the much later Great House on Witney Street and the Jordan mansion on High Street, both town houses squeezed into cramped sites. The Priory, by contrast, stands in secluded grounds on the town's western edge.

The house was probably built soon after Tanfield acquired the site, since his daughter Elizabeth was reportedly born at Burford in 1585 or 1586. Tanfield's predecessor Edmund Harman had been a life lessee only, and though he may have begun the hospital's conversion he seems to have lived mostly at Taynton. He is, therefore, unlikely to have spent much on large-scale rebuilding, and the mansion is probably mostly Tanfield's work. It was known as The Priory by Tanfield's time, reflecting the site's religious origins, and in 1603 was grand enough for James I to stay there three nights on his journey from Scotland.

Figure A: Burford Priory today, with William Lenthall's chapel of 1662 on the left. Only the left-hand bay of the house is original: the porch was reassembled and the north bay rebuilt when it was halved in size in 1808.

Surviving remains and later drawings (Figure 51) show that the mansion had an imposing three-storeyed front made up of seven tall gabled bays. It was built on a conventional E-shaped plan, with projecting north and south wings and a projecting three-storeyed entrance porch (surmounted by a curved gable) in the centre. The existing house comprises only the southernmost three bays, all heavily remodelled. Like many contemporary houses it mixed traditional late medieval or Tudor styles with new classical motifs, most obviously the two surviving tiers of Corinthian columns framing the porch. Early drawings show a highly confused arrangement, however, and may not be fully reliable. Two carved figures flanking the porch appear to represent wild men, one of them possibly Hercules with a lion-skin (left), and the other (with a ragged staff) perhaps associated with Harman.

Little remains of the original internal layout. Entrance was probably into a screens passage at the northern end of a one-and-a-half-storey hall, lit by a tall window shown in early drawings. The principal rooms lay at the south end, where a first-floor drawing room (probably originally the great chamber) still has an impressive plaster ceiling (Figure B). The main staircase was probably in a westward projection (later rebuilt) off the high end of the hall. The present hall bears no relation to the original one, but has a late 16th-century chimneypiece, moved there from elsewhere in the house in 1908.

The Tanfields were followed by the lawyer Sir William Lenthall (1591-1662), whose family owned the house until 1828. Lenthall's chief addition was a handsome freestanding private chapel just south of the house, connected by a gallery with a covered walkway below and an open balustraded walk above (Figures 51 and 108). Its style suggests it was by the Oxford mason-architect John Jackson, who worked at Brasenose College and the University church, and who probably designed a new chimneypiece in the first-floor drawing room. It has been claimed that Lenthall added a new rear (south-west) wing to house his extensive picture collection, which attracted visitors from far afield. In fact the pictures were hung in the principal stairway and great chamber, and the wing (mostly rebuilt c.1922) looks stylistically later, around 1680-1720.

The Priory continued as a country house until the 19th century, occupied by the Lenthalls or by aristocratic tenants. By the late 18th century the Lenthalls were in financial difficulty, and in 1808 John Lenthall (died 1820) reduced the house from seven bays to three with a simple rectangular plan. Only the southern bay and stair projection were kept; the matching north bay was newly built, incorporating an Elizabethan bay window from the north end, and the entrance porch was reassembled between them. Internal planning was conventional, with four rooms on the ground floor either side of the entrance passage.

Figure B: This impressive plaster ceiling of c.1600 survives in a first-floor room on the south, now used as a chapel by the Priory community (below). The chimneypiece was probably added by Lenthall.

The family sold their estate in 1828, and by the late 19th century the house was semi-derelict (Figure 68). It was restored in two stages: first by Colonel de Sales la Terrière from 1908 (using the local building firm Alfred Groves of Milton under Wychwood), and second by the architect Walter Godfrey, commissioned around 1922 by the owner E.J. Horniman (who bought the house in 1912). Horniman was followed by Sir Archibald Southby, and in 1941 the house became the Priory of Our Lady. Initially a women's community, it now admits brothers as well.

The few medieval fragments incorporated into Tanfield's building are insufficient to say anything much about the medieval hospital. The most substantial is a late 13th-century east-west arcade opened up by La Terrière, part of which was reassembled further north to form a screen across the hall (Figure 46). Originally it could have belonged to either a medieval chapel or an aisled hall. The west (back) wall of Tanfield's house made use of an earlier wall, which still has a four-centred arch as a door opening, and a few other re-used fragments were found during the 1908 restoration work. [Report by Nicholas Cooper for VCH (2006); *BR* 257-95; Godfrey, W.H., 'Burford Priory', *Oxoniensia* 4 (1939), 71-88; Skelton, J., *Antiquities of Oxfordshire* (1823)]

Figure C: The development of Burford Priory, showing the various building phases.

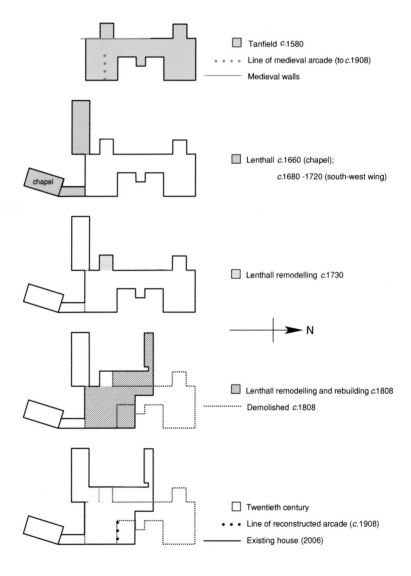

Endnotes

The following abbreviations are used throughout the endnotes.

BL	British Library
Bodl	Bodleian Library
Buildings List	English Heritage (formerly Department of the Environment), List of Buildings of Special Architectural Interest: available online at www.imagesofengland.org.uk
Cal Close	*Calendar of Close Rolls … in the Public Record Office*
Cal Pat	*Calendar of Patent Rolls … in the Public Record Office*
Census	Census returns 1801-2001, published until 1911 as Parliamentary Papers
Dir	Directory
Fisher	Fisher, J., *A History of the Town of Burford* (1861)
Gretton, *Records*	Gretton, R. H., *The Burford Records* (1920)
Hearth Tax	Weinstock, M. (ed.), *Hearth Tax Returns for Oxfordshire, 1665* (ORS 21, 1940)
Jewell	Jewell, A., *Burford in Old Photographs* (1985)
Kelly	*Kelly's Directory of Oxfordshire*
Monk, *History*	Monk, W.J., *The History Of Burford* (1891)
Moody, *BB*	Moody, R. and J., *The Book of Burford* (1983)
Moody, *Churchmen*	Moody, R., *The Churchmen of Burford* (privately printed 2000)
Moody, *Inns*	Moody, R., *The Inns of Burford* (Hindsight, revised edn 2007)
Moody, *Thousand Years*	Moody, R. and J., *A Thousand Years of Burford* (Hindsight 2006)
Moody, *Vicaridge*	Moody, R., *The Burford Book for the Vicaridge Rights* (privately produced pamphlet, no date)
Nash	Nash, J., 'Aspects of a Town in Decline: a Population Study of Burford, Oxfordshire, 1851-1901' (D Phil thesis, University of Oxford, 2006)
NMR	National Monuments Record Centre, Swindon
ODNB	*Oxford Dictionary of National Biography*
OHS	Oxford Historical Society
ORO	Oxfordshire Record Office

ORS	Oxfordshire Record Society
OS	Ordnance Survey
Oxf Jnl	*(Jackson's) Oxford Journal*
Oxon	Oxfordshire
Pevsner	Sherwood, J. and Pevsner, N, *Buildings of England: Oxfordshire* (1974)
PO Dir	Post Office Directory of Oxfordshire
PRO	Public Record Office (in TNA)
TNA	The National Archives, Kew
VCH	Victoria County History
Wills	Weaver, J. R. H. and Beardwood, A.(eds), *Some Oxfordshire Wills* (ORS 39, 1958)

ORO and PRO wills cited in endnotes have been transcribed by the Burford Probate Group; transcriptions are being made available on the Oxfordshire EPE website. Images of PRO wills are downloadable from The National Archives website.

CHAPTER 1 Understanding Burford pp. 1-9

1 **Early descriptions:** Toulmin Smith, L (ed.), *Itinerary of John Leland* (1964 edn), V, 74; Blome, R, *Britannia* (1673), 188; Simpson, S, *Agreeable Historian* (1746), 779. **Decline:** Brewer, J N, *Topographical and Historical Description of Oxon.* (1819), 472; *Gardner's Directory of Oxfordshire* (1852), 499; Blanchard, E L (ed.), *Topographical Dictionary of England and Wales* (c.1860), I, 283-4.

2 *Gentleman's Magazine*, vol. 72 (2) (1802), pp. 924-5; Evans, H A, *Highways and Byways in Oxford and the Cotswolds* (1905), 357; Titchmarsh, P and H, *The Cotswolds* (Ordnance Survey Landranger Guidebook, 1989), 37.

3 **Skelton:** *Antiquities of Oxfordshire* (1823); **Buckler:** Bodl MS Top. Oxon. a 65; **Dryden:** Northants Central Library, Dryden collection; **Taunt:** Oxfordshire Studies, Oxford Central Library; English Heritage, National Monuments Record, Swindon.

4 **Burford buildings:** Laithwaite, M, 'The Buildings of Burford', in Everitt, A (ed.), *Perspectives in English Urban History* (1973), 60-90.

CHAPTER 2 Planning Medieval Burford pp. 13-31

5 **New Winchelsea:** Lilley, K D, 'Urban Planning and the Design of Towns in the Middle Ages: the Earls of Devon and their "New Towns"', *Planning Perspectives,* 16 (2001), 5.

6 **Roman evidence:** Coles, S, Lowe, J and Preston, S, 'Roman and Medieval Occupation at 47-53 High Street, Burford, Oxfordshire', *Oxoniensia* (forthcoming). See also the information in Oxfordshire Sites and Monuments Record.

7 **Place name:** Gelling, M, *Place Names of Oxfordshire* (English Place Name Soc. 23-4, 1953-4), II, 310. **Bampton:** *VCH Oxon.* XIII, 6-17. **River crossings:** Blair, J, *Anglo-Saxon Oxfordshire* (1994), 119.

8 **Anglo-Saxon enclosures:** Blair, J, *The Church in Anglo-Saxon Society* (2005), 196-7, 285-6. **Brewood:** Slater, T R, 'Plan characteristics of small boroughs and market settlements: evidence from the Midlands', in Dyer, C and Giles, K (eds), *Town and Country in the Middle Ages: Contrasts and Interconnections, 1100-1600* (Society for Medieval Archaeology, 2004), 23-42.

9 **Guildenford**: Gelling, *Place Names of Oxfordshire*, II, 310-11.
10 **Burford mill-stream**: Fisher, 26; Moody, R, *The Landscape of Burford* (Tolsey Papers 2, 1980), 18. **Canals:** Blair, J (ed.), *Waterways and Canal-Building in Medieval England* (2007).
11 **Minsters**: Blair, J, 'Clerical Communities and Parochial Space: the Planning of Urban Mother Churches in the Twelfth and Thirteenth Centuries', in Slater, T R and Rosser, G (eds), *The Church in the Medieval Town* (1998), 272-94. **Informal Sunday trading**: Blair, J, 'Small Towns 600-1270', in Palliser, D M (ed.), *Cambridge Urban History of Britain*, I (2000), 251; Morris, R, *Churches in the Landscape* (1997), 212. **Changing market days**: Goodfellow, P, 'Medieval Markets in Northamptonshire', *Northants. Past and Present*, 7 (1988), 310. **Burford's medieval market day**: Moody, R, *The Burford Year* (priv. print. 1998), 4.
12 **Odo and FitzHamon**: *VCH Oxon*. I, 406; *ODNB*. **Burford charter**: Gretton, Records, 5-12, 295-303; Gretton, M S, *Burford Past and Present* (1944), 73. **Descent of Burford manor:** Gretton, *Records*, 80-7.
13 **Course of Sheep Street**: Gretton, *Burford Past and Present*, 32.
14 **High Cross and Tolsey**: Gretton, *Records*, 210. **Date of Tolsey**: dendrochronology from roof timbers (February 2006). **Stocks and whipping post**: Moody, R, *Burford: an Introduction and Guide* (priv. print. 1999), 10. **Removal of cross**: Eddershaw, D, *The Civil War in Oxfordshire* (1995), 163.
15 **Early plots (general)**: Palliser, D M, 'The Topography of Towns, 600-1300', in Palliser, D M (ed.), *Cambridge Urban History of Britain*, I (2000), 169. **Church:** below, chapter 5.
16 **Foundation of Hospital**: *VCH Oxon*. II, 154; Godfrey, W H, 'Burford Priory', *Oxoniensia*, 4 (1939), 72. **Barns etc and Ivy House:** Gretton, *Records*, 260; Gazetteer. **St John's Lane**: Gelling, *Place Names of Oxfordshire*, II, 310-11; Gretton, *Records*, 168.
17 **Claims about extent of town**: Gretton, *Records*, 167. **Medieval burgages**: Palliser, op. cit. 170.
18 **Bridge repair:** *Cal Pat* 1321-4, 307; Gretton, *Records*, 18, which misdates it.
19 **Newlands**: Bond, C J and Hunt, A M, 'Recent Archaeological Work in Pershore', *Vale of Evesham Historical Society Research Papers*, 6 (1977), 23; *VCH Oxon*. XII, 58, 106-7.
20 **Bury Barns**: Gretton, *Records*, refs at 708.
21 **1250 half burgage**: Gretton, *Records*, 668.
22 **John Hannes' property**: Gretton, *Records*, 633; cf. 401-2 and Gazetteer.
23 **Domesday Book:** *VCH Oxon*. I, 406. **1377:** Fenwick, C (ed.), *Poll Taxes of 1377, 1379 and 1381*, II (2001), 290. **Other small towns:** Hilton, R H, 'Towns in English Feudal Society', in Hilton, R H, *Class Conflict and the Crisis of Feudalism: Essays in Medieval Social History* (1985), 175.
24 **Map of Inward and Outward**: OS Map 1:2500, Oxon. XXX.4 (1881 edn).

CHAPTER 3 A Medieval Wool Town pp. 33-52

25 **Functions of small towns:** Dyer, C, 'Small Towns 1270-1540', in Palliser, D M (ed.), *Cambridge Urban History of Britain*, I (2000), 505-37; Hilton, R H, *English and French Towns in Feudal Society* (1992). **Burford trades and occupations:** except where stated, information is derived from: Gretton, *Records*, part III, passim; Bolton, J L and Maslen, M M (eds), *Calendar of the Court Books of the Borough of Witney 1538-1610* (ORS 54, 1985); Burford wills and inventories in ORO, MSS Wills Oxon. Transcripts of Burford wills are being made available on the Oxfordshire EPE website.

26 TNA: PRO E 179/161/8, rot. 5, transcribed in Gretton, *Records*, 594-5.

27 **De Clare:** Gretton, *Records*, 89.

28 **Merchants:** Gretton, *Records*, passim. **Wills:** *Wills*, 24-5, 35, 38-9.
    Pinnock's Burford houses: Gazetteer, 101-103, 105, 118-122 High
    St. **Southampton house:** Kaye, J M (ed.), *Cartulary of God's House,
    Southampton* (Southampton Records Series 19, 1976), 119.
    Southampton trade: Coleman, O (ed.), *Brokage Book of Southampton
    1443-1444* (Southampton Records Series 4 and 6, 1960-61), I, 25, II, 269;
    Hurst, D, *Sheep in the Cotswolds* (2005), 202.

29 **Surnames:** Gretton, *Records*, Part III, passim. **Thomas of Lincoln:**
    Gretton, *Records*, 594.

30 **Origin of market:** Chapter 2 (under Anglo-Saxon Settlement). **Medieval
    market circuits:** Unwin, T, 'Rural Marketing in Medieval
    Nottinghamshire', *Journal of Historical Geography*, 7.3 (1981), 231-51.
    Surrounding markets: Letters, S, Online Gazetteer of Markets and Fairs in
    England and Wales to 1516 (www.historyac.uk/cmh/gaz/gazweb2.html:
    [Oxfordshire; Berkshire; Wiltshire; Gloucestershire] 2006).

31 **1323 grant of tolls:** Gretton, *Records*, 166, 436-8 (misdated); *Cal Pat*
    1321-4, 307.

32 **Medieval shops:** Gretton, *Records*, 333, 400; ORO, MS Wills Oxon. 179,
    f. 34; Chapter 4.

33 **Medieval wool trade:** Bridbury, A R, 'Markets and Freedom in the Late
    Middle Ages', in Anderson, B L and Latham, A J H (eds), *The Market in
    History* (1968), 78-119. **Sheep bones:** Coles, S et al., 'Roman and Medieval
    Occupation at 47-53 High Street, Burford', *Oxoniensia* (forthcoming).
    Wool sales: Gretton, *Records*, 569, 576. **Tolls:** *Cal Pat* 1321-4, 307; Gretton,
    Records, 436-8 (misdated).

34 **Burford fairs:** Letters, op. cit. note 30; Gretton, *Records*, 304. **Letter of
    1403:** Origo, I, *A Merchant of Prato* (1957), 349.

35 **Richard Cely:** Hanham, A, *The Cely Letters* (1975), 150. **Bishop and
    Pinnocks:** Gretton, *Records*, passim; **Wool sales:** Hurst, D, *Sheep in the
    Cotswolds* (2005), 157-8.

36 **Trade through Southampton:** e.g. Stevens, K F and Golding, T E, *Brokage
    Books of Southampton 1477-8 and 1527-8* (Southampton Record Society
    28, 1985). **Bristol ware:** Coles et al., '47-53 High Street', *Oxoniensia*
    (forthcoming).

37 **Wool stores:** Gretton, *Records*, 336 sqq; ORO, MS Wills Oxon. 144/3/23
    (mentioning wool stored in a wood [sic] chamber); Gazetteer, No. 3 Witney
    St.

38 **Dye imports:** Coleman (ed.), *Brokage Book of Southampton 1443-4*
    (Southampton Record Series 4 and 6, 1960-1), I, 28; II, 308. **Pinnock:**
    Lewis, E A, *Southampton Port and Brokage Books, 1448-9* (1993), 161.

39 **John Jones:** Gretton, *Records*, 655-6; TNA: PRO PROB 11/30, f. 271v.
    Cf. ORO MS Wills Oxon. 181, f. 85 (Henry Stringfellow).

40 **Edmund Silvester:** TNA: PRO PROB 11/51, f. 40 and v. **Relative
    wealth:** TNA: PRO E179/161/173, E179/162/223; Gretton, *Records*, 601-3.

41 **Apprenticeships:** Bolton and Maslen (eds), *Court Books of Borough of
    Witney*, 86, 189.

42 **Inns:** below, Chapter 4 and Gazetteer; see also Moody, *Inns*. A later Bear
    Inn was opened in the 17th century.

43 **Court rolls:** Gretton, *Records*, 659-60.

44 **Town charter:** Gretton, *Records*, 301-3. **Animal remains:** Coles et al.,
    '47-53 High Street', *Oxoniensia* (forthcoming), citing the predominance of
    cattle skulls and hooves. **Domestic leather-working:**

ORO MS Wills Oxon. 17/3/48. **Tanneries:** Gretton, *Records*, 423, refs at 715; ORO MS Wills Oxon. 62/3/22; Gazetteer (No. 1 High St).

45 **Henry and Robert Janyns:** *ODNB*, entry for Henry Janyns; Harvey, J, *English Medieval Architects* (1984 edn), 160.

46 **Hedges:** ORO MS Wills Oxon. 179, f. 112. **Silvester:** TNA: PRO PROB 11/59, f. 177v.

47 **Lordship of manor:** Gretton, *Records*, 87. **Honour of Gloucester:** Welch, F B, 'Gloucestershire in the Pipe Rolls', *Transactions of Bristol and Glos Archaeol. Soc.* 57 (1958), 44-109.

48 **Guild:** Gretton, *Records*, 12-65. **Great Almshouse:** Moody, *Thousand Years*, 10; Gretton, *Records*, 361-2. A 19th-century datestone gives the date 1457.

49 **Whitsun procession etc.:** Moody, R, *The Burford Year* (1998), 30-8. **Burford Dragon:** Bloxham, C, *May Day to Mummers* (2002), 200-7. **Drunkenness:** Baker, E P (ed.), *Bishop Wilberforce's Visitation Returns* (ORS 35, 1954), 27; Moody, *Churchmen*, 25-6, 32.

CHAPTER 4 Medieval Secular Buildings pp. 53-71

50 See also Pevsner, 513-20.

51 Cf. Wood, M, *The English Medieval House* (1965), 354; Sturdy, D, 'Houses of the Oxford Region', *Oxoniensia*, 26/27 (1961/2), 319-20.

52 **Ivy House:** Moody, *Inns*, 79-80; Gretton, *Records*, 260.

53 **124 High Street:** *Vernacular Architecture*, 37 (2006), 124-5.

54 **Fireplaces mentioned:** Wood, *English Medieval House*, 267 and plate 42.

55 **Medieval town-house plans:** Pantin, W A, 'Medieval English Town House Plans', *Medieval Archaeology*, 6-7 (1963), 202-39; Grenville, J, *Medieval Housing* (1997), 165-74; Schofield, J and Vince, A, *Medieval Towns* (2003 edn), 79-120.

56 **Calendars:** see *Vernacular Architecture*, 37 (2006), 125.

57 **162 High Street:** see *Vernacular Architecture*, 37 (2006), 126. **Cruck distribution:** Alcock, N W (ed.) *Cruck Construction: An Introduction and Catalogue* (Council for British Archaeology Research Report 42, 1981).

58 **Hill House:** Sturdy, 'Houses of the Oxford Region', 319. **Old Rectory, Westwell:** Buildings List (Images of England no. 420663).

59 **Calendars:** *Vernacular Architecture*, 37 (2006), 125.

60 **Burford stone:** Arkell, W, *Oxford Stone* (1947), 54-78; Powell, P, *The Geology of Oxfordshire* (2005).

61 **Quarries:** Gretton, *Records*, 171; Turner, J, *Quarries and Craftsmen of the Windrush Valley* (1988). **Methodist Church:** Gomme, A, *Smith of Warwick* (2000), 396.

62 **Oxfordshire stone slates:** Arkell, *Oxford Stone*, 128-150. **Removal of slates:** local information.

63 **Medieval shops:** Gretton, *Records*, 333, 400; ORO, MS Wills Oxon. 179, f. 34; Grenville, *Medieval Housing* (1997), 171-74; Clark, D, 'The Shop Within? An Analysis of the Architectural Evidence for Medieval Shops', *Architectural History*, 43 (2000), 58-87.

64 **14th-century urban inns:** Munby, J, 'Zacharias's: a 14th-Century Oxford New Inn', *Oxoniensia* 57 (1992), 303-9. ***New Inn* and *George Inn:*** Gazetteer.

65 **Undercrofts and taverns:** Platt, C, *Medieval Southampton* (1973), 75; Martin, B and D, *New Winchelsea, Sussex: A Medieval Port Town* (2004), 105-27; Munby, 'Zacharias's', 302-3.

CHAPTER 5 Medieval Church and Religion pp. 73-83

66 **Role of minsters**: Blair, J, 'Secular Minster Churches in Domesday Book', in Sawyer, P H (ed.), *Domesday Book: A Reassessment* (1985), 104-42. **Minster sites**: Blair, J, 'Anglo-Saxon Minsters: A Topographical Review', in Blair, J and Pyrah, C (eds), *Church Archaeology: Research Directions for the Future* (1992), 6-18.

67 **Siting of minsters**: Blair, J, *The Church in Anglo-Saxon Society* (2005), 193. **Endowment of Burford church**: *Taxatio Ecclesiastica Anglie et Wallie ... circa AD 1291* (Record Commission, 1801), 32; *Valor Ecclesiasticus, tempore Henry VIII* (Record Commission, 1810-34), II, 179; Moody, R, *Vicaridge*, 2-13.

68 **West Oxfordshire minsters**: Blair, J, *Anglo-Saxon Oxfordshire* (1994), 70. **Fulbrook, Upton, and Signet**: Dugdale, W, *Monasticon*, VI, 453; Lloyd Jukes, H A (ed.), *Articles of Enquiry at the Primary Visitation of Dr Thomas Secker, 1738* (ORS 38, 1957), 32.

69 **Grant to Keynsham Abbey**: Dugdale, *Monasticon*, VI, 451-3. **Vicarage endowment**: *Rotuli H. de Welles*, II (Lincoln Record Society 6, 1913), 28; *Taxatio Ecclesiastica ... 1291*, 32; *Valor Ecclesiasticus*, II, 179, 182; Moody, *Vicaridge*, 2-13; Gretton, *Records*, 139-140. **Vicarage house**: Gazetteer (Cobb House).

70 **Chaunceller**: Emden, A B, *Biographical Register of the University of Oxford to AD 1500* (1957-9), 397. **Other medieval vicars**: Emden, op. cit. 159, 397, 1001, 1251. **Medieval curates**: Moody, *Churchmen*, 10; Salter, H E (ed.), *Subsidy 1526* (OHS 63, 1909), 259-60; Gretton, *Records*, 115; *Valor Ecclesiasticus*, II, 179.

71 **Dawes**: *Cal Pat* 1343-5, 424. **Eymer**: *Cal Close* 1389-92, 522.

72 Gretton, *Records*, 107-114; *Wills*, 24-25, 79, 94-95.

73 **Nevilles and porch**: Gretton, *Records*, 120. **Pinnock and Cakebread**: ibid. 112-13, 420; *Wills*, 38-9.

74 **Merchant guild**: above, Chapter 3. **Lady (formerly guild) chapel**: Gretton, *Records*, 105-6, 112; Clarke, F L, *Burford Parish Church, Oxon: The Nineteenth-Century Repair and Restoration* (1960). **St Peter's chapel**: Gretton, *Records*, 106-7; Street, G E, in 'Excursion to ... Burford', *North Oxon. Archaeological Society*, [10] (1870), 23-4.

75 **Burford dragon**: Bloxham, C, *May Day to Mummers* (2002), 200-7; Plot, R, *Natural Hist. Oxon.* (1705 edn), 356.

76 **Church porch, Pinnock**: above, note 73. **Guild chapel**: Gretton, *Records*, 114. **Janyns**: Harvey, J, *English Medieval Architects* (1984 edn), 160; Colvin, H M, *History of the King's Works*, III (1) (1975), 313-14.

77 **Hospital**: *VCH Oxon.* II, 154-5; Gretton, *Records*, 257-65. **Asthall chantry**: *VCH Oxon.* XV, 67. **Warwick Almshouses**: Gretton, *Records*, 181, 361-2.

CHAPTER 6 Burford in Transition 1500-1790 pp. 85-103

78 **Population**: Chapter 8, p. 121. **1523-5 subsidy lists**: Gretton, *Records*, 599-603. **1544 lists**: TNA: PRO E 179/162/223, E 179/162/234. **Office-holders**: Gretton, *Records*, 96-7, 102-3. **1566 élite**: Gretton, *Records*, 400; occupations identified from Gretton, *Records*, passim and Burford wills.

79 **Silvester**: TNA: PRO PROB 11/51, f. 40 and v. **Hopkins**: ORO MS Wills Oxon. 189, f. 95. Transcriptions of 16th- and 17th-century Burford wills are being made available on the EPE website.

80 **Lollard reading**: Gretton, *Records*, 144-5. **Books in wills**: ORO MSS Wills Oxon. 50/1/42, 69/3/24, 70/1/42 (Myles Paddleford, Thomas Walburg, Simon Walburg).

81 **Cirencester, Solihull:** Howard-Drake, J (ed.), *Oxford Church Courts: Depositions 1589-1593* (1997), 18, 43. **Wales:** names in Gretton, *Records*, Part III, passim. **Wilkins:** ORO MS Wills Oxon. 69/1/5.

82 **Hospital:** *VCH Oxon.* II, 154-5. **Harman:** Balfour, M, *Edmund Harman: Barber and Gentleman* (1988); *ODNB*; ORO Taynton parish register.

83 History of corporation: Gretton, *Records*, 43-50.

84 **Wisdom's almshouse:** Moody, *Thousand Years*, 82; Gretton, *Records*, 200, 359-60. **Jones:** ORO MS Wills Oxon. 37/1/12.

85 **Whitsun hunt:** Moody, R, *The Burford Year* (1998), 31-2. **Football:** ibid. 38. **Racing:** Stawell, J, *The Burford and Bibury Racecourses* (revised edn, 2000), 6-8.

86 **Tanfields:** *ODNB*, entry on Sir Lawrence Tanfield. **1617 and 1628 cases:** Gretton, *Records*, 53-63.

87 **Cary:** Gretton, *Records*, 93, 274-5. **Lenthall:** *ODNB*.

88 **1648 loans:** *Calendar of the Proceedings of the Committee for Advance of Money, 1642-56* (1888), 999. **Events:** Gretton, *Records*, 202-5.

89 **Population:** Chapter 8, p. 121.

90 **Descriptions:** Blome, R, *Britannia* (1673), 188; *Jackson's Oxford Journal*, 26 Jan. 1782; Cooke, G A, *Topographical and Statistical Description of the County of Oxford* (1805), 108. **Cheese, toys, hiring fair, April fair:** Thwaites, L W, 'The Marketing of Agricultural Produce in 19th-Century Oxon.' (Birmingham PhD thesis, 1981), 65.

91 **Mercers:** Burford wills in TNA: PRO (searchable online) and ORO MSS Wills Oxon. (indexed in Cheyne, E and Barratt, D M, *Probate Records of the ... Archdeacon of Oxford, 1516-1732* (1981-5); Barratt, D M, Howard-Drake, J and Priddey, M, ibid. *1733-1857* (1997)). **Addresses:** Gazetteer.

92 **Craftworkers:** wills indexes in previous note. **Tannery:** Moody, *Thousand Years*, 126. **Saddles:** Gretton, *Records*, 219. **Waine and Warner:** ORO MSS Wills Oxon. 74/3/30, 159/1/36; parish register transcript. **Paper-making:** Moody, *Thousand Years,* 124-5, 165.

93 **Apothecaries and surgeons:** Burford wills in TNA: PRO; *Oxf Jnl*, 28 Dec. 1754, 2 Sept. 1758, 17 March 1759 etc. **Scriveners and lawyers:** ORO MS Wills Oxon. 57/1/5; *Oxf Jnl*, 4 July 1767, 25 July 1778, 14 Aug. 1790.

94 **Thames navigation:** Peberdy, R B, 'Navigation on the River Thames between London and Oxford in the Late Middle Ages: A Reconsideration', *Oxoniensia*, 51 (1996), 311-13; Prior, M, *Fisher Row: Fishermen, Bargemen, and Canal Boatmen in Oxford, 1500-1900* (1982), 118-22. **Malt:** Brewer, J N, *A Topographical and Historic Description of the County of Oxford* (1819), 472; Cheyne and Barratt, *Probate Records Oxon. 1516-1732*. **Cumberson and Yeate:** ORO MS Wills Oxon. 163/1/41; parish register transcript; Gazetteer, 47-49 High St. **Competition:** information from D J Gerhold, Putney.

95 **Coach services:** *VCH Oxon.* IV, 290; *VCH Glos.* IV, 128; Gretton, *Records*, 224. **Turnpikes:** Moody, *Thousand Years*, 109.

96 **Inns:** Moody, *Inns*; ORO QSD/V 2; Gazetteer.

97 **Booksellers, wig-makers etc:** ORO MSS Wills Oxon. 16/2/43; 67/4/40; 81/2/20; 250/1/39; 269/1/28. **Clockmakers:** Beeson, C F C, *Clockmaking in Oxfordshire 1400-1850* (Banbury Historical Society 4, 1962), 98, 101, 148.

98 **1662 hearth tax:** TNA: PRO E 179/255/4, pt 3, f. 239 and v. **Bailiffs:** Gretton, *Records*, 99-100. **Under-recording:** based on comparison with Gibson, J, *Oxon. and North Berks. Protestation Returns and Tax Assessments* (ORS 59, 1994), 18-20.

99 **Occupations** derived from probate records and Gretton, *Records*,

passim. **Veysey:** ORO MS Wills Oxon. 68/4/4. **Keble:** Gretton, *Records*, 454, 463. **Hayter:** Gretton, *Records*, 448; TNA: PRO PROB 11/323, ff.167-8. **Payton:** Gretton, *Records*, 353, 355. **Eve:** ORO MS Wills Oxon. 126/1/9. **Ward:** TNA: PRO PROB 11/363, f. 506v. **Haynes:** ORO MS Wills Oxon. 34/1/32. **Hughes:** ORO MS Wills Oxon. 81/2/20. **Smith:** ORO MS Wills Oxon. 61/4/18.

100 **Jordan:** TNA: PRO PROB 11/312, ff. 301-2. **Hopton:** TNA: PRO PROB 11/380, ff. 285-7.

101 **Small towns:** Dyer, A, 'Small Market Towns, 1540-1700' in Clark, P (ed.), *Cambridge Urban History of Britain*, 2 (2000), 440-1. **1758 list:** *Oxf Jnl*, 2 Sept. **1790s bailiffs:** Gretton, *Records*, 102. **Aston:** Moody, *Inns*, 3-4, 17, 23; Moody, *Thousand Years*, 36. **Whitehall:** Gazetteer. **Upston:** Gretton, *Records*, 101; Gazetteer. **Castle:** Gretton, *Records*, 100; Gazetteer. **Chavasse:** Gretton, *Records*, 101-2; Moody, *Thousand Years*, 61, 95.

102 Cf. Clark, P, 'Small Towns, 1700-1840' in idem (ed.), *Cambridge Urban History of Britain*, 2 (2000), 753, 763-6.

103 **Racing:** Stawell, J, *The Burford and Bibury Racecourses* (revised edn 2000). **Events at *Bull*:** *Oxf Jnl*, 1750s-90s; Moody, *Thousand Years*, 63-4. **Cockpit:** Monk, *History*, 162, 182.

104 **Mrs Gast:** Moody, *Thousand Years*, 65-6. **Widow's school:** *Oxf Jnl*, 22 Feb. 1755. **Ladies' and Quaker schools:** Moody, *Thousand Years*, 119-120. **Witney and Banbury schools:** *VCH Oxon*. X, 123; XIV, 161.

105 **Charities:** details to 1702 in Gretton, *Records*, 484-508. **Bread charities:** *8th Report Charity Commission* (1823), 479-80; *Abstract of Returns relative to Charitable Donations* (Parliamentary Papers 1816, 511, xvi), 968-9; *Charities Digest* (Parl. Papers 1871, HC 292-II, lv), 14-15.

CHAPTER 7 Decline and Rebirth: Burford from 1790 pp. 105-119

106 **1812 diversion:** Gretton, *Records*, 228. ***Bird-in-Hand*:** Moody, *Inns*, 110. **Railway:** *VCH Glos*. IV, 172. **Coach services:** *PO Dir* (1847 edn); *Dutton, Allen and Co's Dir Oxon* (1863 edn); Fisher, 13.

107 **Occupations in 1841:** TNA: PRO HO 107/872 (census enumerators' books).

108 **1841 census:** previous reference. **Banks:** Fisher, 18; *Pigot's Dir Oxon* (1830 and 1842); *Melville & Co's Dir Oxon* (1867); Gazetteer. **Insurance agents:** *Pigot's Dir Oxon* (1823-4); *PO Dir* (1847 and 1864); *Kelly* (1887 and 1895).

109 **Burford Brewery:** Moody, *Inns*, 91-8; Gazetteer (Sheep St).

110 Moody, *Thousand Years*, 90.

111 **Poor costs:** Moody, *Thousand Years*, 85; Nash, 109. **Administrative decline:** Gretton, *Records*, 75-8. **Racing:** Stawell, *Burford and Bibury Racecourses* (2000 edn), 21. **Priory and sales:** Fisher, 52-3; Nash, 37; Gazetteer.

112 **Dallas:** Dallas, A B, *Incidents in the Life and Ministry of the Revd Alexander R C Dallas* (1871), 226-32. **Rebuilding, revels:** Moody, *Thousand Years*, 79, 82, 138.

113 **Racing:** Stawell, *Burford and Bibury Racecourses* (2000), 30-1. **Feast:** Fisher, 10.

114 TNA: PRO HO 107/872/17, ff. 5-6, 21-31, 36-46.

115 **Census returns:** see previous note. **Chapman:** Monk, W J, *Guide to Burford* (1929).

116 **Cottage yards:** TNA: PRO HO 107/1731; Chapter 8; Gazetteer.

117 Nash, 40-1, 67, 91, 95.

118 Nash, 45-6.

119 **Leisure:** Nash, 53-6. **Recreation Society:** *Kelly* (1911). **Shopkeepers:** names in Moody, *Thousand Years*, 153; identified from TNA: PRO RG 13/1397 (census returns) and *Kelly* (1911). **Pageant:** Moody, *Thousand Years*, 153; Jewell, 46-7.

120 **Market and fairs:** Gretton, *Records*, 230; *Harrod's Dir Oxon* (1876, omitting July fair); *Oxf Jnl*, 5 May 1877; Moody, *Thousand Years*, 78. **Declining livestock sales:** *Oxf Jnl*, 5 May 1877. **Witney market:** *VCH Oxon.* XIV, 104-5. **Agricultural depression:** *VCH Oxon.* XV, 28, 61, 92, 136, 235.

121 **1871 and 1901 censuses:** TNA: PRO RG 10/1454 and RG 13/1397. **1910:** *Cope's Oxon Dir* (1910). **Garne's brewery:** Moody, *Inns*, 93-5. **Rope factory:** Moody, *Thousand Years*, 129; Gazetteer (142 High St).

122 **1901:** TNA: PRO RG 13/1397. **Beeching, Hutton:** Moody, *Thousand Years*, 144-5; *ODNB.* **Mackenzie, Grettons:** Moody, *Thousand Years*, 145. **Books on Burford:** Cordeaux, E H and Merry, D H (eds), *Bibliography of Printed Works relating to Oxfordshire* (OHS ns 11, 1955), 18, 191-2.

123 **Artistic activity:** Moody, *Thousand Years*, 145. **Jane Morris:** ORO BGS VIII/7; Gretton, M S, *Burford Past and Present* (1920 edn), 122 n; information from Jan Marsh based on Jane's correspondence. **May Morris**: Gretton, M S, *Re-cognitions* (1951), 56, 83-6.

124 **Cycle depot and facilities etc:** TNA: PRO RG 12/1177, entry A30; *Cope's Oxon Dir* (1910); ORO DV Survey of Burford; Jewell, 69; Gazetteer. ***Bull Inn***: *Kelly* (1895).

125 *Kelly* (1939).

126 **Council:** Nash, 97-8. **East:** Moody, *Thousand Years*, 150, 152; Jewell, 26.

127 **1940s, Ayerst, Green:** information from R Moody. **Briggs:** *ODNB.* *Countryman*: Moody, *Thousand Years*, 155.

128 Four paragraphs based on Moody, *Thousand Years*, 129 and biog. note; *West Oxon. Business Dir 2000-1*; information from R Moody. **End of brewing:** Moody, *Inns*, 97-8. **Windlesham:** cf. *House of Lords Biographies.* **Kark:** *ODNB.* **Shops and galleries:** Gazetteer.

CHAPTER 8 Town and Buildings from 1550 pp. 121-147

129 **Population 16th-17th century:** TNA: PRO E 179/161/172, E 179/161/173, E 179/161/179; E 179/255/4, part 3, ff. 239 and v., 249; Graham, R (ed.), *Oxon. Chantry Certificates* (ORS I, 1919); Gibson, R (ed.), *Oxon. and North Berks. Protestation and Tax Assessments 1641-2* (ORS 59, 1994), 18-20; *Hearth Tax*, 215-18, 233; Whiteman, A (ed.), *Compton Census of 1676* (Records of Social and Economic History ns 10, 1986), 417, 423. **Population from 1801**: *Census*, 1801-2001 (combining Burford figures with Upton and Signet after 1931).

130 **19th-century boundaries:** OS Map Oxon. 1:2500, XXX.4 (1881); Dallas, A B, *Incidents in the Life and Ministry of the Revd Alexander R C Dallas by his Widow* (1871). **Medieval shrinkage:** Chapter 2.

131 **Sheep Street diversion**: Moody, *BB*, 32.

132 **Infilling, back plots, cottage yards:** see Gazetteer. **No. 134:** plan in Laithwaite, M, 'Buildings of Burford', in Everitt, A, *Perspectives in English Urban History* (1973), 87.

133 **Reset stonework:** cf. Pevsner, 513-21. **Hill House:** Sturdy, D, 'Houses of the Oxford Region', *Oxoniensia*, 26/27 (1961/2), 319.

134 **Lenthall stone sale:** MacArthur, W, *The River Windrush* (1946), 126. **Shoo Cottage:** Jewell, 55.

135 **Great Rebuilding:** Hoskins, W G, 'The Rebuilding of Rural England,

1570-1640', in Hoskins, W G, *Provincial England: Essays in Social and Economic History* (1963).

136 **Wisdom and rebuilding:** Moody, *Thousand Years*, 15-16, 19; TNA: PRO, PROB 11/71, f. 205v.; Gazetteer.

137 **Mullion shapes and paired lancets:** Wood-Jones, R, *Traditional Domestic Architecture of the Banbury Region* (1963), 255, 258.

138 **Roche House and Kempster:** datestone of 1696, with initials RAS (probably Robert and Sarah Aston); Kempster is known to have made Aston's tomb in Burford church. **Old Rectory:** Pevsner, 519; Gretton, *Records*, 137-8. **Great House:** Gazetteer.

139 **The *Bull:*** Steane, J M and Raines, M, 'Burford: The Bull', *South Midlands Archaeology*, 13 (1983), 86-8; Moody, *Inns*, 20-32; Gazetteer. **111-113 High Street:** Jewell, 12, showing the detailing has been altered since the 1880s.

140 Gomme, A, *Smith of Warwick* (2000), 396, gives a circular argument for the attribution.

141 **Window tax:** Hall, L, *Period House Fixtures and Fittings, 1300-1900* (2005), 79.

142 **Brewery:** Brown, M, *Oxon Brews: The Story of Commercial Brewing in Oxfordshire* (2004), 50-5; Gazetteer (Sheep St). **Tuckwells:** Young, A, *General View of the Agriculture of Oxfordshire* (1813).

143 **Ropery:** Moody, *Thousand Years*, 129.

144 **The Priory:** Godfrey, W H, 'Burford Priory', *Oxoniensia*, 4 (1939), 71; Gazetteer. ***Highway Hotel:*** Building List (suggesting that Horniman may have rebuilt the second floor in 1922). **Other houses:** local information.

145 **20th-century development:** OS Maps 1:2500, Oxon. XXIV.16 and XXX.4 (1899 and later edns); ibid. SP 2411-2511, 2412-2512 (1978 and later edns); Moody, *Thousand Years*, 155-63. **Planning and conservation:** information from Mr R Parkinson, West Oxfordshire District Council.

146 **Houses by Russell Cox:** Gretton, M S, *Burford Past and Present* (1944), 142-3; Jewell, 106; Taunt photograph of Laurence Lane in NMR. **No. 3 Guildenford:** information from R Parkinson (Conservation Officer, West Oxon District Council); photograph in Jewell, 20. **Grettons' restoration work:** Gretton, M S, *Re-cognitions* (1951), 78, 80. **Gretton family:** Chapter 7; Moody, *Thousand Years*, 145.

147 **The Malthouse:** information from Robert Franklin, architect. **Cripps and Filkins:** VCH Oxfordshire (forthcoming, texts available on VCH Oxfordshire website).

148 **Barclays Bank site:** photograph of 1909 in Jewell, 32.

CHAPTER 9 Church and Chapel since the Reformation pp. 149-159

149 **Rectory estate and advowson:** Gretton, *Records*, 135-7, 642-4. 653, 666. **Harman:** *ODNB*; Chapter 6.

150 **Lollard heretics:** Pratt, J (ed.), *Acts and Monuments of John Foxe* (4th edn, *c.*1877), IV, 235-8, 243-4, 584 (including charges against Wisdom); Gretton, *Records*, 144-6. **Late 16th-century vicars:** Spencer Pearce, S, 'Clergy of the Deaneries of Witney and Bicester during the Settlement of 1559 and Afterwards', North Oxfordshire Archaeological Society *Report* (1914), 187. **Roman Catholics:** Moody, *BB*, 99.

151 **Vicars:** Moody, *Churchmen*, 12; Emden, A B, *Biographical Register of the University of Oxford 1501-1540* (1957-9), 25. **Wills witnessed by local clergy:** ORO MS Wills Oxon. 179, ff. 27, 34, 112, 191 (all 1540s); ibid. 189, ff. 294, 354; ibid. 50/1/43, 25/2/1 (1580s-90s). **Tanfield and vicar's rights:**

Moody, *Vicaridge*, 2-13; Gretton, *Records*, 139-40. **Vicarage house:** Gazetteer (Cobb House).

152 **Glynn:** Moody, *Churchmen*, 14. **Dissenting preachers:** Clapinson, M (ed.), *Bishop Fell and Nonconformity* (ORS 52, 1980), 56, n. 135; *ODNB*, under Coppe; Matthews, A G, *Calamy Revised* (1934), 374. **Wills:** ORO MSS Wills Oxon. 51/3/22, 60/1/31, 66/1/19, 115/3/23.

153 **Church damage:** Gretton, *Records*, 110, 117, 121, 206, 255.

154 **Priory pew and chapel names:** ORO MS Oxf. Dioc. c 454, f. 109. **Erection of Tanfield monument:** *Guide to Burford Church* [*c*.2000], citing churchwardens' papers.

155 **Criticism of Knollys:** Dallas, A B, *Incidents in the Life and Ministry of the Rev. Alexander R C Dallas* (1871). **Curate:** ORO MS Oxf. Dioc. c 654, ff. 140-1 (Revd Kipling).

156 **Dallas:** Dallas, *Incidents*, 226-31; Moody, *Churchmen*, 24-8; Chapter 7. **Rearrangement of interior**: contemporary plan and wooden model in church; Gretton, *Records*, 121-2.

157 **Burgess's changes:** Moody, R, *History from the Minutes* (priv. printed 2002), 29; Moody, *Churchmen*, 33-6. **Church services etc:** visitation returns in ORO MSS Oxf. Dioc. c 332, c 335, c 338, c 341, c 344, c 347, c 350, c 356, c 362, c 374. **Church restoration and celebrations:** *Oxf Jnl*, 1 June 1872, p. 8; 'Excursion to ... Burford', North Oxfordshire Archaeological Society *Report* [10] (1870), 22-5; Moody, R, *Victorian Restoration of Burford Church* (priv. print. 1999): copy in Burford church archives; *Kelly* (1920).

158 **Marriott:** church restoration sources cited above. **Declining congregations:** ORO MS Oxf. Dioc. c 332, f. 105.

159 **Neglect and spire:** Fisher, 110; Monk, *History*, 37, 67, 69. **Dallas alterations:** Monk, *History*, 38-9. **Victorian restoration:** *Oxf Jnl*, 1 June 1872; Moody, *Victorian Restoration of Burford Church*; *Kelly* (1920).

160 **Morris:** Kelvin, N (ed.), *Collected Letters of William Morris* (1984-96), I, p. 352; Tolsey Museum, Burford, AN 1671, extracts by A H Swann (1989) relating Cass's account to W J Titcombe.

161 **Enquiry of 1676:** Whiteman, A (ed.), *Compton Census of 1676* (1986), 422-4. **Bishop Fell's enquiries:** Clapinson, M (ed.), *Bishop Fell and Nonconformity* (ORS 52, 1980), refs at p. 86.

162 **Quakers:** Moody, *BB*, 97-8; Moody, *Thousand Years*, 46. **Thomas Minchin:** Clapinson (ed.), *Bishop Fell*, refs at p. 80; Besse, J, *Collection of the Sufferings of the People called Quakers* (1753), 569-74, mentioning two men of that same name. **Elizabeth Minchin:** *Oxf Jnl*, 10 May 1800.

163 **Meeting House:** Quaker Monthly Meeting transcript (1708-9); Stell, C, *Nonconformist Chapels and Meeting Houses: Oxon.* (1986), 172-3; Hartley, B, *Burford's Quaker Meeting House* (1999); Buildings List (Images of England no. 421463); Pevsner, 509; local information.

164 **Baptists:** Clapinson (ed.), *Bishop Fell*, p. xxiv; Monk, *History*, 175-81; Moody, *Thousand Years*, 45. **Chapel:** Stell, *Nonconformist Chapels*, 172; Packer, J, *A History of Burford Baptist Church* (2004); Buildings List (Images of England no. 422183); Pevsner, 509.

165 **Wesley:** Curnock, N (ed.), *Journal of John Wesley* [1909-16], II, 285, 320, 324, 331, 426, 475. **Burford Methodists:** Moody, *Thousand Years*, 46-8 (quoting memorial to Buswell); Wise, D, *Early Methodism in and around Burford* (Tolsey Papers 4, 1986); Monk, *History*, 182-6. **Chapel:** Stell, *Nonconformist Chapels*, 172-3; Buildings List (Images of England no. 419756); Pevsner, 508-9; Jewell, 64; Gazetteer.

166 **Attendance in 1851:** Tiller, K (ed.), *Church and Chapel in Oxfordshire,*

1851 (ORS 55, 1987), pp. 17-18. **Vicars' comments:** Baker, E P (ed.), *Bishop Wilberforce's Visitation Returns, 1854* (ORS 35, 1954), 27; ORO MS Oxf. Dioc. c 332, f. 105. **Plymouth Brethren:** Moody, R, *A Brief Account of the Plymouth Brethren Meeting in Burford* (2000). **Drunkenness:** Moody, *BB*, 98; Baker (ed.), *Wilberforce Visit.* 27; ORO BOQM I/ii/10 (Society of Friends quarterly meeting minute books).

167 **Plymouth Brethren:** Moody, *Plymouth Brethren.* **Quakers:** ORO, BOQM I/ii/8-18. **Roman Catholicism and church:** Worrall, E S (ed.), *Return of Papists, 1767*, II (Catholic Record Soc. occasional publication 2, 1989), 114; Moody, *Thousand Years*, 49; Ellis-Rees, H, *The Church of SS John Fisher and Thomas More in Burford* (2006); information from Mr R Parkinson, West Oxfordshire District Council.

168 **Emeris:** Moody, *Churchmen*, 33-6. **Burford Council of Christian Churches:** papers in ORO MS dd Par. Burford d 16. **Priory:** website (2007); local information. **Combined benefices:** Moody, *Churchmen*, 38; papers in ORO MS Oxf. Dioc. c 1702-3; *Oxford Diocesan Year Book* (1980 and later edns).

Further Reading and Sources

Since the 1970s historians, archaeologists and geographers have studied the historical characteristics of English small towns on an unprecedented scale. Their work has guided and influenced the foregoing account of Burford. The following section provides a selection of publications on the main themes of this book, in the hope that they will encourage local historians to study other small towns. This is followed by details of publications and sources relating to Burford itself.

FURTHER READING

The Victoria County History

The Victoria County History's encyclopaedic coverage of England's towns, villages and parishes includes accounts of numerous small towns, as well as volumes dedicated to major urban centres. Oxfordshire towns already published include Banbury (VCH Oxfordshire X), Bicester (VI), Oxford (IV), Thame (VII), Witney (XIV) and Woodstock (XII). A project on Henley is in progress. Further details are on the VCH Oxfordshire website (*www.victoriacountyhistory. ac.uk/Oxfordshire*) and at British History Online (*www.british-history.ac.uk*), where many VCH histories are available.

Small Towns and Urban History

Beresford, M.W., *New Towns of the Middle Ages: Town Plantation in England, Wales and Gascony* (1967).

Blair, J., 'Small Towns 600-1270', in Palliser, D.M. (ed.), *The Cambridge Urban History of Britain*, vol. 1, *600-1540* (2000), 245-70.

Chalklin, C.W., 'Country Towns', in Mingay, G.E. (ed.), *The Victorian Countryside*, vol. 1 (1981), 275-87.

Clark, P. (ed.), *The Cambridge Urban History of Britain*, vol. 2, *1540-1840* (2000).

Clark, P., 'Small Towns 1700-1840', in idem (ed.), *The Cambridge Urban History of Britain*, vol. 2, *1540-1840* (2000), 733-74.

Clark, P. and Slack, P., *English Towns in Transition 1500-1700* (1976).

Corfield, P., *The Impact of English Towns 1700-1800* (1982).

Daunton, M.J. (ed.), *The Cambridge Urban History of Britain*, vol. 3, *1840-1950* (2000).

Dyer, A., *Decline and Growth in English Towns, 1400-1640* (1991).

Dyer, A., 'Small Market Towns 1540-1700', in P. Clark (ed.), *The Cambridge Urban History of Britain*, vol. 2, *1540-1840* (2000), 425-50.

Dyer, A., 'Small Towns in England, 1600-1800', in Borsay, P., Proudfoot, L.J. (eds.), *Provincial Towns in Early Modern England and Ireland: Change, Convergence and Divergence* (Proceedings of the British Academy, 108, 2002), 53-67.

Dyer, C., 'Small Places with Large Consequences: The Importance of Small Towns in England, 1000-1540', *Historical Research*, 75 (2002), 1-24.

Dyer, C., 'Small Towns 1270-1540', in Palliser, D.M. (ed.), *The Cambridge Urban History of Britain*, vol. 1, *600-1540* (2000), 505-37.

Ellis, J.M., *The Georgian Town, 1680-1840* (2001).

Haslam, J., *Early Medieval Towns in Britain, c.700 to 1140* (1985).

Hilton, R.H., *English and French Towns in Feudal Society* (1992).

Hilton, R.H., 'Towns in Societies: Medieval England', in idem, *Class Conflict and the Crisis of Feudalism* (1985), 175-86.

Palliser, D.M. (ed.), *The Cambridge Urban History of Britain*, vol. 1, *600-1540* (2000).

Patten, J., *English Towns 1500-1700* (1978).

Platt, C., *The English Medieval Town* (1976).

Reynolds, S., *An Introduction to the History of English Medieval Towns* (1977).

Royle, S.A., 'The Development of Small Towns in Britain', in Daunton, M.J. (ed.), *The Cambridge Urban History of Britain*, vol. 3, *1840-1950* (2000).

Swanson, H., *Medieval British Towns* (1999).

Waller, P.J., *Town, City and Nation: England 1850-1914* (1983).

Waller, P.J. (ed.), *The English Urban Landscape* (2000).

Town Layouts

Aston, M. and Bond, J., *The Landscape of Towns* (1976).

Barley, M.W. (ed.), *The Plans and Topography of Medieval Towns in England and Wales* (CBA Research Report, 14, 1975).

Conzen, M.R.G., *Alnwick, Northumberland: A Study in Town-Plan Analysis* (Institute of British Geographers Publication 27, 1960).

Conzen, M.R.G., 'The Use of Town Plans in the Study of Urban History', in Dyos, H.J. (ed.), *The Study of Urban History* (1968),113-30.

Hindle, B.P., *Medieval Town Plans* (1990).

Lilley, K.D., *Urban Life in the Middle Ages, 1000-1450* (2002).

Palliser, D.M., Slater, T.R. and Dennison, E.P., 'The Topography of Towns 600-1300', in Palliser, D.M. (ed.), *The Cambridge Urban History of Britain*, vol. 1, *600-1540* (2000), 153-86.

Slater, T.R., 'The Analysis of Burgage Patterns in Medieval Towns', *Area*, 13 (1981), 211-16.

Slater, T.R., 'Understanding the Landscape of Towns', in Hooke, D. (ed.), *Landscape: The Richest Historical Record* (2001), 97-108.

Economic and Social History

Blair, J. and Ramsay, N (eds.), *English Medieval Industries: Craftsmen, Techniques, Products* (1991).

Borsay, P., *The English Urban Renaissance: Culture and Society in the Provincial Town 1660-1770* (1989).

Britnell, R.H., 'The Economy of British Towns 600-1300', in Palliser, D.M. (ed.), *The Cambridge Urban History of Britain*, vol. 1, *600-1540* (2000), 105-26.

Britnell, R.H., 'The Economy of British Towns 1300-1540', in Palliser, D.M. (ed.), *The Cambridge Urban History of Britain*, vol. 1, *600-1540* (2000), 313-33.

Clark, P., *The English Alehouse: A Social History 1200-1830* (1983).

Clark, P., Gaskin, K. and Wilson, A., *Population Estimates of English Small Towns* (1989).

Clay, C., *Economic Expansion and Social Change, England 1500-1700*, vol.1, *People, Land and Towns* (1984).

Corfield, P.J., 'Small Towns, Large Implications: Social and Cultural Roles of Small Towns in Eighteenth-century England and Wales', *British Journal for Eighteenth-Century Studies*, 10 (1987), 125-38.

Dyer, C., *Making a Living in the Middle Ages: The People of Britain 850-1520* (2002).

Dyer, C., 'Market Towns in the Countryside in Late Medieval England', *Canadian Journal of History*, 31 (1996), 17-35.

Everitt, A.M., 'The English Urban Inn', in Everitt, A.M. (ed.), *Perspectives in English Urban History* (1973), 91-137.

Everitt, A.M., 'The Marketing of Agricultural Produce' in J. Thirsk (ed.), *The Agrarian History of England and Wales*, vol. 4, *1500-1640* (1967), 466-592.

Farmer, D.L., 'Marketing the Produce of the Countryside 1200-1500', in Miller, E. (ed.), *The Agrarian History of England and Wales*, vol. 3, *1348-1500* (1991), 324-430.

Fideler, P.A., *Social Welfare in Pre-Industrial England* (2006).

Hilton, R.H., 'Lords, Burgesses and Hucksters', *Past and Present*, 97 (1982), 3-15.

Hilton, R.H., 'Medieval Market Towns and Simple Commodity Production', *Past and Present*, 109 (1985), 3-23.

Hilton, R.H., 'Small Town Society in England before the Black Death', *Past and Present*, 105 (1984), 53-78.

Miller, E. and Hatcher, J., *Medieval England: Towns, Commerce and Crafts 1086-1348* (1995).

Stobart, J., 'Leisure and Shopping in the Small Towns of Georgian England', *Journal of Urban History*, 31 (2005), 479-503.

Sweet, R., *The English Town 1680-1840: Government, Society and Culture* (1999).

Wrightson, K., *Earthly Necessities: Economic Lives in Early Modern Britain* (2000).

Secular Buildings

Ayres, J., *Domestic Interiors: The British Tradition 1500-1850* (2003).

Barley, M., *Houses and History* (1986).

Brunskill, R.W., *Traditional Buildings in Britain: An Introduction to Vernacular Architecture* (2004).

Chalklin, C., *The Provincial Towns of Georgian England: A Study of the Building Process* (1974).

Clark, D.R., 'The Shop Within? An Analysis of the Architectural Evidence for Medieval Shops', *Architectural History*, 43 (2000), 58-87.

Clifton-Taylor, A., *The Pattern of English Building* (4th edn 1987).

Clifton-Taylor, A. and Ireson, A.S., *English Stone Building* (2nd edn 1994).

Cunnington, P., *How Old is Your House?* (1999).

Grenville, J., *Medieval Housing* (1997).

Hall, L., *Period House Fixtures and Fittings 1300-1900* (2005).

Hallett, A., *Almshouses* (2004).

Harris, R., *Discovering Timber-framed Buildings* (1993).

Hoskins, W.G., 'The Rebuilding of Rural England, 1570-1640', in idem, *Provincial England: Essays in Social and Economic History* (1963), 131-48.

Morrison, K.A., *English Shops and Shopping* (2003).

Pantin, W.A., 'Medieval English Town House Plans', *Medieval Archaeology*, 6-7 (1963), 202-39.

Pantin, W.A., 'Medieval Inns', in Jope, E.M. (ed.), *Studies in Building History* (1961), 166-91.

Prescott, E., *The English Medieval Hospital 1050-1640* (1992).

Quiney, A., *Town Houses of Medieval Britain* (2003).

Steane, J., *The Archaeology of Power* (2001).

Stenning, D.F., 'Timber-framed Shops 1300-1600', *Vernacular Architecture*, 16 (1985), 35-9.

Tittler, R., *Architecture and Power: The Town Hall and the English Urban Community c.1500-1640* (1991).

Wood, M., *The English Medieval House* (1965).

Religious Life and Buildings

Blair, J., *The Church in Anglo-Saxon Society* (2005).

Blair, J., 'Minster Churches in the Landscape', in Hooke, D. (ed.), *Anglo-Saxon Settlements* (1988), 35-58.

Campbell, J., 'The Church in Anglo-Saxon Towns', in idem, *Essays on Anglo-Saxon History* (1986), 139-154.

Chadwick, O., *The Victorian Church* (2 vols., 3rd edn 1987).

Clifton-Taylor, A., *English Parish Churches as Works of Art* (1974).

Collinson, P. and Craig, J. (eds.), *The Reformation in English Towns, 1500-1640* (1998).

Duffy, E., *The Stripping of the Altars: Traditional Religion in England 1400-1580* (2nd edn 2005).

Gilley, S. and Sheils, W.J. (eds.), *A History of Religion in Britain* (1994).

Johnson, D., *The Changing Shape of English Nonconformity 1825-1925* (1999).

Morris, R., *Churches in the Landscape* (2nd edn 1997).

Pounds, N.J.G., *A History of the English Parish* (2000).

Rex, R., *The Lollards* (2002).

Rodwell, W., *The Archaeology of Churches* (2005).

Rosser, G., 'The Cure of Souls in English Towns before 1000', in Blair, J. and Sharpe, R. (eds.), *Pastoral Care before the Parish* (1992), 267-84.

Royal Commission on the Historical Monuments of England, *Nonconformist Chapels and Meeting-Houses in Central England* (1986).

Southall, K.H., *Our Quaker Heritage: Early Meeting Houses* (1974).

Watts, M.R., *The Dissenters* (2 vols., 1978, 1995).

Oxfordshire and the Cotswolds

Arkell, W.J., *Oxford Stone* (1947).

Barratt, D.M. and Vaisey, D.G., *Oxfordshire: A Handbook for Students of Oxfordshire History* (1973).

Blair, J., *Anglo-Saxon Oxfordshire* (1994).

Bond, J. and Rhodes, J., *The Oxfordshire Brewer: Brewing and Malting in the City and County of Oxford* (1985).

Brown, M., *Oxon. Brews: The Story of Commercial Brewing in Oxfordshire* (2004).

Eddershaw, D.G.H., *The Civil War in Oxfordshire* (1995).

Emery, F.V., *The Oxfordshire Landscape* (1974).

Finberg, J., *The Cotswolds* (1977).

Foreman, W., *Oxfordshire Mills* (1983).

Garne, R., *Cotswold Yeomen and Sheep* (1984).

Gelling, M., *The Place-Names of Oxfordshire* (English Place Names Society, vols. 23-24, 1953-4).

Greensted, M., *The Arts and Crafts Movement in the Cotswolds* (1996).

Hill, M. and Birch, S., *Cotswold Stone Houses* (1994).

Paine, C. and Rhodes, J., *The Worker's Home: Small Houses in Oxfordshire through Three Centuries* (1979).

Pilling, J., *Oxfordshire Houses: A Guide to Local Traditions* (1993).

Porter, E., *Yeomen of the Cotswolds* (1995).

Portman, D., 'Vernacular Building in the Oxford Region in the Sixteenth and Seventeenth Centuries', in Chalklin, C. and Havinden, M. (eds.), *Rural Change and Urban Growth* (1974), 135-68.

Postles, P., 'Markets for Rural Produce in Oxfordshire 1086-1350', *Midland History*, 12, 14-26.

Powell, P., *The Geology of Oxfordshire* (2005).

Rhodes, J., *Oxfordshire: A County and its People* (1980).

Rodwell, K. (ed.), *Historic Towns in Oxfordshire: A Survey of the New County* (1975).

Sherwood, J. and Pevsner, N., *Oxfordshire* (Buildings of England series, 1974).

Steane, J.M., *Oxfordshire* (1996).

Turner, J., *Quarries and Craftsmen of the Windrush Valley* (1988).

Victoria History of Oxfordshire (15 vols 1907-2006; in progress).

SOURCES FOR BURFORD

Secondary Publications

Fisher, J., *A History of the Town of Burford, Oxfordshire* (1861).

Godfrey, W.H., 'Burford Priory', *Oxoniensia*, 4 (1939), 71-88.

Gretton, M.S., *Burford Past and Present* (1920; revised edns 1929, 1945, 1950).

Gretton, M.S., *Re-cognitions* (1951).

Gretton, R.H., *The Burford Records: A Study in Minor Town Government* (1920).

Harley, B., *Burford's Quaker Meeting House* (1999).

Hutton, W.H., *Burford Papers: Letters of Samuel Crisp to his Sister at Burford and Other Studies, 1745-1845* (1905).

Jewell, A., *Burford in Old Photographs* (1985).

Laithwaite, M., 'The Buildings of Burford: A Cotswold Town in the Fourteenth to Nineteenth Centuries', in Everitt, A.M. (ed.), *Perspectives in English Urban History* (1973), 60-90.

Monk, W.J., *Burford* (1897).

Monk, W.J., *Burford: The Official Guide* (1934; also three revised edns).

Monk, W.J., *Guide to Burford* (1929).

Monk, W.J., *History of Burford* (1891).

Monk, W.J., *The Story of Burford* (1909).

Moody, J., *Burford's Roads and Rogues*, pt 1, *Turnpikes, Traffic and Travellers* (1998).

Moody, J., *Burford's Roads and Rogues*, pt 2, *Vagabonds, Villains and Highwaymen* (2000).

Moody, J., *The Great Burford Smallpox Outbreak* (2nd edn, 1996).

Moody, R., *A Burford Celebration in Camera* (1990).

Moody, R., *Burford, The Civil War and the Levellers* (2nd edn, 1999).

Moody, R., *Burford: An Introduction and Guide* (2nd edn, 2001).

Moody, R., *The Burford Year: Markets, Fairs, Festivals and Seasonal Life* (1998).

Moody, R., *The Inns of Burford* (2nd edn 2007).

Moody, R. and Moody, J., *The Book of Burford* (1983).

Moody, R. and Moody, J., *A Thousand Years of Burford* (2006).

Nash, J., 'Aspects of a Town in Decline: A Population Study of Burford, Oxfordshire, 1851-1901' (University of Oxford, D.Phil. thesis, 2006).

Paintin, H., *Burford Priory and the Lenthall Family* (1907).

Stawell, J., *The Burford and Bibury Racecourses: A History* (2nd edn, 2000).

Wise, S., *Discovering Burford* (1971).

Printed Sources (except maps)

Gretton, R.H., *The Burford Records: A Study in Minor Town Government* (1920).

Kelly's Directory of Oxfordshire (1883-1939).

Oxfordshire Record Society publications (1919-).

Post Office Directory of Oxfordshire (1847-77).

Warner, R., 'Memoirs of a Twentieth-century Antique Dealer', *Regional Furniture*, 17 (2003), 1-175.

Maps

The earliest large-scale map of the town is the 1:2500 Ordnance Survey map of 1881 (Oxfordshire, sheets XXIV.16 and XXX.4). Earlier reliable maps of the Burford area are: T. Jefferys, *The County of Oxford* (1767); R. Davis, *A New Map of the County of Oxford* (1797), and 1" Ordnance Survey, 1st edn (sheet 45, 1833). A map of the parish in 1823, showing areas inclosed in 1773 and 1795, is reproduced in Gretton, *Burford Records*, 227; the originals are in Oxfordshire Record Office and the Tolsey Museum in Burford.

EPE Website

The England's Past for Everyone (EPE) project is developing an interactive website which makes available a wide range of complementary material. The Burford pages include fuller accounts of buildings covered in the Historical Gazetteer, incorporating names of all known owners and occupiers; related image galleries, including photographs by English Heritage and volunteers; and transcripts by the Burford Probate Group of nearly a thousand wills and other probate documents. Resources for other counties include maps and images, digitised documents, oral histories and audiovisual material. Access to each county is from the EPE website at *www.englandspastforeveryone.org.uk*.

Unpublished Sources (by location)

Burford, The Tolsey. Several collections of town records, belonging to individuals and corporate bodies, are stored in Burford's 'town hall'. The records of the former town corporation survive in the Cheatle Collection and in the collections of the Charity Trustees and School Foundation Governors. The Cheatle Collection includes royal charters, deeds, wills, and memorandum and account books. The Trustees' collection includes deeds, rent rolls, borough court records, charity accounts, apprenticeship indentures, constables' and overseers' book. The School collection comprises 20 items of the 16th-18th centuries. Many documents have been published in summary form in *The Burford Records* by R.H. Gretton (1920). The Tolsey also holds the records of the parish council (1894 onwards) and a small collection accumulated by the Tolsey Museum.

London, The National Archives (Public Record Office). Numerous items relating to Burford are held by TNA (PRO) and can be most easily found by searching TNA's electronic catalogue. A selection of important records has been published in Gretton's *Burford Records* (pp. 565-665), including assessments for lay subsidies, inquisitions, and a survey of 1552. Important sources used for this book include the Burford sections of national censuses (1841-1901), wills proved in the Prerogative Court of Canterbury (PROB 11), copies of which can be obtained online, and the 1662 Hearth Tax (E 179/255/4, Part 3, ff. 239-239v.).

Oxford, Bodleian Library. The Bodleian's collection of Oxfordshire manuscripts includes miscellaneous material relating to Burford, such as a 16th-century survey of lands once belonging to the guild (MS Top. Oxon. d 169, f.iv). The Bodleian also holds drawings of Burford buildings by J.C. Buckler (MS Top. Oxon. a. 65).

Oxford, Brasenose College. The College holds charters, leases and other material relating to two tenements. Many of the documents have been calendared and published in Gretton's *Burford Records* (pp. 668-73).

Oxford, Oxfordshire Record Office. The ORO holds important collections of Church records: the Oxford archidiaconal and diocesan records (including visitation returns for Burford) and Burford's parish records (including parish registers, churchwardens' accounts, vestry and select vestry minutes, church rate books). Other relevant collections include records of the Wesleyan Methodists, probate records, and quarter sessions records (including victuallers' recognizances, which list Burford's inns). There are also deeds for some Burford properties.

Oxford, Oxfordshire Studies. The centre holds a transcript of Burford's parish registers, copies of census returns on microfiche, photographic collections (including pictures by Henry Taunt), pamphlets, sales catalogues, and the schedule of Listed Buildings in Burford. The collections are partly searchable online through Heritage Search, accessible from the Oxfordshire County Council website, *www.oxfordshire.gov.uk*.

Oxford, Sites and Monuments Record (at Oxfordshire Studies). The SMR holds archaeological data for the county, including the Burford area.

Swindon, National Monuments Record (English Heritage). The NMR holds extensive buildings and photographic collections for Burford and elsewhere. The schedule of Listed Buildings is available (with photographs) on English Heritage's Images of England website, *www.imagesofengland.org.uk*.

Index

Picture Credits

The authors and publishers wish to thank the following for permission to reproduce their material. Any infringement of copyright is entirely accidental: every care has been taken to contact or trace all copyright owners. We would be pleased to correct in future editions any errors or omissions brought to our attention. References are to page numbers except where stated.

Ashmolean Museum, Oxford, 95
Bodleian Library, Oxford, 10, 38, 42 (Fig. 18), 76-7, 90, 101 (Fig. 62), 202 (Calendars)
James Bond, 18 (right)
British Library, 35, 41 (Fig. B), 45 (Fig. D), 148
English Folk Dance and Song Society, 116 (Fig. B)
English Heritage (Mike Hesketh-Roberts), 2, 4, 7, 39 (Figs B-C), 50 (Fig. 24), 54
     (Fig. 29), 58-9, 64, 68 (Fig. B), 70, 72, 81-2, 84, 92 (Fig. 52), 100 (Fig. 60), 101
     (Fig. 61), 110, 120, 130, 132 (Fig. 88 left), 133, 152-3, 156, 174 (99 High St), 199
     (Bank), 210 (Great House), 212-13 (Priory); (James Davies), 79 (Fig. D)
English Heritage (NMR), 23-4, 49 (Fig. A), 91, 94, 96-7, 104, 137 (Fig. 93), 179
     (1885 photo)
Daniel Miles, 63 (Fig. D)
Monumental Brass Society, 42 (Fig. 19)
Raymond and Joan Moody, 11 (Fig. C), 27, 100 (Fig. 59), 107, 109, 111 (Fig. 71),
     114, 116 (Fig. C), 117 (Fig. 77), 135 (Fig. 91), 158, 166 (7 High St)
Museum of London Picture Library, 102
The National Archives: Public Record Office, 99
National Portrait Gallery, 92 (Fig. 53)
Newsquest Oxfordshire, 93 (Fig. B)
Northamptonshire Central Library (Sir Henry Dryden collection), 8, 208 (Bull
     Cottage 1840)
Ordnance Survey: © Crown Copyright. All rights reserved. Licence number
     100020457, 141-2
Österreichische Nationalbibliothek (ONB/Wien BA1NR00026), 12
Oxfordshire Architectural and Historical Society, 69
Oxfordshire County Council Photographic Archive, cover, 45 (Figs B and C), 66,
     113, 181 (1922 photo), 207 (foundry)
Oxfordshire Record Office, 43 (right), 87, 154
Society of Antiquaries of London, 155
Sonia Halliday Photographs, 32
John Steane, 49 (Fig. B)
Tolsey Museum, Burford, 25, 112, 170 (24 High St), 172 (Titcomb), 184-5
     (College, 66-70 High St), 200 (Brewery and Garne), 202 (Temperance Hotel)
Trowbridge Museum, 45 (Fig E)
University of London (Ann Atkinson), 197 (184-92 High St); (Jessica Brod),
     6, 46, 54 (Fig. 28), 68 (Fig. A), 119, 182 (George), 186-9 (78-124 High St); (Mark
     Casson), 175-6 (75-97 High St); (Antonia Catchpole), 18 (left), 41 (Fig. A);
     (David Clark), 39 (Fig. A), 43 (left), 55-7, 60-2, 67, 68 (Fig. C), 78 (Fig. B),
     103, 116 (Fig. D), 128, 131, 132 (Fig. 89), 134, 138 (Figs 95-6), 140, 146,
     160, Gazetteer except as stated; (David Fielding), 126-7; (Heather Horner),
     129 (right), 173-4; (Michael and Rosemary Howden), 11 (Fig. B), 48 (right),
     137 (Fig. 94), 150, 169-71 (colour photos); (Brian Scholes), 117 (Fig. 76);
     Richard Shaw), 157; (Simon Townley), xii, 20-1, 51, 78 (Fig. A), 79 (Fig. C),
     89, 111 (Fig. 72), 118, 125, 132 (right), 138 (Fig. 97), 143, 145, 151, 159,
     Gazetteer except as stated; (Bernice Williamson), 48 (left), 129 (left)
V&A Images/Victoria and Albert Museum, London, 116 (Fig. A)

New maps were drawn by Cath D'Alton (Maps 1-20) and Alan Fagan (Fig. 45, p.
214 Fig. C), using Ordnance Survey 1st edition maps except as listed above.
© University of London.